THE VALLEY OF THE KINGS

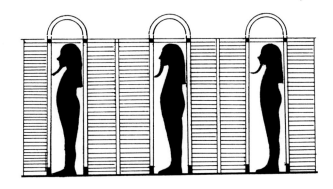

ERIK HORNUNG

THE VALLEY OF THE KINGS

HORIZON OF ETERNITY

TRANSLATED BY DAVID WARBURTON

TIMKEN PUBLISHERS

Publisher's Note

I wish to thank Professor Erik Hornung for making his knowledge of Egyptian religion available to a wider public and for everything he has done to facilitate the preparation of this edition. I also thank David Warburton for the translation of *Tal der Könige* and for preparing the list of abbreviations, the references and further readings, and the glossary. I am grateful to Christine Lilyquist who gave so generously of her time and whose editorial supervision made this English-language edition possible. In addition Dr. Lilyquist suggested and oversaw the preparation of the tomb plans and the expansion of the maps and the chart in the appendix. Working with these three scholars has been an entirely rewarding experience.

Jane Timken

German edition copyright © 1982 by Artemis Verlag, Zurich and Munich

English-language translation copyright © 1990 by Erik Hornung

Text arrangement and material new to the English-language edition copyright © 1990 by Timken Publishers, Inc.

First U.S. edition of *The Valley of the Kings* published in 1990 by Timken Publishers, Inc., 225 Lafayette Street, New York, N.Y. 10012

Library of Congress Cataloging-in-Publication Data

Hornung, Erik
   [Tal der Könige. English]
   The valley of the kings / Erik Hornung: translated by David
Warburton.
     p.   cm.
   Translation of: Tal der Könige.
   Includes bibliographical references.
   ISBN 0-943221-07-2
   1. Valley of the Kings (Egypt)   2. Mural painting and decoration.
Egyptian—Egypt—Valley of the Kings.   I. Title.
DT73.B44H6713 1990
932—dc20   90-10909
                                                         CIP

Copyedited by Anna Jardine
Printed and bound by South China Printing Company, Hong Kong

Frontispiece: The tomb of Sety I on the left and the tomb of Ramesses I on the right in the main branch of the Valley, with the pyramid-shaped Qurn towering above.

Page 6. View from the first to the second corridor in the tomb of Sety I.

CONTENTS

FOREWORD

Preface to the German Edition Much that was copied in vivid colors by visitors to the Valley of the Kings in the last century is lost to us today, having simply disappeared or been damaged beyond recognition. One of the most interesting monuments visited by almost every traveler, the tomb of Sety I, was closed in 1979, but this alarm signal went virtually unheeded. The crowds of tourists are now directed into other tombs, which are likewise consigned to gradual destruction. More significant than the inadequate protection of these monuments however is the remarkable lack of appreciation and goodwill shown by visitors to the Valley, the largest open-air museum in the world. If the masterpieces in our museums were daily touched by as many hands as are the reliefs and paintings of these tombs, the works of Raphael and Rembrandt would be known to us only from photographs and descriptions. The portable objects found in the Valley's tombs would appear to have been saved, standing as they do, well protected in the showcases of the Egyptian Museum in Cairo. However, the most valuable treasures are still in the Valley, where they are seriously endangered, and the emphasis of that danger is one of the purposes of this book.

The results and problems of decades of work in the Valley of the Kings are assembled here for the first time. Attention is directed primarily to the religious texts and illustrations with which the tombs are decorated, but the architectural development with its carefully graded canon of proportions is not ignored. The slow work of deciphering, translating, and interpreting constantly leads to new and previously unimaginable interpretations of the perceptual forms and vividly presented conceptions of an earlier people's reflections on death and the Beyond, terrifying and comforting visions of poets of the second millennium B.C. Long rows of hieroglyphs and unusual, extremely intricate sequences of pictures cover the stucco and limestone tomb walls. Whoever draws the curtain and reveals what was hitherto unknown may be overwhelmed with the same feeling that struck the archaeologists peering at the glittering treasures in the small chamber of the tomb of Tutankhamun.

The traveling treasures of Tutankhamun's tomb will be discussed only marginally here, as we are concerned with other treasures of the Valley. What was previously reserved for a limited audience in the form of text editions, translations, and commentaries will now be offered to the wider public, supported by the broadest possible selection of illustrations from scenes and motifs that remain almost unknown, even in scientific circles. This would have been impossible without the indefatigable Andreas Brodbeck, who has selflessly served our Valley of the Kings project with his photographic and epigraphic skills since 1969, and who has placed at my disposal most of the photographs reproduced here. I am also grateful to Artur Brack, Hans Hauser, Gunther Lapp, Lotty Spycher, and Frank Teichmann, as well as to the British Library in London and the City Museum and Art Gallery in Bristol (home of the Belzoni drawings), which gave me additional pictures. My talented colleague Elisabeth Staehelin supported my efforts in many ways, and I am likewise obliged to the students of our seminar for their close assistance and to other professional colleagues concerned with the royal tombs with whom I had a profitable exchange. I also benefited from the interest shown in the progress of my work by Hans and Gretel Wagner and Martin L. Schneider. Those Egyptian friends who helped as conditions became increasingly difficult have earned special thanks, as have, for their hospitality and help, the German Archaeological Institute and the Swiss Institute for the Study of Ancient Egyptian Architecture and Civilization in Cairo.

If the ancient Egyptians were more interested than any other people in the secrets surrounding death and the hereafter, this does not mean they found the final answers to these age-old questions of humanity. They did, however, try to be consistent and pursued the problems of the quality of life in the other world with nearly scientific dedication. Their thoughts have the added fascination that they have not been diminished by popularization, so that these fresh and unexpected speculations can touch each of us directly and forcefully in vivid color. Anyone crossing the thresholds of the royal tombs is confronted with the hoards of the dead passing by on the walls of the sloping corridors, and beholds the threatening and painful powers of disintegration before his eyes; but he also experiences death as a necessary renewal of all existence, and understands the Beyond as the reflection of the depths of the human soul, whose language was always that of the image.

For almost 500 years the most gifted artists of Egypt worked in the Valley of the Kings. It is thanks to their ability that the content and form of these brave and vivid visions of the Beyond fall so perfectly together, easing our access to a strangely alien perspective. What remains of these 4,000-year-old works of art is a precious heritage. Despite all losses, they are preserved in brilliant colors that make them seem as if they were completed yesterday. Yet they are seriously threatened today. If the damages from modern tourism are allowed to continue, there will be nothing of the splendor of the reliefs and paintings left for our descendants. As most of these tombs have not even been published (or scientifically preserved) at present, I have attempted to document the broadest possible spectrum of the pictures in color. That this was possible despite high costs is due to subsidies, for which we thank the Georg Wagner Foundation and the Freiwillige Akademische Gesellschaft, Basel, as well as private supporters.

Basel, January 1981   Erik Hornung

Preface to the English Edition

The English-speaking world is generally familiar with the Book of the Dead, which records the hopes and fears of the ancient Egyptians concerning death and the Beyond. However, the complementary world of the royal funerary books remains practically unknown, although these are among the most creative works inspired by the religion of the New Kingdom.

The Book of the Dead, a collection of texts written in the New Kingdom (ca. 1600 B.C.), belongs to a tradition dating back to the late Old Kingdom (ca. 2300 B.C.), when kings had their burial chambers inscribed with spells known as the Pyramid Texts. After the fall of the Old Kingdom (ca. 2100 B.C.), these royal spells were adopted by commoners and inscribed on their coffins; these Middle Kingdom works are thus known as the Coffin Texts. This corpus of spells includes modified versions of older spells as well as many new ones. In the New Kingdom, commoners contemporary with the pharaohs whose tombs are in the Valley of the Kings were buried with papyrus scrolls inscribed with numerous spells, many of them evolved from Coffin Texts. The collection of spells on these scrolls is known today as the Book of the Dead. The ancient Egyptian name, Book of Going Forth by Day, indicates the desire to "come forth living from the Beyond." The spells, guaranteeing a happy afterlife and protection against all danger, were used by everyone, sometimes even by the king.

During Dynasty 18, however, these popular spells do not appear on the walls of the royal tombs; in their place are the newly created Books of the Netherworld and related compositions, such as the Litany of Re. Their purpose was to provide the king with a systematic description of the world beyond death, one that followed the path of the sun after sunset through the twelve hours of the night. The two Dynasty 18 Books of the Netherworld, the Amduat and the Book of Gates, are divided into twelve parts corresponding to the twelve hours of the night. The later Ramesside texts have a more flexible structure. Still more texts were created until the end of the New Kingdom. Private tombs and sarcophagi of the Late Period were also decorated with copies of these works, and it is not improbable that even early Christian texts were influenced by ideas and images from the New Kingdom religious books.

The illustrations in these royal books are not restricted to individual complementary illustrations, as in the Books of the Dead. Instead they achieve a unity of word and image. The Egyptian love of imagery opened up almost unlimited possibilities of religious expression using pictorial symbolism, which reached a climax in the epoch of Akhenaton and his immediate successors. It is this sophisticated imagery that produces the particular impact of the wall decoration of the New Kingdom royal tombs—these compelling visions of the world beyond death reach the modern beholder directly. This is where the visions of the unconscious meet the world of dreams and the archetypes of modern Jungian psychology.

The Valley of the Kings is meant as an introduction to this world of ancient visions as preserved in paintings and reliefs of the walls and ceiling of the New Kingdom royal tombs. The material is arranged neither chronologically nor by tomb, nor even by funerary book, but instead thematically and in keeping with the ancient Egyptian mentality. Chronology, glossary, architectural plans, and further information about the individual books and tombs can be found in the appendix. In order to group the explanation of texts in the middle of the book with introductory and ancillary chapters framing it, the order of chapters in the English edition has been changed from that in the German edition, and the order of the illustrations has been adjusted accordingly. My thanks are due to David Warburton, who not only translated the text and prepared the glossary and bibliography for the English edition, but also made many useful suggestions that improved the text in many places. For suggestions and help I am grateful also to Christine Lilyquist. To the unflagging interest and support of Jane Timken we owe the appearance of this English edition.

The dangers mentioned in the preface to the German edition have not been averted: modern tourism is worse than ever, threatening and even destroying these documents of human heritage. The tomb of Sety I, once reopened, has been closed again. The tomb of Nofretari is now being restored and conserved by the Getty Conservation Institute and further protective measures are envisioned. But what is required now is a new attitude toward these tombs and their decoration; we hope that this book will aid in the development of a new point of view.

Basel, January 1990   Erik Hornung

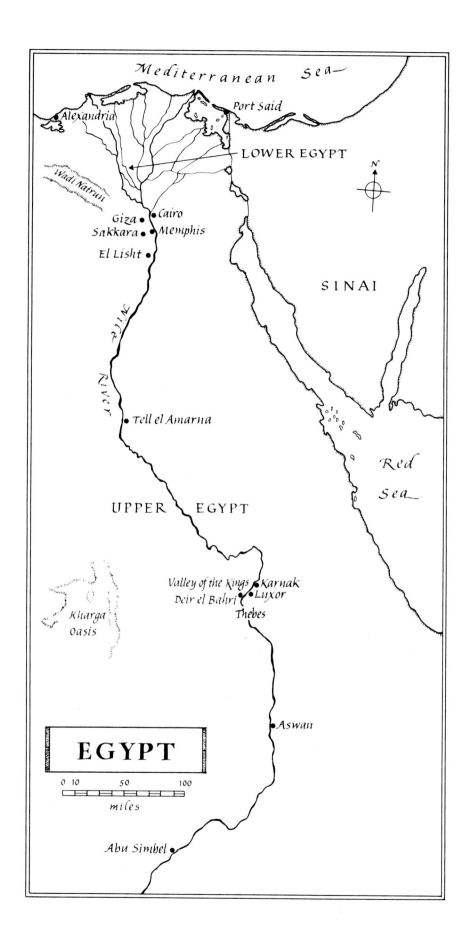

C H A P T E R 1 **EXPLORING THE VALLEY**

From the luxurious valley, from the gardens along the east bank of the Nile, the traveler's eye wanders across the river defining the landscape, where sails and blossoms come into view, and beyond, to the distant silhouette of the desert mountains. Here are the tombs, and here begins the realm of the dead who repose in the ''beautiful west.'' Out of the depths of the human soul many cultures conjure up a broad stream dividing the world they know from the world beyond, a simile for the removal and alienation brought about by death. But in Egypt this borderline was not a mere image or simile, it was the ever-present Nile. And just as the river of the hereafter could not be crossed by a ford or bridge, the Nile is not spanned by a bridge at Luxor, the ancient Thebes, even today, despite repeated efforts.

Now as then, another timeless image of the human soul provides the agent uniting the two shores: the mythical ferryman performing his gloomy task on the edge of the river or the world, carrying his weightless freight from one shore to the other. Having troubled the ferryman today and crossed the border, one reaches an unfamiliar world. As the fields and gardens are left far behind, the path blends into the borderless desert, which is not flat and sandy, but rough and mountainous with cliff upon cliff as far as the eye can see. Here, where the corpses of the dead lie, is the home of the departed souls, and the silence of the kingdom of the dead rules supreme, as heavy as the midday heat. A land of no return, borne within each of us, is now visible before us: the Beyond.

Near the line where the fields and the desert meet—between the sugar cane and grazing sheep today—stand two huge throned statues. Originally towering more than sixty feet above the plain, each was cut out of a single block of sandstone and erected in honor of the third Amenophis—the father of the heretical monotheist Akhenaton. The similarity of his name to that of a hero led the Greeks to name the statues after Memnon, son of Eos, slain by Achilles before Troy. And thus the pair of stone guardians are introduced to the modern traveler as the Colossi of Memnon. They face the east from where we have journeyed: the ancient capital of the New Kingdom, where the god Amun was worshipped in the extensive temple precincts at Karnak and Luxor. Spread out to the west behind the statues is the largest cemetery created by human hands, save that of the pyramid fields near Memphis, the northern capital. The three groups of tomb structures rise gradually from the valley into the craggy desert, with funerary temples on the edge of the green fields, the tombs of officials on the mountain slopes, and finally the tombs of the kings, queens, and royal children in the valleys and gullies behind the first ridge, in the Valley of the Kings, the Valley of the Queens, and numerous other ravines.

Only a fraction of the originally abundant monuments dating to the 2,000 years before the beginning of the Christian era is preserved today, but these are nevertheless quite enough to catch the eye. Even the tourists of antiquity, who first made their way to Egypt under the Persian emperors, found the temples and tombs of Thebes a central attraction and arrived in swelling numbers after Alexander the

Great. According to the graffiti of Ptolemaic and Roman times, the Colossi of Memnon and the tombs of the Valley of the Kings were among the spots favored even by hurried travelers. The oldest dated Greek visitor's inscription—cut into the walls of the tomb of Ramesses VII—takes us back to 278 B.C., but it was doubtless preceded by many undated inscriptions. Most of the Greek and Latin graffiti are found in the easily accessible tombs of Ramesses IV and Ramesses VII, but also in the more remote sepulchers of Merneptah, Sety II, Ramesses XI, Ramesses IX, Ramesses II, Amenmesse, and Ramesses III. The other tombs, including the splendid tomb of Sety I and those of Dynasty 18, were then lost and inaccessible.

Diodorus, who visited the Valley of the Kings in the 180th Olympiad (60–65 B.C.), probably visited only these open decorated tombs. But he refers to the notes of priests that contained a list of forty-seven royal tombs, which corresponds with the actual number (including some nonroyal tombs) relatively well. Precise records must have been kept, for the geographer Strabo mentions "around forty," a number derived from similar sources. At that time, however, no one even considered the possibility of excavating in order to find the lost tombs.

In the age-old manner, visitors left their names, places of origin, and occasionally their dates, but they almost never hinted at the feelings aroused during their visits. We are better informed by those who visited the northerly of the two Colossi of Memnon, which began to whistle when struck by the early-morning rays of the sun, as a result of an earthquake in the first century B.C. that left cracks in the stone. For two centuries this attraction amused travelers, including Hadrian, who came to Upper Egypt with his entourage in A.D. 130. A subsequent imperial visit by Septimius Severus in 199 led to the reconstruction of the damaged statue, ending this singular phenomenon and returning the royal tombs to center stage.

The tourists of antiquity were followed by Christian hermits, who turned to the desert seeking new paths to God in the unruly days of the late Roman world. Alongside the older Greek and Latin graffiti, they added Coptic writing, and they defaced or destroyed images they found to be particularly offensive. The tombs of Ramesses IV and VI were especially coveted for their spaciousness; the former was even turned into a church.

With the Arab conquest of Egypt in 642 and the beginning of the Islamic epoch, the Theban tombs vanish from history. Even educated Arab travelers, geographers, and authors say nothing about Luxor's ancient past. Only the Armenian Abu Salih mentions the ancient ruins of the city in the thirteenth century. Early European travelers visiting Egypt after the rediscovery of its ancient past contented themselves with the ruins of Alexandria and those in the immediate vicinity of Cairo. Their reports refer to the pyramids and the sphinx at Giza but contain nothing of the wonders of Upper Egypt. The temple at Karnak was first seen and described by an unknown Italian who found his way to Philae, the "Pearl of the Nile," at the first cataract, in 1589; but apparently he did not cross over to the Theban west bank.

Egypt was visited more often in the course of the seventeenth century, and 1668 brings the first recorded visit to the Valley of the Kings by European travelers, two Capuchin friars, Protais and François, whose report was published by Thévenot four years later. Aside from Karnak, they mention "biban el melouc," the modern Arabic name for the Valley. More precise are the notes of the Jesuit Claude Sicard, who was in the Valley in 1708 and found ten tombs open; the gigantic granite

Ancient Greek graffito of the poet Mikkalos in the tomb of the pharaoh Merneptah, dating probably to the reign of the Emperor Trajan (A.D. 104).

The Theban necropolis as Richard Pococke saw it in 1738: the Colossi of Memnon (M, N), Medinet Habu (K), and the Ramesseum (D) are on the plain below the tombs on the slopes.

Pococke's schematic plan of the Valley of the Kings: Ramesses IV (A); Merneptah (B); Ramesses V/VI (C); Tausert/Sethnakht (G); Sety II (H); Ramesses III (K); Amenmesse (L).

sarcophagus of Ramesses IV and the brilliant colors of the decoration, ''as fresh as on the first day,'' particularly impressed him.

Credit for the first scientific description of the Valley and its tombs is given to the Anglican clergyman Richard Pococke. In Thebes twice in 1738, he made the first serviceable plan of the Valley, although he—like many of those who followed in his footsteps—was threatened by the notorious thieves of Qurna. Pococke also mapped the easily accessible tombs (Ramesses IV and VI, Sety II, Tausert) and described part of the decoration of that of Ramesses IV: the picture above the entrance and the Litany of Re in the first two corridors. He noted fourteen tombs altogether, only nine of which were really accessible, the others being blocked. Like Sicard, he was quite taken by the vivid colors, but he made no copies. When James Bruce visited seven tombs in 1769, he copied the two harpists in the tomb of Ramesses III and was prevented from continuing, as he intended to do, only by the natives. His copies appeared in 1790 and deeply impressed the contemporary world with the first samples of the imagery of the royal tombs, which until then had been seen by only the select few.

Visitors of the following decades brought nothing new. In 1792 William George Browne noted that the natives of the village of Qurna already enjoyed living in the tombs: ''The first village one comes to . . . is called Qurna. It lies on the west side and consists of only a few houses as most of its inhabitants live beneath the earth.''

It was only with the disembarkation of Napoleon's Egyptian expedition at Alexandria in July 1798 that a new period of scientific interest began, as the fascination aroused by ancient Egypt around the time of the French Revolution could now be indulged with proper study. When General Desaix was entrusted with the pursuit of the Mamluks and the conquest of Upper Egypt, the indefatigable Vivant Denon was in his entourage and accompanied the French troops as far as Aswan and Philae, while Napoleon carried out his unsuccessful expedition to Palestine. Although his view was occasionally obscured by the dust of battle, Denon's pencil continued to record the monuments of Upper Egypt. But while he

Vivant Denon's drawing of the ruins of the Ramesseum, the funerary temple of Ramesses II.

was able to realize his dreams and even visit Thebes seven times, war left him little time for his work. And conditions had not changed very much since the days of Pococke and Bruce: from the depths of the tombs, visitors could be "greeted by a hail of stones and javelins, preventing further discoveries," and a real counteroffensive against the villagers subsequently became necessary. Other members of the Institut d'Égypte, founded by Napoleon in Cairo, soon followed Denon, exploring the ruins of Upper Egypt and especially the Valley of the Kings. It was thus that the first discovery of a hitherto unknown tomb was made, in fact the first one dating to Dynasty 18; until then only the Ramesside tombs with their large and representative entrances were known. While scouting around, the engineers Jollois and de Villiers found the hidden tomb of Amenophis III in a western branch of the Valley; and although they could not identify the original owner—having no knowledge of the hieroglyphs—they remarked on the similarity of the mural decoration in the burial chamber to that of writing on papyrus. It was still impossible to read the mysterious texts, but the impression that they contained profound wisdom was inevitable. Jomard and Costaz provided the most detailed contemporary description of the royal tombs when the results of the mission were published in 1821, in the monumental *Description de l'Égypte*. But the opportunity was missed, and the *Description* offers only a few sad glimpses of the decoration, while devoting more attention to the architectural plans. Costaz's sketch plan listed eleven accessible tombs and five others that were either blocked or left unfinished.

After the defeat of the French expedition, with its political implications, it was left to the British to take up the joys of travel and leave accounts of the Valley. The attitude of villagers had changed so profoundly that in 1814 Henry Light was actually able to organize a kind of "excavation" to look for royal mummies. But only a bit of earth was shifted, and without results. The first real and truly successful excavations followed two years later, when Giovanni Battista Belzoni practically stumbled on the tombs of Sety I and Ramesses I.

Belzoni is one of the most fascinating and successful personalities in the history of exploration. Born in 1778, the son of a barber, he fled the political chaos of Italy in 1803 and found a new home in England. In London he joined the Sadler's Wells theater as a "strongman": the high point of his act was the "human pyramid," consisting of ten to twelve persons whom he carried around the stage on an iron frame. Belzoni had studied engineering in Rome and was persuaded to go to the

14

court of the new Egyptian ruler Mohammed Ali, who aspired to modernize his country with European aid. In June 1815, Belzoni entered plague-stricken Alexandria; he was welcomed by the khedive in August, but the irrigation machine he brought was not well received. With the assistance of the Swiss explorer Johann Ludwig Burckhardt, the penniless engineer entered the service of the new British consul, Henry Salt, who was to make a significant contribution to the British Museum with its first major collection of ancient Egyptian monuments.

Belzoni's first highly successful accomplishment was to move the colossal head of a statue from the Ramesseum, the funerary temple of Ramesses II in Thebes. After this, he went on to visit Nubia, including the temples at Abu Simbel, which Burckhardt had discovered a few years earlier, and to his first discovery in the western branch of the Valley of the Kings, the tomb of Pharaoh Aye, the successor of Tutankhamun. A year later, in October 1817, Belzoni's success story continued as he found, in the space of a few days, first the tomb of a late Ramesside prince (Montuherkhepeshef); then that of Ramesses I; and finally, as the crowning glory, ''Belzoni's Tomb,'' actually that of Sety I, which remains today the most significant Egyptian royal tomb of the New Kingdom. This tomb had been emptied of its treasures, and there remained but a few pitiful scraps of the original funerary furnishings; even the royal mummy had been displaced. But the quality and wealth of the colorful decoration were the creations of the most glorious phase of Egyptian relief work in the New Kingdom, overwhelming Belzoni and all those who followed him. The discoverer felt as if the tomb ''had just been completed on the day that we entered it.'' Some 160 years of a steadily increasing flow of tourists—even thousands in the course of a single day—have left little of the original pageant intact, however, and in the winter of 1978–1979 this most important attraction had to be closed to visitors; it has been reopened only occasionally since then.

It is thus very fortunate that Belzoni, together with the artist Alessandro Ricci, copied the tomb completely. All the decoration was recorded in drawings and watercolors, for a model to be exhibited in London in 1821. Belzoni published only a few samples in his narrative, and most of the originals eventually came to the City Museum in Bristol. Belzoni and Ricci deserve our admiration for the fidelity with which they copied while unable to read even a single sign; despite their occasional errors and reversals, the drawings can still be studied with profit today to reconstruct the decoration of the damaged walls, and they prove more reliable than many later copies.

In London, with the model, Belzoni displayed the most valuable original object removed from the tomb itself: the royal sarcophagus of translucent alabaster. It is the first royal stone sarcophagus to depart from the conventional box shape and approach the mummiform, and is decorated on all sides with the complete text of the Book of Gates, several parts of which can be seen also on the tomb walls. This precious sarcophagus came into the possession of the architect Sir John Soane in 1824 and can be seen among the numerous art treasures in the small but packed private museum he founded at Lincoln's Inn Fields in London.

The discovery of the tomb of Sety I disproportionately increased the attractions of the Valley of the Kings and channeled the interest of subsequent travelers, artists, and scholars primarily to this tomb. And Belzoni's conviction that there was nothing more to be found in the Valley remained valid until the close of the century, when a new series of discoveries followed each other in quick succession.

Drawing of a scene in the tomb of Ramesses III taken from Pococke's Description de l'Égypte *(1821) with restorations. A harpist plays before the god Shu, son of Re, who wears the ostrich feather spelling his name on his head.*

With the increasing interest in the royal tombs during the nineteenth century, the number of copies of individual motifs grew. Even if the same unusually striking scenes were repeatedly reproduced, and the drawing of entire tombs not even attempted, the copies made between 1820 and 1840 are collectively of great value, sometimes being the only record of scenes that have since been destroyed completely. The copies by Robert Hay (after 1824) are distinguished by their unusual fidelity and sure grasp of style, but even John Gardiner Wilkinson (after 1821), James Burton (after 1824), and Nestor l'Hôte (1838–1839) did a far better job than their immediate successors.

After 1822, Jean-François Champollion's extraordinary decipherment of hieroglyphs assured that these texts could finally be read and the illustrations better understood. Champollion himself spent three months of his long Egyptian journey, from March to June 1829, in the Valley of the Kings, sharing the tomb of Ramesses IV—the best "hotel" in the country—with his companions. Vague speculations about the significance and meaning of the decoration were replaced by the first reasoned insights in the thirteenth of Champollion's *Lettres écrites d'Égypte et de Nubie, en 1828 et 1829*. Up to that point, it had been assumed that the texts on the tomb walls contained reports on the life and deeds of the pharaohs. Champollion realized, however, that these were exclusively concerned with the pharaoh's afterlife, his crossing the lower hemisphere like the sun, in order to be born again. At the same time, Champollion sensed that the descriptions of the other world were analogous to those of Dante's Inferno, and that the texts and pictures of the royal tombs revealed "the entire cosmological system and general physical laws of the Egyptians." In the symbolic representations of this most refined mysticism were "ancient truths concealed, considered by us to be very recent." Champollion was the first to recognize that certain textual and pictorial cycles appeared in almost every tomb; he described these religious texts in detail and even provided long translations accompanied by careful copies of the illustrations and hieroglyphic texts; these are still an indispensable aid for work on the Books of the Netherworld.

The next major expedition to arrive in the Valley of the Kings was financed by the Prussian king Friedrich Wilhelm IV and led by C. R. Lepsius. In the winter of 1844–1845 this group surveyed the entire Valley, cleared the debris from a number of tombs, and copied many examples from the decoration, which Lepsius published shortly thereafter in the monumental volumes entitled *Denkmaeler aus Aegypten und Aethiopien*. However, like Adolf Erman after him, Lepsius found it difficult to appreciate these religious works. Only Gaston Maspero's research built on that of Champollion, and brought new insights and more precise translations.

Maspero's name is eternally bound up with that of the royal mummies. His term of office as director of the Egyptian Antiquities Service began with two major discoveries in 1881. The oldest existing collection of religious spells, the Pyramid Texts of the Old Kingdom, was discovered when the pyramids of Dynasties 5 and 6 were opened in Saqqara. And in Thebes, Maspero succeeded in discovering the origin of certain grave goods that had turned up on the antiquities market after 1874.

A few years earlier, villagers had found a tomb in the steep walls of Deir el-Bahri that had originally served as the tomb of the family of the high priest Pinudjem II (ca. 980 B.C.), but that was also used as a cache for the mummies of most of the pharaohs of the New Kingdom. Lengthy interrogations eventually led to the revelation of the secret of this cache, and a quickly assembled commission of the Antiq-

While accompanying Jean-François Champollion in Egypt, Nestor l'Hôte drew this scene; the original is now damaged. Amenophis III and his ka face the goddess Nut, who greets the king with a sprinkling of purified water.

Royal mummy from the cache at Deir el-Bahri, decorated by priests with garlands of flowers and lotus blossoms, as drawn by Schweinfurth at the time of its discovery in 1881.

uities Service was completely overwhelmed by a dreamlike vision: some forty coffins containing the remains of—according to their ancient labels—not only queens, princes, and high priests, but also some of the most important pharaohs of the New Kingdom, including Ahmose, the founder of the New Kingdom; the martial Tuthmosis III; Sety I and his son Ramesses II; and even Ramesses III, the last great Ramesside, who fended off the so-called Sea Peoples. Until then the numerous pyramids and rock tombs had not produced a single royal mummy, and now one find had brought a full dozen to light.

News of the royal cache so aroused the imagination of the villagers—there were rumors of whole coffers filled with gold and gems—that it was imperative to act swiftly to ward off an attack on the tomb. In July 1881 it was emptied as quickly as possible, and the royal mummies started their last voyage, in a Nile steamer bound for Cairo; the riverbanks were thronged and the journey became a real funeral procession, with women clad in black raising the shrill call of mourning intended for the last voyage of the deceased.

Meanwhile, progress on the interpretation of the religious texts in the royal tombs proceeded apace. Édouard Naville published several texts (the Litany of Re, the Book of the Celestial Cow) in complete and reliable copies before producing what would become the standard edition of the Book of the Dead, a collection of funerary texts used by commoners. Eugène Lefébure supplied a first translation of the Book of Gates for the series Records of the Past. Accompanied by Bouriant and Loret, he returned to the Valley in February and March 1883, and in a matter of weeks took a basic inventory of as much of the necropolis as was then known. He also drew the tombs of Sety I and Ramesses IV in exemplary fashion and made more or less detailed descriptions of the remaining tombs. Unfortunately this material, which Lefébure presented to the public in his *Hypogées royaux de Thèbes*, has the limitations of work done quickly and cursorily; it is advisable to turn to the earlier, far more reliable copies wherever possible.

Maspero also returned frequently to the Valley, attempting to find his way further into the bizarre world of the Books of the Netherworld on the tomb walls. His studies, initially published in 1888–1889 in the *Revue de l'histoire des religions*, proceeded for the first time beyond Champollion's basic premises. Maspero produced an early, almost complete translation of the oldest of the Books of the Netherworld, the Amduat, and encouraged his pupil Gustave Jéquier to edit a short version of this book (1894). Maspero was the first to grasp the significance of many motifs and passages in the Amduat and other descriptions of the Beyond. His researches led Chantepie de la Saussaye to identify the Books of the Netherworld as "the most important source for knowledge about the contemporary solar theology" in *Lehrbuch der Religionsgeschichte* (1897). Previous interpretations of this text genre suffered from the fact that aside from the tomb of Amenophis III, no other Dynasty 18 version was known. The Ramesside copies that were used bristled with errors and were disfigured by misunderstood passages.

This situation changed in 1898–1899, when Victor Loret discovered in rapid succession the tombs of Tuthmosis I, Tuthmosis III, and Amenophis II, the three earliest decorated tombs in the Valley. A considerably improved basis for textual criticism was thus available, but several decades passed before it was put to proper use. The next sensation was Loret's discovery of a second cache of royal mummies in the tomb of Amenophis II. Resting here, aside from the owner of the tomb, were his two prominent successors Tuthmosis IV and Amenophis III, as well as Merneptah, the son of Ramesses II and supposed pharaoh of Exodus. Amenophis II was left in the relative peace of his open sarcophagus while the other pharaohs were taken to a family reunion in the old Bulaq Museum, the first Egyptian Museum in Cairo, where they joined the others from the Deir el-Bahri cache, who had already been somewhat pestered by insects. The whole twin discovery was later placed in a mausoleum, where the pharaohs underwent further sufferings due to the dampness of the place, to which they were unaccustomed. Since 1959 the mummies of these once great rulers have been housed in a special hall of the Cairo Museum and improved storage for them is now being planned. The mummies constitute not only unique ''anthropological material'' but also the remains of personalities who determined the course of human history more than 3,000 years ago.

Loret's discoveries were only the prelude to a number of further finds in the Valley of the Kings. New York businessman Theodore M. Davis received an excavation concession for work there in 1902; his first excavation director was Howard Carter, who had come to Egypt as a draftsman and served as a local inspector for the Antiquities Service. Having become thoroughly familiar with the Theban necropolis in this capacity, Carter found another Dynasty 18 tomb (Tuthmosis II). In Davis's service, Carter made a series of discoveries, among them the tomb of Hatshepsut built after she declared herself king, those of Tuthmosis IV and Siptah, and the rich funerary treasure of Yuya and Tuya, Amenophis III's in-laws.

In 1907 Carter entered the service of the fifth Earl of Carnarvon. His extensive collection of notes, plans, and collations kept today at the Griffith Institute at Oxford testifies to his continuing interest in the royal tombs. At that point Davis worked with Edward Ayrton in the Valley of the Kings, and on February 25, 1908, his previous successes were crowned with a further discovery—the royal tomb begun by Haremheb after his accession, intended to replace his hardly less significant private tomb in Saqqara (rediscovered in 1975). Thus the most perfect reliefs of a New Kingdom royal tomb were brought to light, and with them the earliest known version of the Book of Gates. Further, the unfinished parts of the tomb offered insights into the entire process of making a royal tomb. Four years later Davis published photographs of the entire tomb.

Davis and Maspero now shared the opinion that every nook and cranny had been explored and that this discovery exhausted what the Valley had to offer. Lord Carnarvon, who was given Davis's concession in 1914, supported Howard Carter's desire to continue the search after 1917. Their object was the tomb of a king who had died at a tender age, Tutankhamun. Carter's intensive, determined efforts were rewarded on his final attempt in November 1922. Just below the frequently visited tomb of Ramesses VI, his workers came across a series of steps cut into the rock, leading to the sealed tomb entrance.

Ever since that winter of 1922–1923, the world has repeatedly suffered from ''Tut fever,'' and since 1967, when ''King Tut'' went traveling, millions have marveled at the treasures recovered by Carter. It was of course pure luck that the tomb had not been discovered earlier, and its recovery and conservation posed difficult enough problems for its finders. But Carter was immediately offered the aid of specialists from the Metropolitan Museum of Art in New York, who were working nearby, as well as the expertise of many prominent Egyptologists. The somewhat distant tomb of Sety II was hurriedly turned into a provisional laboratory

View into the tomb of Ramesses IV. The airy corridors served as a ''hotel'' for Champollion's expedition and for others later. The sarcophagus of the pharaoh, 8 feet, 6 inches high, is visible at the end of the corridor.

and the Metropolitan's excellent photographer Harry Burton recorded each stage of the work; gratitude is also due to him for the unpublished series of photographs of the entire tomb of Sety I.

One always meets with disbelief when remarking that most of this popular treasure remains unpublished. Not even the famous gold mask, the very signet of every Tutankhamun exhibition, has been the subject of a scientific publication, and only recently were the first useful photographs of the reverse made available. Taking second place behind the enthusiastic treasure-hunting in the Valley of the Kings conducted by Ali Abd el-Rassul even as late as 1960, the analysis of this abundant material has received short shrift and proceeded slowly.

After the interest expressed by Maspero and E. A. W. Budge in the world of the royal tombs, the next generation was deterred by Adolf Erman, whose authority as the best Egyptian philologist gave weight to his condemnation of this "philistine geography of the Beyond"; in his standard work on the religion of the ancient Egyptians he is more emphatic, stating that "whoever stumbles into the gaping corridors of these giant tombs finds himself surrounded on all sides by the figures of the Amduat, as if the ancient Egyptians had nothing more serious to say about life after death than these masks." In 1936 Herman Kees still found that the Amduat and the Book of Gates belonged to "the least sympathetic aspects of all Egyptian literature," but he added prophetically that "perhaps even this will change."

In fact it was assumed for quite a while that the impressive decoration of these tombs built during the most glorious period of Egyptian history could be traced back to the fantastic speculations of magicians and sorcerers, and was thus unworthy of further attention. The intellectual treasures of the Valley, already remarked on by Champollion and Maspero, were thus buried beneath the debris of prejudice, incomprehension, and the extension of modern values and ways of thought; strenuous efforts to free them once again for contemplation were required.

Decisive impulses came from Alexandre Piankoff, a Russian scholar who had left his country after the 1917 revolution to pursue studies in Germany and France. From 1930 until his death in 1966 he spent most of his time in Egypt. After taking part in an expedition to Coptic monasteries near the Red Sea, he was completely entranced by the irresistible spell of the Valley of the Kings and was fascinated by the hitherto neglected texts and representations on the walls of the royal tombs. The Book of Gates, the first fascicle of which he published with Charles Maystre in 1939, served as the beginning of a rich series of texts he published in the following years. Supported by an appreciation for and interest in unfamiliar forms of religious expression, Piankoff attempted to take the illustrations of the Books of the Netherworld seriously, and to explain them step by step in terms of the rest of Egyptian religious literature. His editing and interpreting brought this previously misunderstood literature to the attention of his professional colleagues, even if it has not yet assumed its deserved place in any explanation of Egyptian religion.

New possibilities were realized by Piankoff's cooperation with N. Rambova and with the Bollingen Foundation, who photographed the interior of the tomb of Ramesses VI for him in 1949–1951. When *The Tomb of Ramesses VI* appeared in 1954, it was the first complete publication of a royal tomb, with excellent photographs, as well as an inventory, description, and translation of each element of the decoration. A few years later we began investigating the tomb of Amenophis III and formed a

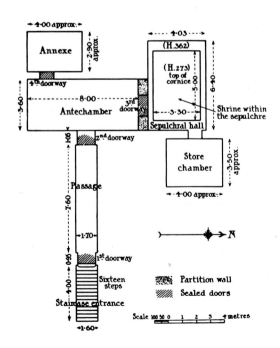

Howard Carter's ground plan of the tomb of Tutankhamun.

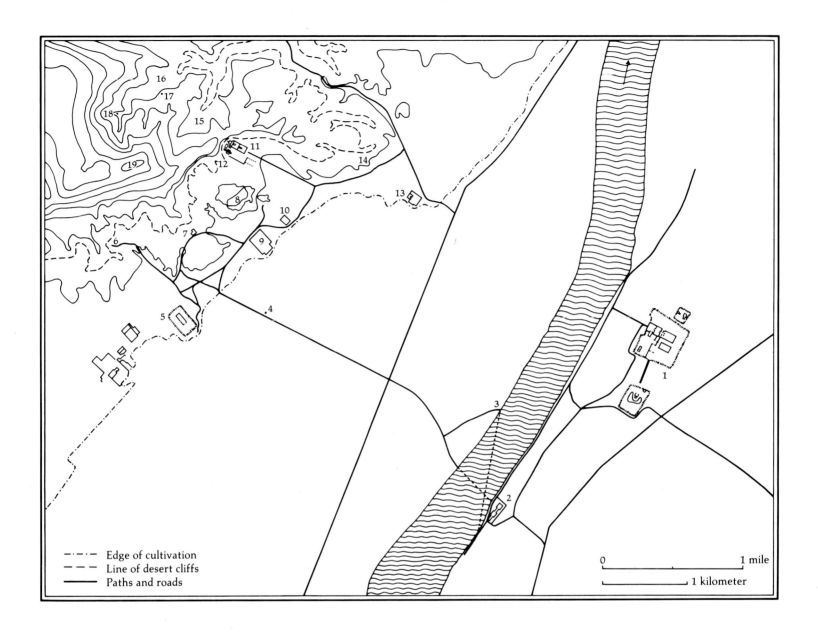

MAP OF THEBES

1	Temples at Karnak	11	Deir el-Bahari with funerary temple of Hatshepsut
2	Temple at Luxor		
3	Landing on west bank of Nile	12	Royal cache
4	Colossi of Memnon	13	Funerary temple of Sety I
5	Medinet Habu, funerary temple of Ramesses III	14	Dra abu'l Naga
6	Valley of the Queens	15	Valley of the Kings, main branch
7	Deir el-Medina	16	Valley of the Kings, west branch
8	Qurna tombs and village	17	Tomb of Amenophis III
9	Ramesseum, funerary temple of Ramesses II	18	Tomb of Aye
10	Funerary temple of Tuthmosis III	19	el-Qurn, the peak called "the horn"

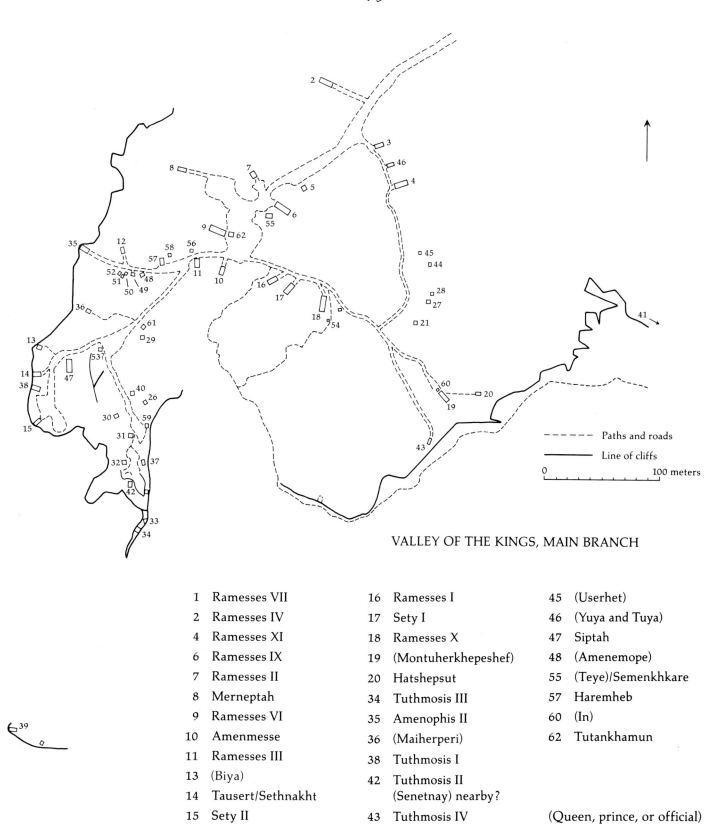

VALLEY OF THE KINGS, MAIN BRANCH

- - - - Paths and roads
—— Line of cliffs

0   100 meters

1	Ramesses VII	16	Ramesses I	45	(Userhet)
2	Ramesses IV	17	Sety I	46	(Yuya and Tuya)
4	Ramesses XI	18	Ramesses X	47	Siptah
6	Ramesses IX	19	(Montuherkhepeshef)	48	(Amenemope)
7	Ramesses II	20	Hatshepsut	55	(Teye)/Semenkhkare
8	Merneptah	34	Tuthmosis III	57	Haremheb
9	Ramesses VI	35	Amenophis II	60	(In)
10	Amenmesse	36	(Maiherperi)	62	Tutankhamun
11	Ramesses III	38	Tuthmosis I		
13	(Biya)	42	Tuthmosis II (Senetnay) nearby?		
14	Tausert/Sethnakht				
15	Sety II	43	Tuthmosis IV		(Queen, prince, or official)

plan to tackle the rest of the still unpublished tombs in the Valley. This project was brought to an abrupt halt by Piankoff's death. Until now only *Das Grab des Haremhab*, produced jointly by Frank Teichmann and myself, has provided color publication of a king's tomb. Most of the tombs in the Valley still await a scientific analysis, including even such prominent tombs as those of Tutankhamun and Sety I; these projects are condemned to compete with gradual decay.

Herman Grapow and Siegfried Schott also devoted attention to the texts of the royal tombs, which were called "Guides to the Beyond" in the earlier literature but can now be called, more appropriately, Books of the Netherworld. Both Grapow and Schott encouraged me as a young student to continue along the way paved by Piankoff's text editions, and publish an edition of the Amduat available in about twenty (mostly incomplete) versions from the New Kingdom, and more frequently on funerary papyri thereafter.

I have not been freed from my work in the Valley of the Kings since then. After the Amduat, other religious works required new, improved editions and in many cases even a first interpretation in terms of content. These texts testify to the almost scientific interest in that far-off age to study the fate of the dead. While including powerful images of the Egyptian visions of the Beyond, the books also involve ruthlessly sober analyses, without their equals in depth and detailed precision. Forcing our way into the imagery of these royal funerary texts leads to a new adventure of exploration; it changes or enhances many of our ideas about Egyptian religion, and allows surprising glimpses into the depths of the world contained within ourselves.

The analysis of texts and pictures is not the only "treasure hunt" taking place in the Valley of the Kings today. Elizabeth Thomas and John Romer have recently studied the practically disregarded undecorated tombs, as well as the larger decorated ones, creating a new basis for the study of the architecture. Much remains to be done here, and it is likewise to be expected that the promising researches of Friedrich Abitz will lead to the comprehension of other details in the construction and decoration of the tombs. Precise measurements and observations have been made by our team from the University of Basel that has allowed us to identify the canon of significant measurement and proportions used during the New Kingdom for the architecture and pictorial cycles in the royal tombs. It is clear that every detail was carefully thought out in advance, and one can pursue the development of the tomb plan from one reign to the next, in light of a simple basic law governing the architecture of the royal tomb: "the extension of the existing." With these insights into the New Kingdom, a different perspective emerges for both royal and private tombs of earlier periods as well. The next chapter is intended to place the tombs of the New Kingdom Valley of the Kings in their historical context.

THE ARCHITECTURE OF
THE ROYAL TOMBS

CHAPTER 2

The history of the Egyptian royal tomb spans more than 3,000 years, from the kings of the Archaic Period to the Ptolemies of Hellenistic Alexandria. The visible form of the tomb easily permits the division of this long period into four phases. The first phase (ca. 3000–2600 B.C.) was characterized by the mastaba, the second (ca. 2600–1500 B.C.) by the pyramid, the third (ca. 1500–1100 B.C.) by the rock-cut tomb, and the fourth (after 1100 B.C.) by the temenos tomb. In each phase, a hierarchy assured that the royal tomb be preeminently distinguished from all others in shape, size, or position. Although this book is concerned primarily with tombs of the third phase, the rock-cut tombs of the Valley of the Kings, this chapter surveys the development of the royal tomb from its origins.

The Egyptian state emerged from its prehistoric background with the unification of the two kingdoms of Upper and Lower Egypt around 3000 B.C. A number of early kings contributed to the political unification of the country. These kings were then transformed by the Egyptians of the New Kingdom 1,500 years later into a single idealized pharaoh, Menes, who personified the historical beginning, the transfer of sovereignty from gods to men. Contemporary sources identify Narmer and Aha as the first significant pharaohs; their tombs still exist today, and the tombs of their immediate predecessors are most probably in the first cemetery at Abydos, north of Thebes.

The earliest tombs are rather modest brick-lined rectangular chambers sunk into the earth (about 10 by 13 to 15 by 25 feet); these introduce a new phase of tomb construction when compared with simple prehistoric tombs. Their superstructures cannot be restored with certainty, but we may assume that they were mastabas:

Ground plan and cross-section of a royal tomb from Dynasty 1 at Saqqara.

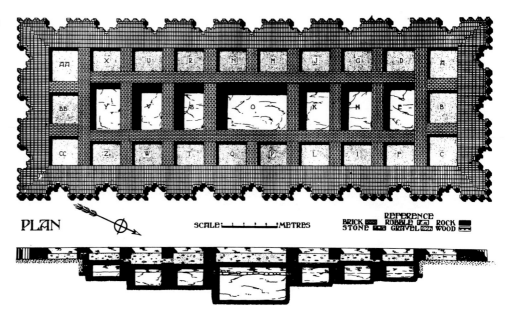

PLAN

SCALE ⌐⌐⌐⌐⌐ METRES

REFERENCE
BRICK ▓ RUBBLE ▨ ROCK ▉
STONE ▦ GRAVEL ▨ WOOD ▤

rectangular crude brick barrows with slanting sides. It appears that from the beginning the early royal tombs were double tombs in which the superstructure covered two chambers arranged side by side. This twinning can be pursued throughout the entire history of the Egyptian royal tomb. Another example of duality is the founding, under Pharaoh Aha, of a second cemetery at Saqqara, across the river from Memphis.

At the start of Dynasty 3 (ca. 2600 B.C.), Pharaoh Djoser and his chief architect, Imhotep, united previously separate elements of the royal tomb into a single monumental complex, employing for the first time stone, a durable material particularly well suited for the eternity of the Beyond. Pharaoh Den of Dynasty 1 had already laid a granite pavement in his Abydos burial chamber, but that was the most ambitious project in stone attempted by the pharaohs of the Early Dynastic Period. Now, from one generation to the next, the dead ruler was supplied with a complete residence in stone. More than a mile long, Djoser's bright white limestone walls rose 33 feet above the desert, enclosing a rectangular complex of almost 45 acres complete with two tombs. The southern tomb was oriented toward the setting sun, and the northern was transformed into a stepped pyramid almost 200 feet high, oriented to the north and surrounded by abundant religious structures of solid stone, including a court and chapels for the gods, to be used in celebrating the festival of renewal. Some subterranean chambers stored grave goods, while others were decorated with relief representations of the pharaoh himself. This first pyramid thus became the symbol of the necropolis at Memphis—it dominates the horizon even today—as it never fell beneath the shadow of the neighboring constructions erected by Djoser's successors.

At the transition to Dynasty 4, royal architects sought new forms, filling in the pyramid steps with solid material, as at the Meidum pyramid, and transforming the southern tomb into a smaller second pyramid not intended for interment. Only in the reign of Cheops did the whole complex reach its ultimate fourfold form, under the direction of the royal chief architect Hemiun and his staff. The pyramid tomb, built between 2550 and 2530 B.C. at Giza, was accompanied by funerary temples and a causeway as well as monumental boats buried in their own stone-lined pits around the pyramid; these guaranteed the deceased king freedom of movement in the heavenly Beyond. The afterlife is likewise indicated by the northward orientation of the entrance corridor, which ascends at an angle of 26 to 27 degrees and creates a direct line from the circumpolar stars to the burial chamber. The pharaoh could thus climb to the "indestructible" stars of the northern sky who accepted him in their number and prevented him from sinking into the depths of the Netherworld.

At 480 feet, the incredible Cheops pyramid towers above all others, and yet it belongs to the experimental period at the start of Dynasty 4. Instead of a subterranean burial chamber and a separate second tomb in the south, both were built into the core of a single pyramid, reviving the ancient principle of duality in a different way; this solution was attempted only once, however. The stupendous grand gallery with its splendidly joined blocks does not appear in any other pyramid, and it is understandable that the pyramid of Cheops is always assigned a special role permitting its exploitation in terms of mystical numbers. But all speculations concerning mysterious and prophetic proportions and the reflection of cosmic

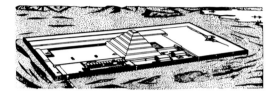

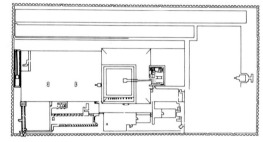

Ground plan and reconstruction of Djoser's pyramid in Saqqara. (Plate 6.)

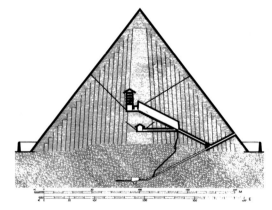

Cross-section of the pyramid of Cheops. The main chamber is not underground as in other pyramids, but within the core of the building. The lower scale refers to Egyptian cubits. (See plate 9.)

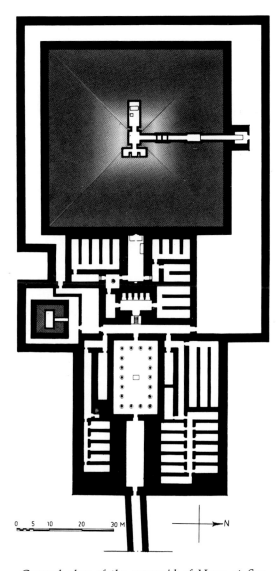

Ground plan of the pyramid of Unas at Saqqara, with the adjoining funerary temple and second pyramid.

0 5 10   20   30 M   ►—N

dimensions in the pyramid are doomed to failure: they are based on imprecise, obsolete measurements. The ancient Egyptians were not the least bit concerned with the precise value of pi to the nth decimal place or with the distance between the earth and the sun. Important to them were clear, comprehensible proportions governing the size of chambers and corridors. Thus, the larger chamber is 10 by 20 Egyptian cubits (1 cubit = seven palms, or about 20⅝ inches), and the 2-cubit-wide corridors have the same breadth as the pillars in the chapel rooms outside the pyramid.

Chephren, who built the second large pyramid at Giza, created a balanced organization reflected in later complexes. After Mycerinus, who erected the third pyramid of the Giza trio, new changes in the conception of the royal tomb become apparent, and at the end of Dynasty 4, Pharaoh Shepseskaf and Queen Khenty-kaus completely abandoned the pyramid-shaped tomb. The pharaohs of Dynasty 5 erected pyramids of quite modest dimensions.

The last two pharaohs of Dynasty 5, Izezi and Unas, brought the development of the royal tomb complex of the Old Kingdom to an end. While the burial chambers of Unas's predecessors had been free of ornamentation, the ceiling of his chamber was decorated with stars, and cut into the walls was a collection of the most varied spells imaginable, all related in one way or another to the royal burial. They guide the procedures of necessary rituals, the pharaoh's ascent into heaven, and provide for his general welfare in face of dangers and uncertain supplies in the Beyond. The aspiration of the deceased is royal: acquiring sovereignty among the gods in the Beyond and becoming the supreme god. The demands of this role grow until the dead pharaoh hunts and violently devours the gods and their magical powers (spells 273–274). At the same time, the deceased appears as Osiris, the suffering, murdered, and resurrected ruler-god, husband and brother of Isis. These spells are of enormous significance, as they are the oldest known group of religious texts.

Political disintegration and economic chaos at the end of Dynasty 6 forced a change of course in tomb construction and in the material aspects of the funerary cult. In the northern part of the kingdom the royal tomb retained the pyramid form, but the Dynasty 11 Theban princes in the south preferred different forms based on local traditions. Mentuhotep II, who succeeded in uniting the entire country around 2040 B.C. and whose reign marks the beginning of the Middle Kingdom, crowned this provincial development at Thebes with a highly original tomb in the basin of Deir el-Bahri. Before the impressive cliffs rose a terraced superstructure, furnished with magnificent columned halls and pillared passages, but without a crowning pyramid, according to the most recent reconstruction. Below, sunk into the earth, two corridor tombs emphasized the ancient duality of the royal tomb in a novel manner. The inclusion of the cult of the Theban god Amun here anticipates the funerary temples of the New Kingdom.

When Amenemhat I, who founded Dynasty 12, returned the royal residence to the north, the Middle Kingdom quite deliberately took up the traditions of Dynasty 6 as seen in the pyramid complex of Pepy II: the new tomb complexes are essentially copies of the pyramid precincts of the late Old Kingdom, with minimal adjustments. Most important is the absence of decoration in the interior rooms. The Pyramid Texts were abandoned, to be freed for use by private people. After undergoing many changes they reappeared on the wooden coffins of officials and their dependents as the Coffin Texts. And the Beyond of the Coffin Texts no longer lies in the heavens; it is bound up with Osiris, the sovereign of the Kingdom of the Dead in the Netherworld.

This fundamental shift from sky-oriented to Osiris-oriented funerary reliefs soon affected the royal tomb complex. Around 1890 B.C. Senwosret II abandoned the conventional north orientation of the pyramid entrance, which was thereafter not governed by the cardinal points. At the same time, the single straight passage leading to the burial chamber was transformed into a complicated system of winding passages: a veritable labyrinth beneath the pyramid, which was intended not (or at least not primarily) to deceive tomb robbers but to embody the basic precepts of the new Beyond. And the profound transformation of the royal image under Senwosret III, which approaches the realism of portraiture for us, did not so much reflect the actual appearance of the ruler as bring the pharaoh closer to Osiris, the divine ruler who suffered and died. However, the late Middle Kingdom retained the pyramid shape for the kings, and even the tomb superstructures of the Theban princes during the Hyksos rule should probably be imagined as having had this form.

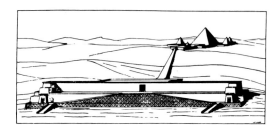

Reconstruction of the pyramid precinct of Pepy II, with the valley temple, causeway, funerary temple, small pyramids, and larger royal pyramid.

Thus we find ourselves at the dawn of the New Kingdom, when the use of the pyramid for the royal tomb was abandoned forever. The location and form of the earliest Dynasty 18 burials are unknown. The temples as well as the mummies that have been discovered suggest that they were in Thebes (although Ahmose possessed a second tomb at Abydos). After Tuthmosis I (ca. 1500 B.C.), rock tombs were excavated in the Valley of the Kings and separate funerary temples were erected nearby in the cultivated area at the edge of the desert where the king would be worshipped after his body had been placed in the tomb and the tomb sealed.

We can only speculate on why this remote valley was chosen as the new burial site, although there were probably a number of different reasons. As far as a religious motive, there may have been an association with Hathor, who was worshipped in the basin of Deir el-Bahri on the east side of the mountain and who since the Middle Kingdom was associated with rejuvenation. An architectural reason was

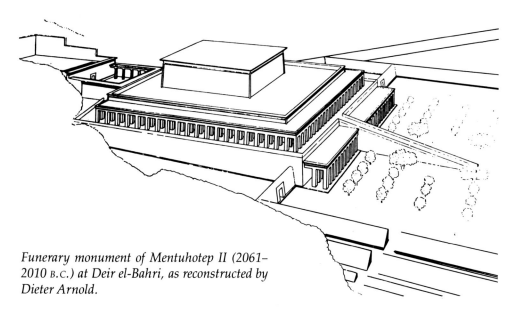

Funerary monument of Mentuhotep II (2061–2010 B.C.) at Deir el-Bahri, as reconstructed by Dieter Arnold.

the pyramid shape of the peak of the mountain towering above the valley. Finally, the remoteness of the valley meant that it could be easily sealed off and guarded. The earliest tombs known were well concealed at the base of steep cliffs wherever possible.

The tombs we associate with these early Dynasty 18 pharaohs are very simple structures when compared with the historical importance of the pharaohs themselves: Tuthmosis I was the first to cross the Euphrates; Tuthmosis III was a great conqueror and, after his death, a guardian for the living and a figure of legend. The long axis of Tuthmosis I's chamber is 33 feet, 9½ inches (just under 20 cubits). The plans for all the tombs in the Valley of the Kings are gathered in the appendix. The crooked lines of the Beyond are observed in the gently curving—later sharply turning—axis of the tomb, which can be traced back to the change in the principles of late Dynasty 12, but were now carried with a rhythmic alternation of stairs and sloping passages descending steeply into the bowels of the earth, as in the tomb of his descendant Amenophis II. Tuthmosis II and Tuthmosis III both had oval burial chambers, corresponding to the oval end of the Amduat—the earliest Book of the Netherworld—illustrating the curvature of the Beyond and recalling the oval form of the royal cartouche.

Tuthmosis III interrupted the sloping passages and stairs with a shaft or well. The shaft was subsequently incorporated into the canonical architecture of the royal tomb and then disappeared at the end of Dynasty 19. Streams from the infrequent but devastating desert rainstorms were thereby prevented from reaching the burial chamber and its valuable contents, and an obstacle for tomb robbers was simultaneously created. But as far as we can tell, the Egyptians never undertook architectural changes out of mere practicality or desire to profit from some technical advance. That this shaft served some other purpose—aside from the collection of rainwater—is clear from the simple fact that it is one of the few decorated parts of the tomb; the corridors of the tombs of this period were normally devoid of decoration. Distinctions in the inscriptions hint that the room was a passage from this world to the Beyond, serving the resurrection of the deceased. The other focal points plastered for subsequent painting in the tomb of Tuthmosis III were the burial chamber and the antechamber. In royal tombs after Tuthmosis III, the shaft was followed by an upper pillared hall related to the lower one, intended for the reception of the royal sarcophagus and apparently recalling the ancient duality of the royal tomb. The pillars were also plastered, but before the reign of Sety I, only those in the burial chamber were painted.

The distribution of decorative motifs over the available surfaces in these early tombs was clearly defined. Up to Haremheb at the end of Dynasty 18, the only text used on the walls of the main burial chamber was the Amduat. At first all twelve hours of the Amduat were placed on the walls, with the summary version in line hieroglyphs, imitating precisely the signs and figures on the papyrus original. After Amenophis III parts of the Amduat were excerpted for use in the burial chamber. The remaining plastered surfaces showed the pharaoh before divinities who were to play an important role in his afterlife, and the ceilings of the shaft, antechamber, and burial chamber were painted for the most part blue with yellow stars, depicting the heavens.

The plan, decoration, and measures employed were all part of an elegant development dominated by what I see as the principle of growth; the new canon of

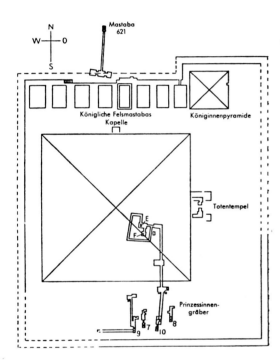

Ground plan of the pyramid complex of Senwosret II (ca. 1890 B.C.) at Illahun.

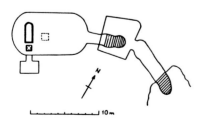

Ground plan of the tomb of Tuthmosis I. A pillar (now destroyed), the sarcophagus, and the canopic chest are shown in the burial chamber.

measures and decorative elements governing both royal and private tombs of the New Kingdom was continuously extended. Each royal tomb was a deliberately larger complex, regardless of the length of the reign. This law of the "extension of the existing," was equally applicable to tomb and temple, and governed all acts of the pharaoh; the king could reenact the deeds of the Creator, returning the world to its pristine state, but he was also obliged to go beyond all that preceded. For hundreds of years, the beginning of each reign was marked by an attempt to add some new element to the plan of the royal tomb (new corridors, side chambers, or pillars); to embellish the decoration itself with new motifs; or to increase progressively the length of a cubit whereby chambers were larger, corridors broader and higher (although not necessarily longer), and the royal sarcophagus larger.

Only Akhenaton, the great reformer in other areas, opposed the steady enlargement and the propensity for the gigantic, which triumphed in the funerary temples of his father, Amenophis III, and its incredible colossal statues (the later Colossi of Memnon). Structures of the Amarna Period are deliberately built with handy small stone blocks, and the royal tomb at the new residence of Amarna was kept within relatively modest bounds with very few modules. An important and enduring change introduced by Akhenaton was the return to a single axis in the royal tomb. This was not however, as in the Pyramid Age, directed at the circumpolar stars; it opened the tomb to the rays of the sun, Aton, the god of light. The new development continued to its logical conclusion in the late Ramesside tombs of Dynasty 20, which were flooded with light and did not seek the depths.

Despite his efforts, Akhenaton did not succeed in reforming the spiritual world of ancient Egypt. This failure was followed initially by a period of uncertainty; his immediate successors, Tutankhamun and Aye, resorted to highly provisional changes in the royal tomb, mixing previously separate elements of private and royal tombs. A new concept is reflected in the tomb of Haremheb. Its straight, slightly displaced axis differed substantially from that of the prototype, the tomb of Amenophis III. Another variation was the return of the tombs to the Valley proper from the west branch of the Valley, which had been used by Amenophis III and Aye. And for the first time, the Amduat was not used to decorate the burial chamber—not even in excerpts, as in the tombs of Tutankhamun and Aye. In its place was a new Book of the Netherworld, the Book of Gates, but even this was not complete; thereafter the Books of the Netherworld were cut up and their various divisions distributed around the most different rooms of the tomb like theater backdrops; in the end, Ramesses IX put sections of the most disparate works side by side on the walls of his tomb.

Another of Haremheb's decisive innovations was the switch from mural paintings to painted reliefs. His royal tomb in Thebes was left unfinished and thus is very instructive for studying the excavation and decoration of a royal tomb. The finished wall surfaces offer us painted bas-relief of a quality and sculptural perfection never seen again.

After the death of Haremheb, Ramesses I founded Dynasty 19. The aging pharaoh was granted only a year and a half of earthly kingship, and his staff did not even plan a full-scale royal tomb, being content with a burial chamber bereft of pillars at the end of a single short corridor. The dimensions and decoration of the burial chamber comprise the basic elements of the royal tomb; however the decora-

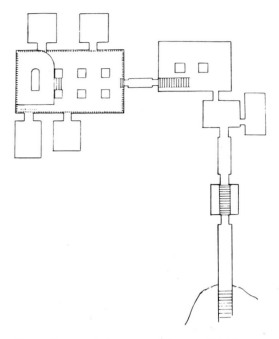

Ground plan of the tomb of Amenophis II, son of Tuthmosis III. For the first time the burial chamber includes a deeper area for the sarcophagus. The walls of the burial chamber were decorated with texts from the Amduat.

tion included new divine scenes and motifs. But because of the pressure of time the paintings were not executed in relief. Even the sarcophagus was only painted in this exceptional case.

While Sety I, Ramesses's son, certainly took part in planning his father's tomb, his own took the evolution of the royal tomb to its climax: decoration was not sparingly reserved for certain selected parts of the tomb, but every interior surface was decorated in color. The tombs of Sety I and Ramesses II were also completely decorated in bas-relief—except for the ceilings, which were merely painted. As in the central axis of a temple, the ceiling of the first corridor here was adorned with flying vultures, which protected the way into the tomb, and the vaulted ceiling of the deep-set part of the burial chamber imitated the heavenly vault, with constellations replacing simple yellow stars on a blue background. Sety I's alabaster sarcophagus was the first royal sarcophagus to be covered with decoration on all its surfaces.

Architectural additions permitted the creation of a pictorial program that would have been impossible with the previous scheme. The adequate wall surface of Sety's tomb allowed both the Amduat and the Book of Gates (although incomplete) to be placed side by side, along with the complete Litany of Re (only part of which

Development of the canon of measurements in the royal tombs. (Figures are in meters; 1 Egyptian cubit is about 52.3 cm.)

	Corridor width	Corridor height	Doors
Thutmosis I	2.30	1.70	1.27/1.45
Hatshepsut	1.80/2.30	2.05	
Thutmosis III	2.05/2.16	to 1.96	1.01/1.88
Amenophis II	1.55/1.64	1.99/2.30	1.30/1.42
Thutmosis IV	1.98/1.99	2.10/2.20	1.72/1.83
Amenophis III	2.51/2.56	2.54./2.83	2.01/2.08
Tutankhamun	1.68	2.05	1.49/1.50
Aye	2.60/2.64	2.47	2.12
Haremheb	2.59/2.64	2.59/2.64	2.04/2.11
Ramesses I	2.61/2.62	2.58	2.05/2.10
Sety I	2.61	2.61	2.07/2.10
Ramesses II	2.62	2.62	1.99/2.10
Merneptah	2.60	3.10/3.27	as corridor
Amenmesse	2.70/2.71	3.15	2.16/2.19
Sety II	2.82	3.25/3.29	2.17/2.28
Siptah	2.61/2.62	3.24/3.34	2.03/2.09
Ramesses III	2.64/2.69	3:32/3.36	2.10/2.18
Ramesses IV	3.12/3.17	3.94/4.18	2.55/2.76
Ramesses VI	3.15/3.19	3.60/4.05	2.61/2.80
Ramesses VII	3.13	4.10	2.75
Ramesses IX	3.24/3.25	4.09	2.77/2.78
Ramesses X	3.17	4.01	2.72
Ramesses XI	3.18/3.30	4.10	2.80/2.86

had appeared on the pillars of the burial chamber of Tuthmosis III), the Book of the Celestial Cow, the ritual of the Opening of the Mouth, and dozens of divinities, for which extra pillars in the side chambers provided additional space. The sarcophagus itself provided space for another, complete copy of the Book of Gates.

Ramesses II adopted the changes from his father's tomb and elaborated on them. While Sety I equipped his pillared halls much as his predecessors had done, Ramesses II chose a new path, which subsequent pharaohs followed. The double row of pillars in the deepest hall containing the royal sarcophagus was perpendicular to the entrance, its middle part cut deeper. This left three aisles, the middle one vaulted. The combination of ramp and stair inserted into the upper aisle was maintained until the reign of Ramesses VI. Quantitative changes included increasing the number of pillars from six, as in the tomb of Amenophis II, to eight, and the number of side chambers from six to ten. In the turn of axis, found here for the last time, I am inclined to see Ramesses II's reaction to the Amarna Period as an attempt to remove all the traces of Akhenaton's revolution.

Ramesses II's son and successor, Merneptah, revived the single straight axis, removing the slight shift visible in the tombs of Haremheb and Sety I. He emphasized the axis by reducing the number of side chambers and supplemented this with a symmetrical unit behind the burial chamber. Merneptah's innovation was a significant increase in the dimensions of his tomb: the height of the corridors rose from 5 to 6 and even 7 cubits; the royal sarcophagi assumed colossal proportions—his outer sarcophagus was over 15 feet long. The programmatic scenes at the entrance were executed in bas-relief, and in quality they approach those in the tomb of Sety I; but the rest of the tomb was executed in sunken relief, a quick method characteristic of the Ramesside construction mania.

Merneptah did not hide the entrance of his tomb in the floor of the Valley, and it is surprising that the tendency to provide the royal tomb with a proper façade for a suitably monumental entrance increased precisely in the unstable years at the end of Dynasty 19. The corridors no longer fell steeply into the depths but were almost horizontal even by the time of Sety II; stairs and shafts were abandoned, making the transport of gigantic sarcophagi easier. Corridor ceilings having already been raised, walls were now set back and corridors correspondingly broadened; the monumental impression of the royal tomb was thus accentuated. The decoration was enriched with newer, more modern Books of the Netherworld, namely the Book of Caverns and the Book of the Earth.

Ramesses III contributed to tomb development by adding painted niches in the first and second corridors, extending the pictorial program with numerous new and unusual motifs, and bringing the number of portals in the tomb axis to a maximum of ten. In contrast, however, the quality of the reliefs and paintings was miserable, and the planning was slipshod from the beginning; the first corridors cut into the neighboring tomb of the usurper Amenmesse, and as a result the axis was shifted several cubits to the right. The tomb of Ramesses III represents the end of the evolution of the royal tomb insofar as the application of the rule of the "extension of the existing" met its limits and had to be reconsidered. The two following reigns were challenged to continue on a completely different basis, with new routes and new solutions.

Ramesses IV responded with a consistent shortening of the plan, while completely abandoning side chambers and pillared halls, except for two extended

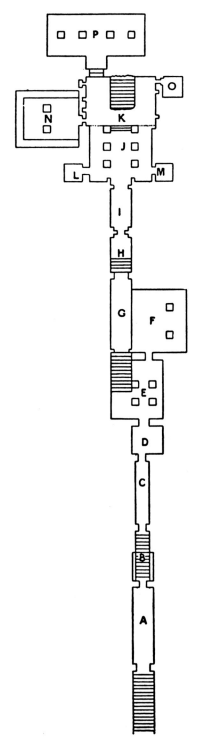

Ground plan of the tomb of Sety I.

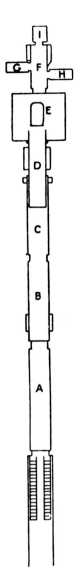

Ground plan of the tomb of Ramesses IV.

niches behind the burial chamber, intended for shawabty figures. With less wall space, the literature of the Beyond was limited to the Litany of Re, the Book of Gates, and spells from the Book of the Dead; the Book of Heaven replaced the constellations in the burial chamber. As with the diminishing size of the pyramids after Chephren, however, the practiced self-limitation signified not an overall reduction in the tomb complex but merely a shift in accent.

The final phase in the formation of the rock tomb was thus reached, and the next tomb, built by Ramesses V and Ramesses VI, maintained the enlarged dimensions of Dynasty 20 while reviving the pillared halls and the full-length plan of Dynasty 19 (although without side rooms). The decoration reached another climax: walls and ceilings show us parts of practically every known Book of the Heavens and the Netherworld, some chapters from the Book of the Dead, and divine representations; only the Litany of Re is missing. The last rock tombs of the Valley of the Kings offer more variations: Ramesses XI's exceeded the obligatory pillar measurement of 2 by 2 cubits, and excavation of a shaft in his burial chamber was begun, although it was not completed.

After the death of Ramesses XI, the Valley of the Kings was no longer the burial place of the pharaohs. Since the Amarna Period, the residence of the pharaohs had been in the north, in Memphis or the Delta, where some kings of the Ramesside period had a cenotaph. The kings of Dynasty 21 built their tombs in their residence at Tanis in the East Delta; a new tomb type, the temenos, developed there. Its origin lies in the small funerary chapels built in the forecourt of the Temple of Amun at Karnak at the close of Dynasty 19 (Sety II): the tomb complex was transferred into the temple precinct. In Tanis, only the rather modest stone substructures are preserved; the largest of these, belonging to Psusennes I, who ruled for half a century, measures a mere 60 by 35 feet. The substructure often consisted of a single chamber, presumably beneath brick. The decoration developed no special forms and merely reproduced brief excerpts from the Books of the Netherworld.

This temple burial was taken up in Thebes shortly thereafter, when the nominally reigning consorts of the god Amun—unmarried princesses of the royal household—erected stone or brick tombs in the Medinet Habu precinct, and probably at the Ramesseum as well. One must suppose that the complexes of Psamtek I and his successors in Sais were similar, as described by Herodotus (II; 169). None of these tombs has, however, survived. Compared with the earlier royal tombs, or indeed the often gigantic and richly decorated private tombs of the Late Period, these were very simple structures, distinguished by their position in the temple precinct. Of the tombs of the last kings of Egypt, Alexander the Great and the Ptolemies, nothing at all survives.

1. *View from the remote valleys southwest of the Valley of the Kings, looking east to the Nile.*

2. *View from the Nile to the fields and gardens of the west bank and to the mountainous desert with funerary temples and tombs.*

3. *The Qurn, or "horn," above the main branch of the Valley of the Kings. Modern masonry walls mark the entrance to Ramesses VI's tomb (ascending walls, middle right) and Tutankhamun's (lower right).*

1

2

3

4

5

4. *Looking toward the mountains to the east of Thebes, from across the Nile flood plain. The bed of the Nile is beyond the trees in the distance. The Colossi of Memnon are at the right.*

5. *The modern houses of the village of Qurna and the porticoes of ancient nobles' tombs above on the hill.*

6

7

6. *Step pyramid of Djoser at Saqqara, the oldest extant manmade stone building, ca. 2610 B.C. In the foreground is the court for the* sed *festival, the royal ceremony of rejuvenation.*

7. *Mastaba with niches in the tomb of Queen Meretneith in the royal cemetery of Dynasty 1 to the north of Saqqara. No stone was used, only mud bricks with mortar.*

8. *Dynasty 5 pyramids of Niuserre and Neferirkare at Abusir, with the remains of Sahure's pyramid temple in the foreground.*

9. *The three great pyramids of Dynasty 4 at Giza: that of Mycerinus in the foreground, with three small pyramids for his queens; Chephren's in the middle, with its original casing near the top still in place; and Cheops's in the background.*

10. *Amenemhat III's brick pyramid at Hawara in the Fayum. Of its pyramid temple, Herodotus's ''Labyrinth,'' only mounds of rubble remain.*

9

10

11. *Modern road leading to the tomb of Amenophis II in the Valley of the Kings. Like all the tombs of the early Dynasty 18 kings, this grave was concealed at the base of a sheer cliff. The later Ramesside kings reversed this custom and provided visible entrances.*

12

12. *Hall-like burial chamber of Ramesses VI's tomb, with the remains of his granite sarcophagus. Representations and text from the Book of the Earth decorate the walls; the Books of the Heavens cover the vaulted ceiling.*

13. *Burial chamber of Amenophis II. The six pillars have scenes of the king before divinities; the walls are painted with the Amduat, the ceiling with stars of the night sky.*

13

THE CONSTRUCTION OF THE VALLEY'S TOMBS: THE WORKERS OF DEIR EL-MEDINA

CHAPTER 3

The biographical inscription in the private tomb of Ineni, a project manager at the Temple of Karnak and mayor of Thebes, relates that during the reign of Tuthmosis I he not only was responsible for the erection of the red granite obelisks in the Temple of Karnak but also "supervised the excavation of His Majesty's rock tomb, in complete solitude, unseen, unheard." Ineni is one of a number of officials identified as having supervised construction on the royal tomb of his pharaoh, but we know next to nothing about the other officials, artists, and craftsmen who planned and executed the royal tombs of Dynasty 18. At the end of the dynasty our material increases in scope, but even then it remains rather vague about the actual tasks of the officials.

On the other hand, thanks to the unusual documentation from the village of Deir el-Medina, we are very well informed about the workmen who actually worked in the Valley of the Kings during the Ramesside period. The excavations of the Institut Français d'Archéologie Orientale found not only tombs, funerary objects, and houses, but also thousands of inscribed sherds and fragments of limestone, called ostraca, on which daily notes were made. Everything was systematically recorded on these ostraca: supplies for the workers, their monthly pay, and more. Proudly calling themselves "Pharaoh's team," the workers at Deir el-Medina were divided into a "right side" and a "left side," each directed by a foreman and a deputy with daily responsibility for the work, while the nominal project director, the vizier, appeared only occasionally to inspect the work. The workers were aided by the "scribes of the royal tomb," who were kept very busy, as is evident from the number of papyri and ostraca preserved today dealing with administrative and judicial procedures. Except for unusual events, the scribes noted only that work took place and that certain workers were absent (with their excuses). We thus learn that the strength of the work force varied from fewer than forty to more than 120 workers. In the Valley of the Kings, it would have been rare that more than sixty men were active at one time, and during the final touching up of a tomb, the number would have been even more restricted. Other ostraca concern tools and lighting, and a number of short graffiti on the cliffs of the Theban necropolis can also be attributed to these scribes.

Regrettably, however, these sources are insufficient for the reconstruction of the entire process of creating a royal rock tomb, and we are obliged to turn to archaeological sources for the rest. Every tomb in the Valley of the Kings has unfinished parts which taken together illustrate the general procedures and course of work in a royal tomb. Especially useful in this respect are the tombs of Haremheb and Sety II; both show every stage of work from the roughly cut walls of the shaft to finished

Statue of the treasurer Maya and his wife, Meret, now in Leiden. Maya was in charge of building Tutankhamun's tomb and overseeing his burial.

and painted reliefs; they thus allow us to describe the basic process leading to the creation of such a monument.

The death of a pharaoh was announced to workers by an official who repeated the ancient formula "The Falcon has flown up to heaven," recalling the role of the king as a manifestation of Horus. Immediately thereafter the accession of his successor was reported; a new era was begun, the Creation was renewed, and the joyous event could be celebrated for days on end. Funerary arrangements for the departed king would be made over the ensuing months, for the royal mummy had to be brought from the residence in the distant north and could be interred only after the traditional mummification process, which lasted seventy days. Consequently, there was adequate time to put the finishing touches on certain elements of the decoration, although one has the impression that in the tombs of Haremheb and Sety II the artisans stopped in the middle of their labors.

Work on the new pharaoh's tomb began immediately after the funeral of his predecessor, if not before. The role of the pharaoh himself in planning his tomb is not clear; we do not know the extent to which it was left to the professionals to determine the form and general principles of the decoration and the offerings. But we have seen that each tomb required a new variation and a new element in accord with the dynamics of the concept of the "extension of the existing." The plan and elevation of the tomb were sketched on a papyrus, with notes on the dimensions, purpose, and decoration of each room. Copies of such plans and more precise plans of specific rooms were transferred onto other papyri or ostraca which could be used daily in the Valley itself. Aside from the famous "Turin Plan" (first associated with the tomb of Ramesses IV by C. R. Lepsius) and a large ostracon in Cairo (for the tomb of Ramesses IX), a number of others are preserved, as are notes on the dimensions of various royal tombs. Not one of the existing plans corresponds precisely to an existing tomb; this is not surprising however, as sketches were not binding and many changes—to deal with unforeseeable variations in the quality of the rock, for instance—were necessary as work progressed.

The tomb plans give us names for the various rooms: corridors are "the god's passages," referring to the sun god, and the complete name of the open descent is "the first god's passage of Re, which is upon the sun's path." The room corresponding to the shaft is "the hall of separation," as the space was intended to break the axis. The royal chariots gave their name to "the chariot hall," and the burial chamber with the golden shrines is called "the house of gold wherein one [the deceased pharaoh] rests." The treasuries and other side chambers all have their own names as well.

Naturally, a suitable location for the proposed tomb had to be found before construction. A full year elapsed after Ramesses IV assumed the crown for the royal commission under the vizier Neferrenpet to begin seeking a place to excavate the tomb of the king. On the other hand, workers were in Sety II's tomb three months after he took over. These commissions must have used reliable plans of the Valley in order to avoid collisions, although one did occur under Ramesses III, when the tomb of the usurper Amenmesse was cut into by a new royal tomb and a change in orientation was necessitated.

When a site had been selected, the two sides of the work crew could begin to cut out the descent and the first corridor. The fissured limestone could be broken with simple stone tools, while flinty beds required spikes of copper or bronze, the traces

Ground plan of the workmen's village at Deir el-Medina.

of which are clearly visible today; iron tools were not common, but wooden hammers were. A slightly rounded chisel was used for finer work and has left quite distinctive traces. Large flint nodules remained in place, as in the tomb of Merneptah. A good deal of debris was simply left, but scribes noted the amount of stone that was removed from the tomb in baskets and sacks. The rooms were cut irregularly from above with little or no attention paid to precise verticality, and there is considerable variation. It was only immediately after the Amarna Period that precision was actually attempted, as in the tombs of Haremheb and Sety I.

The next tasks followed quickly and were closely supervised by the two foremen. Part of the work crew continued to tear into the rock deeper down. Practically on their heels, some of their fellows prepared the walls by polishing with stones and plastering gaps and cracks; the surface was then quickly covered with a uniform thin layer of plaster, as long as the rock still retained its natural moisture. Unfinished parts of corridors, as in the tombs of Ramesses IX and that of his son Montuherkhepeshef, display all three phases of this type of work, while the tombs of Haremheb and Sety II indicate the same type of cooperation in the decoration.

The documents of the draftsmen usually noted that certain divisions of the Books of the Netherworld should be oriented according to predefined cardinal directions, to ensure that the tomb conform as faithfully as possible to the vision of the Netherworld. Such notes are preserved in the burial chamber of Haremheb, detailing even "northeast" and "rear [wall], north." The intended decoration of the various rooms had been determined at the start, but only at the time of the actual execution were the scenes assigned to particular walls.

Guidelines divided the walls at appropriate places. A string dipped in red ink was pulled taut and released against the wall to produce the straight, slightly diffuse lines separating, for example, the registers and hours of the Book of Gates in Haremheb's burial chamber. The outlines of the human figures within each register were carefully delineated by the leading scribe: a line for the top of the head, another for the neck, another for the belt or hand, and so on. Animal figures, gates, and shrines were similarly sketched. A grid was used for the scenes with the gods on the sides of pillars, so that the originals could be reproduced exactly. Ceilings were delineated with red lines defining the central axis, the locations of the pillars, and the rows of stars. Flexibility was important, as the actual proportions of the tomb usually demanded considerable alterations to the texts and figures of the religious books. Registers were shortened or subdivided, and occasionally duplicated. Difficulty with the texts led to inversions. Sometimes whole paragraphs were drawn in reverse order.

Draftsmen drew the figures freely on the grid. Scene for scene, a few sure strokes outlined the figures in red; black lines defined the form. The certainty with which these perfect lines were drawn never ceases to command our admiration. Once the figures were drawn, the accompanying hieroglyphic inscriptions were likewise done quickly in red, followed by the definitive black ink. Occasionally the direction of the signs and their ordering in vertical columns was changed at the last minute. High walls required a scaffolding, and here it would appear that the same draftsman drew the red sketch and the black corrected version after comparison with the draft versions. In the tomb of Sety II, the second version also was done in red.

At first, figures and texts in the tombs were left in black, with merely the decorative background, the red solar disks, and other ornamentation painted in

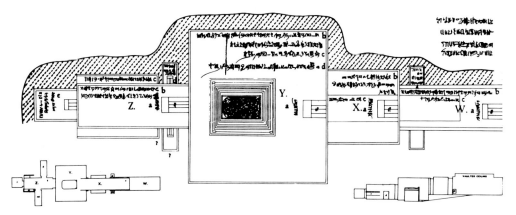

Restored papyrus fragment, now in the Egyptian Museum in Turin, showing a plan of the inner part of Ramesses IV's tomb. On the lower left and right are a modern ground plan and elevation of the tomb. The ancient Egyptian designations of the rooms and the sarcophagus with its gold shrine are shown on the papyrus.

color. Then beginning with the tomb of Tuthmosis IV, every detail in the divine scenes was painted in color, while the Amduat was done in the same cursive strokes that appear on the original papyrus.

In the tomb of Haremheb, the mural frescoes were transformed into relief, sculptors following the draftsmen. Working from the base upward, they chiseled away at the background, leaving the black outlines to be completed in detail later. The shallow relief was then smoothed along with the background, covered with plaster, and whitewashed again. Colors were applied to this finished surface.

The colors themselves were dictated by a firm canon which left the craftsmen little freedom. Virile dark red-brown was stipulated for male beings, and a light yellow tone for the female ones. Wigs were blue or black and kilts bright white. Wooden objects were red, and vegetable elements green. The background was usually done in a dull white, but Haremheb and Ramesses I used blue-gray, which may have been intended to suggest visually the acceptance of the deceased pharaoh among the gods. Sety I used this color only in the shaft of his tomb; the walls and pillars of the burial chamber (or "house of gold") in this and later tombs have an intense yellow background. The other rooms use a neutral white, the third background tone in this tomb.

In those tombs with complete decoration, not only the background and figurative representations but every single hieroglyph is painted in color. The Egyptian writing system is probably unique in defining not just a particular form for each sign but also a color. The painter thus had to have detailed knowledge of the script and the very difficult religious texts in order to give each sign its proper color; there are in fact a few hieroglyphs with identical forms but different colors. The painter could paint correctly signs that the sculptor had carved erroneously.

Besides black and white, only yellow, green, blue, and red were used, and mixtures were strenuously avoided. Where necessary, the prime color could be varied to permit nuances such as a blue sign on a blue background. On a yellow or red ground, signs of the same color were changed to be more distinct, and the valid canon was determined according to the background color. On some unfinished walls, certain colors are lacking; the colors were apparently prepared and applied consecutively rather than simultaneously. A thin layer of varnish was also applied to individual images in the tomb of Sety I.

In the first corridor light was no problem, but farther on, workers and scribes alike were obliged to rely increasingly on artificial lighting. Numerous ostraca note

Stonemason at his work. Sketch on a limestone ostracon in the Fitzwilliam Museum, Cambridge.

Stonecutting made by pointed (left) and flat (right) chisels in the tomb of Haremheb.

Plaster fills in a wall that has already been smoothed, in the tomb of Haremheb.

the use of fat, oil, and wicks; as with the tools, their quantities were carefully recorded in order to avoid misuse of state property. Records show that the amounts distributed to the "left" and "right" sides differed considerably according to the place and type of work. The type of lamp is illustrated in one of the Deir el-Medina tombs: a simple flat clay vessel with several wicks burning fat to give a uniform smokeless light.

Finally, probably after the burial, wooden doors were put in place to divide the various rooms from one another; like the walled-up entrance, these were closed with the seal of the necropolis: the jackal above nine captives, a symbol of visible triumph over all hostile powers, which should not approach the "secret place" of the necropolis.

From the Deir el-Medina texts we know that enemies kept their distance until the time of Merneptah. But then, in the final days of Dynasty 19 (ca. 1200 B.C.), an unruly period began for the workmen. A member of the royal family, the prince and viceroy of Nubia, Amenmesse, revolted against Sety II and ruled Upper Egypt for two years. Work at the royal tomb was interrupted, and the usurper started his own tomb in the Valley: three corridors, a shaft, and a pillared hall were cut to an astounding depth and partially decorated, with incredible swiftness. After recovering Luxor, Sety II had the Litany of Re carefully chiseled away in the first corridor, in order to injure his adversary in the Beyond as well.

This political contest was mirrored in the small world of Deir el-Medina. The foreman of the right side, Neferhotep, forfeited his life shortly after the occupation of Luxor without leaving a son and heir. His brother Amennakht hoped for the job, which had been in the family for three generations. But an outsider, the worker Paneb, was able to obtain the position by presenting the vizier with a "gift" of five slaves. The vizier may have had other motives; Paneb's machinations had led to his own predecessor's dismissal. Despite the indignation, there was no open opposition to Paneb, who already had a reputation for being unscrupulous and violent, and for tyrannizing the entire work force for several years.

The disappointed Amennakht then eagerly noted all of Paneb's misdeeds in a wide-ranging indictment, which he intended to turn over to the vizier at the proper moment. This document, today in the British Museum, reveals that Paneb was a kind of Egyptian Don Juan to whom nothing was sacred. He used the work area and its tools for his own private purposes while enjoying other workers' wives and daughters; broke all oaths he made; repeatedly stole state property and even certain objects from the royal burial; openly threatened to kill his predecessor, Neferhotep, and his colleague Hay; threw bricks and stones at other workers; and repeatedly inflicted bodily injuries on others. He forced his way into private tombs and would appear even to have desecrated the royal burial of Sety II.

It is clear that a certain amount of exaggeration and slander is to be expected from a jealous opponent, but a complementary set of notes from the village confirms certain points and makes it probable that the others were essentially justified. Paneb functioned ex officio as a judge, settling disputes in the community and punishing offenders. In one case the court protocol records his reaction to slanderous rumors concerning Hay; Paneb ordered that the guilty ones be punished with a hundred strokes each, and that their ears and noses be cut off if the offense were repeated. Despite this unsettling side of his character, we know from official documentation that Paneb was in fact a very competent and active foreman. The incredible progress made in the tomb of the usurper Amenmesse is ample testimony to his ability as leader of the work crew, and he retained his office after the restoration, supervising the resumption of work in the tomb of Sety II. It was only after the death of this pharaoh that the complaints and claims against Paneb were pressed home. Amennakht replaced him as the foreman, and Paneb's eldest son, Aaphti, whom he had groomed with a view to the succession, disappeared from the sources.

The injured pride of a professional can be seen in a letter from the time of Paneb: "The draftsman Parahotep greets [one of] his chief[s], the scribe in the Place of Truth, Qenherkhepeshef: In life, prosperity, and health! What do you have against me? I am to you like an ass. If there is work, the ass is brought; if there is banqueting, an ox. If there is beer, you seek [me] not. If there is work, you seek me. . . . Don't look [for me anymore]."

This sounds like a resignation, and only a couple of decades later, we learn that all the workers put down their tools and demanded that they be paid punctually. A scribe noted on an ostracon that they had not received their grain rations for twenty days, and arranged that on the twenty-third day a delivery would finally be made. On another ostracon, the vizier was informed: "We are in dire straits. Supplies have ceased for us from the treasury, the granary, and the storehouse. Stones are not light to carry. Six measures of corn have been taken from us, and six measures of earth given. Let our lord do something, that we may live. Indeed, we are really dying. We are hardly living. Nothing whatsoever is given to us."

Governmental negligence made the workers' situation increasingly precarious, and in the twenty-ninth year of the reign of Ramesses III (1156 B.C.) it led to the first known strike. Neither a pay raise nor worker participation was the issue, but rather the incapacity of the bureaucracy to deliver the workers' wages punctually and

Directional notations for northwest (left) and southeast (right) in the sarcophagus chamber of Haremheb.

Unfinished wall with carved and partly painted relief in the first corridor of the tomb of Sety II.

regularly. The ''Turin Strike Papyrus'' is a detailed record of the events by the scribe Amennakht. When their patience reached its limit, the entire crew crossed ''the five walls of the necropolis'' and sat crying ''We are hungry'' in front of an official building on the west bank until nightfall. They received nothing except promises of appeasement, and on the following days they paraded to the Ramesseum, the main administrative center, even pressing into the inner sanctum of the temple. The police chief, Montumes, turned to the mayor of Thebes in vain: ''The storehouses are empty, there is nothing available''; it was only with great difficulty that a single day's ration could be extracted from the temple reserves: fifty-five loaves of bread. On the advice of the police chief, wives and children were included in the peaceful procession on the following morning; the police chief himself led the marchers to the funerary temple of Sety I, where large reserves were at hand. The workers received an entire month's salary. During the ensuing months the administration repeatedly offered partial payment, but the vizier was apparently unable to fulfill the workers' expectations amid general corruption.

Unfinished wall in the sarcophagus chamber of Haremheb, with the fourth hour of the Book of Gates. In the lower register the sculptor had already begun to carve the relief.

The leisure hours and lack of payment would have encouraged the striking workers to use their precise knowledge of the necropolis to sack the older tombs (though probably not in the closely guarded Valley of the Kings). Under Ramesses IX (ca. 1112 B.C.) a scandal broke out when the two mayors of Thebes, Pawero of the west and Paser of the east, indulged their mutual hostility by simultaneously passing on accusations to the vizier. Paser claimed that even the tomb of the local "patron saint," the deified pharaoh Amenophis I, had been violated. Pawero then led a police inspection of the necropolis, accompanied by policemen, priests, and reporters (scribes). Ten royal tombs dating to Dynasties 11 and 17 in the area of Dra abu'l Naga and el-Tarif (outside the Valley of the Kings) were examined. Only one of these had been broken into and sacked; the rest, including that of Amenophis I, were intact. The situation of the private tombs was, however, disturbing; almost all of them had been violated. Pawero immediately produced a list of eight suspected thieves, who confessed under duress.

The next day, the vizier himself went to the Valley of the Queens, where everything was in order and the suspicion that a certain Pakharu had plundered a queen's tomb proved groundless. The workers were thus cleared, and they came together for a spontaneous parade, expressing their relief while pointing a finger at their accuser, Paser. The disappointed mayor then threatened to go directly to the pharaoh, while his counterpart Pawero wrote a report about the demonstration for the vizier, demanding that the accusations be followed up.

The High Court then met for two sessions, the first of which found Pakharu innocent and ended with a statement to the effect that all the accusations against Pawero were groundless. In the second session, the eight confessed "big thieves" of Dra abu'l Naga were tried, and dramatically described how they broke into the tomb of Pharaoh Sobekemsaf and his consort, Nubkhas, and reached their richly adorned mummies: "We opened their sarcophagi and their coffins, finding the noble mummy of this king equipped with a scimitar; many golden amulets and jewels lay about his neck, and his golden mask was upon him. The noble mummy of this king was completely bedecked with gold, and his coffins adorned with gold and silver inside and out and inlaid with all kinds of precious stones. We gathered the gold we found on the noble mummy of this god, together with his amulets. . . . Finding the queen to be similarly adorned, we gathered all that we found and set fire to the coffins. We also took all the offerings of gold, silver, and bronze and divided them among ourselves. And we made eight portions from the gold . . . coming from these two gods, leaving twenty deben for each of us."

Each robber thus received a stately sixty-five ounces of gold, but the testimony revealed that they parted with some of this to bribe various officials. We also learn that fences were already plying their trade, and that other gangs were active in the necropolis. The proceedings touched only the tip of the iceberg—if one can use the expression in Egypt, where "pyramid of corruption" may be more suitable. The eight thieves were convicted and turned over to Amenhotep, high priest of Amun at Karnak, until the pharaoh decided about their punishment (death or mutilation). But too many people lived off the trade for this to have brought an end to graverobbing.

With the death of Ramesses XI and the end of the New Kingdom (ca. 1070 B.C.), it became increasingly difficult to keep things in the Valley under control. Workers outlived their task for a time, as the tomb of Ramesses XI is the last royal rock tomb.

Representation of a simple lamp with three wicks, held by the personification of Eternity, from private tomb no. 5 at Thebes. Such lamps were used to light the inner spaces of the tombs.

Seal of the necropolis showing Anubis and nine bound prisoners.

Letter of Parahotep to his superiors, as transcribed in hieroglyphs by J. Cerny from the cursive hieratic original.

But the pharaohs in the Valley were not left in peace when the last tomb remained unfinished: the priests of the Theban ''divine state,'' having realized that the tombs simply could not be protected in the long run, started a series of transfers. A number of mummies were initially placed in the tomb of Sety I, others in a side room of the burial chamber of Amenophis II, while the tombs of Ramesses XI and other pharaohs probably also served as temporary tombs. Only Tutankhamun was left forgotten in the Valley, since his tomb had long been buried. It is possible that the clerics took advantage of the opportunity offered by necessity and secured valuables in the tombs as they were opened, to prevent their falling into the hands of the various gangs of thieves. The Nubian gold mines were lost at the end of the New Kingdom, and with them the necessary ''hard currency'' for dealing with the Levantine coast. While conscious of their responsibilities, the new governors must have understood the importance of using the Valley as a source of precious metals and stones.

Under Dynasty 22, the Libyan Sheshonq I (945–924 B.C.) laid the last royal mummies to rest. Most of them arrived in the family sepulcher of the high priest Pinudjem II at Deir el-Bahri, where some lost their royal coffins and shrouds in exchanges with various members of the high priest's family. This cache proved a good choice, as it was sealed in 945 B.C. and discovered countless generations of thieves later in 1871 or shortly thereafter. The papyri and objects from the cache appeared on the market almost a decade before Gustave Maspero finally tracked them down in 1881 and transferred the remaining contents (including all the coffins and mummies) to Cairo. The royal mummies in the tomb of Amenophis II had not been moved, and they were still there when Victor Loret discovered and emptied the tomb in 1898.

The assembly of the accessible royal mummies was recorded in notes on some of the coffins and represents the very last work in the ''place of secrecy,'' and the end of an epoch. This is particularly well documented by the finds of Deir el-Medina. Not just the endless everyday scribblings but also the small monuments with their very personal texts and confessions permit us to look deeper into the hearts of the craftsmen and scribes than is usual in antiquity. Struck by the economic collapse, they put their trust in the gods of Egypt, turning directly to Amun or Ptah, whose oracles spared men painful decisions.

14

14. *Deir el-Medina: below, the settlement in which artists and craftsmen employed in the tombs lived; on the slopes, the entrances to their tombs, and the long home of the French excavators; at the top, ascending to upper right, the path that leads to the Valley of the Kings.*

15

18

16

17

15. *Red- and black-ink preliminary layout of the eleventh scene of the Book of Gates in the sarcophagus chamber of Haremheb.*

16. *Red preliminary drawing for the third hour of the Amduat, with corrections also in red, in the tomb of Sety II.*

17. *In the tomb of Haremheb, text and image are sketched and arranged in red, while the final writing, disposition, and corrections are in black.*

18. *Pillar in the sarcophagus chamber of Amenophis II, with schematically executed figures of the king and the goddess Hathor, who holds the sign of life to the king's nose. Hathor wears a black wig, and is called "the one who is over the Western Desert" (a reference to the cemeteries); the king wears a striped linen headcloth. Only the borders of the scene and the goddess's sun disk with pendant uraeus are fully painted.*

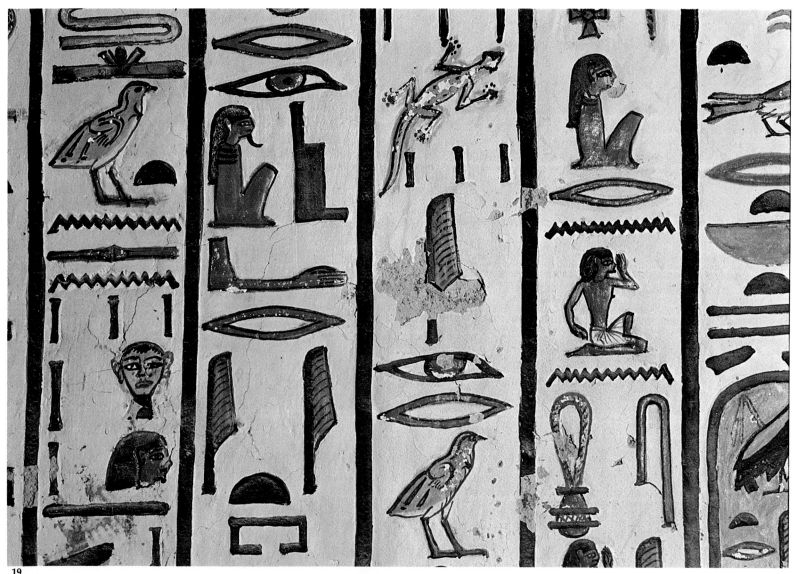

19

20

19. *Completed hieroglyphs in the tomb of Queen Nofretari.*

20. *Unfinished scene from the eleventh hour of the Amduat in the tomb of Sety I.*

21. *Completed relief in the shaft of Haremheb's tomb. The king wears headcloth, uraeus, and ceremonial beard, and offers jars of wine to Hathor. The goddess wears cow horns and sun disk, and holds the* ankh *and the staff of prosperity.*

21

22. *Finished relief on a pillar in the tomb of Queen Tausert, showing Hathor wearing a menit (a necklace with a counterweight, used in religious ceremonies).*

23. *Detail of a relief in the tomb of Haremheb. The king offers wine to Isis, who wears Hathor's headdress, cow horns, and a sun disk with pendant uraeus.*

22

23

24. *Painted hieroglyphs from the text of the Opening of the Mouth in the tomb of Sety I.*

25/26. *Hieroglyphs naming Anubis and Osiris in the tomb of Haremheb.*

EGYPTIAN DIVINITIES:
THE PHARAOH FACES THE
CHAPTER 4 LORDS OF THE BEYOND

On one of the two pillars in his burial chamber, Tuthmosis III is depicted with the members of his family, and in a sketch at the beginning of this scene is an unusual motif: a stylized tree offering its breast to the pharaoh, with the legend: ''He sucks on [the breast of] his mother Isis.'' As Tuthmosis's real mother was the ''Royal Mother Isis'' who is depicted crossing the fields of the Beyond in a papyrus skiff on the same pillar, one might think that this vignette with the king and the tree was intended to show the deceased pharaoh's return to his mother, who gives him suck once again as to a small child, a sort of rejuvenation in the tomb.

But the tree portends another goddess, usually identified as Nut or Hathor, appearing in many of the private tombs as a female form growing out of the tree and offering the deceased and his *ba* (soul) cool water and food. Visualized in the relationship between humans and gods is the trust in the strengthening powers of the gods. The tree offers shade, moisture, and sustenance, and the birdlike human soul likewise finds all that it requires. The tree goddess offers a stream of life that does not cease in the Beyond.

The tomb of Tuthmosis III is the only royal one that contains this scene; indeed it is the first instance of a divine scene in a royal tomb. That this pharaoh had an Isis as his earthly mother almost certainly led to the use of her name in place of that of Hathor or Nut. At the same time, the king as Horus on earth is able to return to his heavenly mother Isis, who tended and reared him in the myth, guarding him against all dangers.

Hathor is the only goddess appearing on the pillars of the tomb of Tuthmosis III's successor, Amenophis II, along with the gods, Osiris and Anubis. On the walls of the tomb of the latter king's son and heir, Tuthmosis IV, Hathor is depicted as often as both the other gods together. The classic trinity of the most important gods of the dead has thus been established, each related to a very different aspect of the Beyond. Each raises the same *ankh* sign, symbolizing life, to the pharaoh's nose. This gesture incorporates the gods' powers of animation, sustaining life in the Beyond and bringing about repeated resurrections, true to the promise of the Pyramid Texts: ''Rise, for you are not dead!''

Initially, the pharaoh remained passive before the gods who offered life in the Beyond. Haremheb is the first to pray before them, even offering jars of wine to improve their spirits; Sety I gives other presents long familiar in the temples. Promises are then attributed to the gods, intensifying the reciprocal exchange between god and man. More moving are the earlier scenes where only a touch of the hand or an embrace of the king signifies his entry into the circle of the gods, where the simple hieroglyph of ''life'' before his nose shows that life in the Beyond, has been awarded him.

The tree goddess offering bread and cool water to the deceased and his wife. The lotus blossoms on her tray signify the desired renewal of life; the ointment cones on the heads of the deceased, continual pleasant scent. From the tomb of Sennedjem at Deir el-Medina. (See plate 28.)

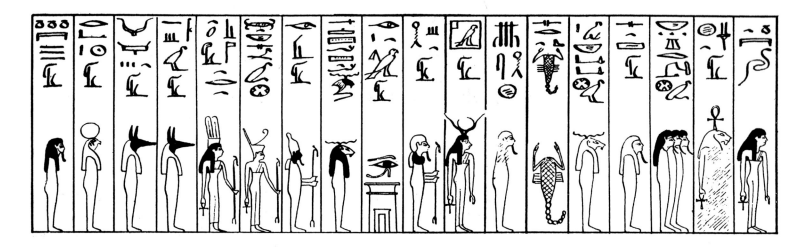

Detail from spell 42 of the Book of the Dead, concerned with the deification of each part of the body.

Egyptian belief placed the gods beyond the confines of this earth. Our reality can know them only in picture and parable, never directly; their apartments are in the heavens and the Netherworld, the two spheres of the Beyond. Only the dead can have the extraordinary experience of direct contact with the gods, encountering them face to face. Whoever has crossed the dark threshold is "introduced" into the world of the gods, as in the later mystery cults. These divine scenes and the descriptions of the pictures of the Beyond in the New Kingdom royal tombs are the initiation into the mysteries of another world, an initiation that demands death and is open to all.

Pharaoh's familiarity with the gods, as shown on the walls and pillars of the royal tombs, confirms his acceptance into the fields of the Beyond, which are intimately portrayed in the second part of the decoration, in the Books of the Netherworld. His hand is lovingly grasped, as he is led from god to god before the throne of the sovereign of the dead, Osiris, the king of eternity. Pharaoh had indeed already had divine roles on earth, where he was the image of the god of creation, but he is now accepted in the divine sphere in a much more profound sense. Death removes all the limits impinging on his divinity while on earth. The Pyramid Texts of the Old Kingdom describe the pharaoh's ascent to heaven, and how he violently forces his way in if he is not peacefully accepted. His divine apotheosis peaks when he has incorporated the magical powers of all of the denizens of heaven, thus bringing his divine power to its absolute maximum. His complete divinization is expressed in a ritual by which every part of the royal body—from head to heel—was identified with a particular divinity.

> My face is a falcon,
> The top of my head is Re,
> My two eyes . . . are the two sisters,
> My nose is Horus of the Netherworld,
> My mouth is the Sovereign of the West.
>
> My ribs are Horus and Thoth,
> My buttocks are the great flood,
> My phallus is Tatenen,
> My toes are divine cobras.

The individual gods named change from text to text with neither rhyme nor reason, but the intention is that the deceased be identified—utterly and absolutely, to the skin of his fingertips—as a god, and he exclaims to his "brothers": "I am one of you." In the New Kingdom Litany of Re, the pharaoh's detailed divinization climaxes in general affirmations:

> My members are gods,
> I am entirely god.
> No member of me is free of god.
> I enter as god,
> I depart as god,
> The gods have transformed themselves into my body.

In the tomb of Tausert (an exceptional queen who ruled Egypt in 1190–1184 B.C. and was buried in the Valley) a number of male divinities are assigned female epithets, which were earlier ascribed to slovenliness; we have now learned to pay more attention to such oddities. As with the feminine endings of the royal titulary, these forms indicate that this ruling queen has entered into the being of the god in question, herself becoming, Osiris, Ptah, and so on. That she is standing before and praying to the very god whom she has entered into did not particularly disturb the Egyptian; he had already seen a number of Egyptian kings (Amenophis III, Ramesses II) worshipping their own statues. A god could appear in many forms simultaneously, even in that of the ruling monarch. In the Beyond, the true realm of the gods, the king is accepted in the form of each and every divinity; this guarantees his everlasting life.

We now return to the trinity of Hathor-Anubis-Osiris, which is at the beginning of this development. Osiris dislodged an ancient god as lord of the West toward the end of the Old Kingdom and became sovereign of the Netherworld. As for Anubis, he belongs to a much older generation of zoomorphic gods, dating back to the prehistoric epoch. His head, derived from that of a jackal or similar beast, was a prototype that permitted the early Church Fathers and others to amuse themselves over contemptible and ridiculous dog-headed gods and other mixtures of the human body with an animal head. The head is, however, just one of many possibilities used by the Egyptians to signify the nature or function of a divinity with an attribute.

Anubis as the desert hound who takes care of the bodies is also the god of mummification, who assures the bodily integrity of the dead. A common image in the Ramesside tombs, private and royal alike, is that of Anubis before the bier laying his hand on the mummy, accompanied by Isis and Nephtys kneeling beside the bier; a similar scene appearing prominently on coffins of the Late Period places the canopic jars with the mummy's innards beneath the bier. Everything related to corporeal existence is entrusted to Anubis, "Lord of the Secluded Land" and thus chief guardian of the necropolis; on the royal necropolis seal he guards and masters nine bound "enemies."

The third member of the triad, Hathor, is worshipped even in the royal monuments of the Old Kingdom where she appears beside the sun god Re as a guarantor of continued life in the Beyond. In the New Kingdom royal tombs at Thebes she was much closer to home, as Hathor in cow form had been worshipped at Deir el-Bahri since Dynasty 11, at the latest, with Hatshepsut and Tuthmosis III merely continu-

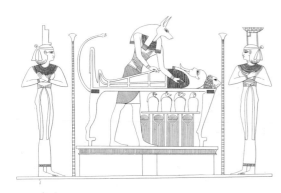

Anubis between Isis (left) and Nephthys (right) at the bier of the mummiform deceased in the tomb of Tausert. Under the bier are four canopic jars, each above its box. The jars held the internal organs that had been removed for separate mummification; the jar lids are shaped like the heads of Horus's four sons. (See plate 35.)

ing the tradition in Dynasty 18. From a mountain or a papyrus thicket, she would take the dead under her motherly protection. New Kingdom Books of the Dead, such as the famous Papyrus of Ani in the British Museum, frequently close with such a scene of "The Cow in the Western Mountain," and this motif belongs to the basic decoration of Ramesside private tombs, as well as to the painted coffins and decorated papyri of Dynasty 21. In the Coffin Texts and the Book of the Dead (spell 103), the deceased aspires to be in the entourage or beside the goddess, sharing the role of the shady and refreshing tree goddess with the heavenly Nut.

Where Hathor rules, love, music, dance, and blessed intoxication are all present, and a person can become regenerated and rejuvenated. Since the goddess also rules as "Lady of the West" and "Mistress of the Western Desert" and thus over the domain of the dead, people may hope to enter this realm of general joy and regeneration beyond death. Hathor brings the dead and the living together, as is signified by subtle distinctions on the pillars of the tomb of Amenophis III. The eastern faces of the pillars show Hathor in her conventional form with cow horns and a solar disk adorning her head, while on the western faces she takes the form of goddess of the West, with the hieroglyphic sign for "west" on her head, although still addressed as a particular manifestation of Hathor. After the time of Amenophis III, Hathor appears regularly in the Valley of the Kings, and later on the floors of Dynasty 21 coffins as the counterpart of Nut, the goddess of the heavens who already protected the dead of Dynasty 18 on the inner face of coffin lids.

On the walls descending into the tomb shaft of Amenophis III, the painted decoration shows Hathor leading the divinities on the left while Nut leads those on the right, testifying to Pharaoh's acceptance in both spheres of the Beyond, the heavens and the western realm of the dead. The goddesses embrace him as mothers, as they do the sun god, who sinks into the western desert each evening, entering the body of the celestial goddess. Uninviting and threatening, the desert is the mere skin of the Beyond, beneath which are concealed the sustaining and rejuvenating depths of the world. This is the domain of the goddess who embraces the dead, and reaches out of the desert mountains to draw the sun to herself each evening in the scenes of the solar cycle.

If Hathor holds sway over the endlessness of the desert and its precipitous depths, how does she relate to Isis, the sister-wife of Osiris, who awakens him from death? Although Isis played a very important role in the Osiris myth and in the burial of the dead, the older Egyptian traditions never accorded her a major role as the partner of Osiris in ruling the Netherworld—perhaps because Hathor was already in the west and Nut in heaven. Osiris rules alone here, and his daily resurrection is achieved by the sun god descending into the Netherworld, not by Isis.

In fact Isis, in her human form, is incorporated into the decoration of the royal tombs only after the Amarna Period. She appears for the first time in the burial chamber of Tutankhamun, and is then represented four times in the tomb of Haremheb—twice with her own hieroglyph (the throne) on her head, and twice with cow's horns and a solar disk of Hathor. Both Isis and Hathor have the same epithets, "Lady of Heaven" and "Sovereign of the Gods," and only Isis's title "Mother of the God" distinguishes them. Isis also becomes the "Mistress of Western Thebes," and—when assuming the black wig of the goddess of the dead, another aspect of Hathor—she is increasingly identified with the goddess of the West; she appears in the tomb of Haremheb under the name of Hathor, but in

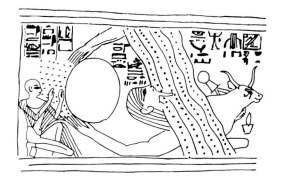

Hathor as a cow emerging from the Western Mountain on the right, joined with a scene of the sun's course on the left. From the Dynasty 21 papyrus of Amenemwia, in Berlin.

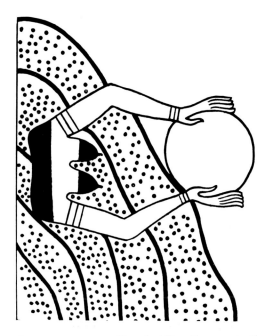

An anonymous goddess holding the sun in the Western Mountain.

different guise, as she wears the ''west'' symbol instead of the cow's horns. The names, representations, epithets, and functions of the three goddesses—Isis, Hathor and the goddess of the West—overlap, without the goddesses losing their identities: they are actually aspects of a single goddess, however distinct. The Egyptian theologian has carefully left their relationship vague, avoiding a dogmatic and ''correct'' solution; he is conscious that the delicate and complex fabric of the tangible divine world is full of overlaps and contradictions. In later tombs only the caption with the name permits us to distinguish Isis from Hathor. There is always the other Isis, standing with her sister Nephtys behind the throne of Osiris, or kneeling with her beside his bier, as they were earlier depicted at the ends of the royal sarcophagus, guarding the pharaoh as Osiris; Hathor and the goddess of the West never intrude into this context. And Isis and Nephtys flank the sun god in his disk at the entrance to the Ramesside tombs, their presence emphasizing the nightly meeting of Re and Osiris. Nephtys appears only as the helper and sister of Isis and Osiris, her own nature so completely submerged that it is for us unfathomable—a divine example for those who serve silently and selflessly.

In the tomb of Haremheb, Harsiese—''Horus, the son of Isis''—appears for the first time, but not in the form of Horus, the ancient god of the heavens, whose wings spread over the whole earth; it is Horus as the son and helper of Isis and Osiris, and thus of the deceased pharaoh, whom he guides across the threshold of death to his father. As Osiris's heir, Horus assures the continuity of earthly rule, but he supports his father in the Netherworld as well, so that Osiris—weakened by death—will not succumb to the attack of his hostile brother, Seth. The tomb of Aye introduced more members of this family into the Valley of the Kings: the sons of Horus—Imsety, Hapy, Duamutef, and Qebehsenuef, a foursome dictated by the cardinal directions, guaranteeing complete protection. Their origins lay in the ceremonies of mummification, and they appear as guardians of the dead in the most diverse contexts; in the Books of the Netherworld they aid the sun god in his conflict with the Apophis serpent. The Egyptian did not concern himself with the genealogy of these four, however, so that either Osiris or Horus can appear as the father of the four, their mother remaining anonymous. In spell 151 of the Book of the Dead they place themselves as guardians beside the deceased, and then Osiris announces:

> I am your son Osiris!
> I am come that I may be your protection,
> I have strengthened your house, that it last,
> As Ptah commanded, as Re himself decreed.

The Ptah named here appears regularly in the royal tombs from the end of Dynasty 18. In the tombs of Haremheb and Sety I, Ptah and his ''son'' Nefertum, holding the djed pillar and Isis-knot amulets, are notably conspicuous as they close the tomb decoration at the passage into the burial chamber. Nefertum's role is an ancient one. He is known since the Old Kingdom as the god of salves, fragrances, and pleasant odors in general, and wears a lotus blossom on his head. Cosmetics and their receptacles were important offerings even in prehistoric times for refreshing and maintaining the dead in the Beyond. These goods lost nothing of their importance with the advent of mummification, continuing to function as preservatives and agents of reawakening and deification. Scents invariably signify the presence of the gods. In the tale of the divine origin of Hatshepsut, her mother is overwhelmed by the god's fragrance as he approaches in the form of her royal husband. Egyptian tomb paintings frequently have the owners holding a lotus blossom or even a jar of perfumed oil before their noses, symbolizing their re-awakening, and Nefertum takes part in the daily regeneration of the sun god as ''the lotus at Re's nose.'' Typical of pictures in New Kingdom private tombs are the conical lumps of scent depicted on the heads of the deceased and his family, intended to envelop the dead person in a divine odor, protecting him against the powers of death, disintegration, and putrefaction. Nefertum's lotus blossom has the same function.

Isolating the role of Nefertum's father, Ptah, in the Beyond is more difficult. A hymn praising Ptah for attending to the Netherworld and the dead confirms that as a universal creator god he has assumed various responsibilities of the sun god, and, like him, ''goes down in the Western Mountain,'' to the dead. As Ptah-Sokar-Osiris he shares the sovereignty of the Realm of the Dead: Sokar, the Memphite god of death in falcon form, provides the link here, with his worship in Theban tombs and temples taking on new proportions in the New Kingdom. In spell 82 of the Book of the Dead, ''Assuming the Form of Ptah,'' Ptah is involved only very generally with the apotheosis of the deceased; but in the ceremony of the ''Opening of the Mouth,'' whereby the dead regain their senses, he plays an important part. And his real significance in the world of the dead is in his relations to the oldest gods—the primeval waters, Nun, and the barren earth, Tatenen. For in his creative qualities, Ptah aids the resurrection of the dead.

Another role of Ptah in the Beyond is as the lord of *maat*, that is, world order as established at the Creation. *Maat* does not lose its importance in the Beyond. Accomplishing justice is a constant refrain there, since each of the deceased faces judgment in the Hall of the Two Maats. This dual *maat* refers to the entire, complete *maat*, valid in this world as well as the next. Maat, the goddess with the feather in her headband, doubled as two Maats accompanies the sun god on the solar bark in the first hour of the Amduat. With the tomb of Haremheb Maat gains entrance to the Valley of the Kings as the visible guarantee that justice is not for this earth alone. On each side of the passage into the burial chamber, she greets the pharaoh, to guide him securely on the paths of the Beyond. Later, in Dynasty 19, Maat awaits the deceased at the entrance of the tomb, adorned with protective wings ready to aid her protégé.

Haremheb's successor, Ramesses I, assumed the crown at an advanced age, and his hurried preparation of a tomb in the Valley of the Kings permitted only the provision of basic necessities. However, this ''summary'' of a royal tomb is particularly valuable for us, as it shows the essentials of the decorative program, despite the urgency and limitations of the project. Only one room was decorated. On its side walls are two divisions of the Book of Gates, representing the pictorial cycles of the Books of the Netherworld. The entrance wall was reserved for the depictions of Maat goddesses and other divine scenes, as in the tomb of Haremheb. But the back wall introduces new patterns and divinities into the program of the royal tombs. Throned back to back are Osiris and the sun god in his morning form, Khepri, with a scarab beetle in place of a head. Osiris and the sun god are united here as the two most important gods governing the destiny of those in the Beyond. Ramesses I is led before Osiris by Harsiese, Atum, and Neith. On the other side,

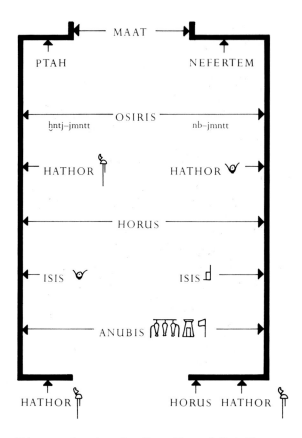

Diagram showing the disposition of divinities in the antechambers of the tombs of Haremheb and Sety I.

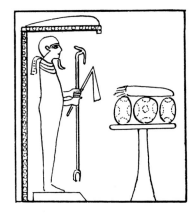

Ptah in a vignette from spell 82 of the Book of the Dead.

The Iunmutef priest wearing panther skin and side-lock, his raised hands holding cult implements. Before him is an ibis standard with the jubilating souls of Buto and Hieraconpolis.

Divine beings in the antechamber of Ramesses III, as drawn by Champollion.

the king consecrates four chests of clothing before the sun god, half kneeling among the "souls of Buto and Hieraconpolis," and rhythmically pounding his breast and praising the god. This ancient motif of jubilation, suggesting the rejoicing of all creation, is taken up with a new twist in the tomb of Sety I. In Sety's burial chamber, the pillar faces along the central axis to the left bear the jackal-headed souls of Hieraconpolis, and those to the right, the falcon-headed souls of Buto. They face the entrance, so that the sun god and the king look toward this joyful crowd in the course of their daily journey.

With the transition to the completely decorated tomb under Sety I, the decorative program of the royal tomb was considerably enlarged to include a whole new series of gods. The scenes in the shaft and antechamber were traditional, but the fourteen pillars of the upper pillared hall offered space for many new representations. The four protective goddesses—Isis, Nephthys, Selket, and Neith—are represented with Atum, Shu, and Geb. They are joined by the moon god, Thoth; Ptah as Ptah-Sokar-Osiris; the sun god in all of his main forms (Khepri, Atum, Harakhty), and Anubis in an unusual ram-headed manifestation that Ramesses I had already placed in the Osiris niche. Then comes Iunmutef (literally, "pillar of his mother"), wearing a panther skin and identified here as the eldest son of Sety I. Iunmutef will later be presented as a manifestation of Horus, son of Osiris.

In this same pillared hall, female divinities alone face the central aisle (the goddess of the West and Hathor, with Isis and Nephthys at the rear); they are completely absent from the pillars in the lower part of the tomb. This striking contrast can perhaps be explained in terms of contemporary scenes of the solar cycle where the sun disk moves between two pairs of arms: from below, the arms of a god push the disk up from the depths, and the arms of another goddess grasp it from above. As the decoration of a royal tomb was frequently determined by the daily course of the sun, one may assume that this program reflected a basic principle whereby the powers of the depths were masculine, and those of the heavens were feminine.

The tomb of Ramesses II is heavily damaged but one of the few innovations that can be identified there also suggests a reference to the solar cycle on the decorations of the pillars in the burial chamber. The sides of the pillars in the burial chamber facing inward apparently all bore the image of a *djed* pillar, an image that frequently served as the basis for scenes of the solar cycle and also represented Osiris, who remained in the depths.

The rest of the royal tombs of Dynasty 20 are either too damaged or unfinished to pursue the development of the divine scenes easily. However, the relatively well-preserved tomb of Queen Tausert shows one basic innovation, which distinguishes it from the tombs of Sety I and all earlier pharaohs. The king and the divinity no longer appear together but are on different faces of the pillar.

The further expansion of the pictorial cadre of divinities is visible in Dynasty 20 in the tombs of Ramesses III and his successors. Here the general tendency is for "important" gods to step aside, permitting lesser or purely local divinities to offer Pharaoh succor and protection. Ramesses III brought quite unexpected gods into the Valley of the Kings. In his tomb the provincial divinities Shepsi of Middle Egyptian Hermopolis and Horus-Khentekhtai of Athribis in the Delta accompany the special goddess Meret, who embodies the world of tones and is thus related to the royal *sed*, or festival of renewal. Sopdu and Onouris appear to take us to the borders of the Egyptian world: as lords of the desert they are well placed to aid and protect the pharaoh in the wastes of the realm of the dead. The serpent-formed Meretseger, responsible for the Theban desert, was the incarnation of the highest peak above the workers' village at Deir el-Medina, and its inhabitants were particularly attached to her. This purely local divinity who gazes over the Valley of the Kings was added to the royal tomb decoration during the reign of Ramesses VI, and later appeared even in the entry scene in the tomb of Ramesses IX. Bearing the "west" sign on her head, she assumes the form of the goddess of the West, and thus that of Hathor.

Other divinities were pictured in the antechamber before Ramesses III's burial chamber. They are almost completely lost today, but watercolors of the last century show them to have been intact. Here we encounter the dwarfish and grotesque Bes, a popular source of hope often found on widely distributed amulets. We also encounter divinities with snakes and lizards in their hands, or with animal heads. Tar-covered wooden statues of similar forms were found by Giovanni Battista Belzoni in the tomb of Sety I. Snakes, lizards, and turtles being symbols of regeneration in the Beyond, the representations of these singular divinities surrounding the dead pharaoh would have assisted him at the resurrection.

The purpose and function of these divine figures influenced the text and illustration of spell 182 of the Book of the Dead for commoners, where the vignette depicts numerous friendly spirits around the mummy on a bier. The preamble reveals that the spell was intended to cause Osiris to endure, to let him breathe (and thus to reawaken him), and to drive off his enemies—in brief, "to provide protection, aid, and support in the necropolis." The text of the spell states it concisely:

> Protection and Life surround him,
> This god, guarding his ka soul, the king of the Netherworld,
> Who rules the West, and triumphantly conquered the heavens . . .
> Who shall endure for all eternity.

Such words may be used as the comprehensive motto for all divine scenes in the Valley of the Kings, as these are the two hopes bound up with the help of the gods in the Beyond: protection in the face of danger, and new rejuvenating life. Since the time of Sety I's tomb, flying vultures protectively span the ceilings of the first corridor. While falcons, serpents, and scarab beetles alternate with the vultures, the winged solar disk at the passage leading to the next corridor sets the tone for all. The endless lines of these creatures flying into the interior of the tomb drove away all hostile powers, and their beating wings provided the life-giving air for the dead pharaoh to breathe. Between the outspread vulture wings and the walls at the edge of the ceiling are two parallel lines of text in which the sun god as Harakhty, "Horus of the Horizon" on the left and Osiris, "King of the Living," on the right greet the pharaoh as their loyal son, promising him a pleasant life in the hereafter. The pharaoh is placed under the protection of the two gods who determine his destiny in the other world from the very entrance of the tomb, where they hail him as son and heir of all the gods in the tomb.

Book of the Dead, spell 182. The upper and lower registers contain divine beings who protect and revive the deceased; the middle register depicts Isis, Nephthys, and the sons of Horus.

27. *Tree goddess on a pillar in the burial chamber of Tuthmosis III. She extends her breast to the deceased king, and the hieroglyphic legend reads: "Menkheperre [the throne name of Tuthmosis III] suckles his mother Isis."*

28

29

30

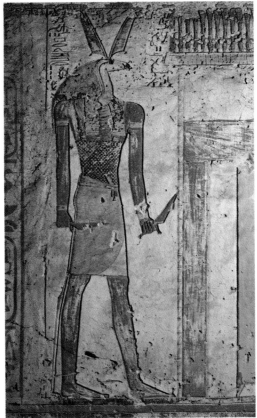

31

32

33

28. *Wall painting in the Theban tomb of the priest Pannehsi (reign of Ramesses II) with the tree goddess, a scene which was very popular in private tombs. She offers the deceased food and cool water, and her branches shade not only the deceased but also his bird-formed* ba *as they drink.*

29. *The antechamber of the tomb of Tuthmosis IV. Left to right: the king before Osiris, Anubis, Hathor as Lady of the West, and Hathor as ''the one who is over the Western Desert.'' In each case the deity offers an* ankh, *the sign of life, to the nose of the king.*

30–32. *The antechamber of the tomb of Tausert. Along with other divinities are the gatekeepers of the Netherworld taken from spell 145 of the Book of the Dead: (30) the keeper of the fifteenth gate; (31) the keeper of the sixteenth gate; (32) the keeper of the fourteenth gate with King Sethnakht, who appropriated Tausert's tomb.*

33. *Sarcophagus hall of Tausert. On the faces of the pillars are Geb (left) and Anubis (right); on the dado, representations of burial gifts; and on the walls, details from the Book of Gates.*

34. *Detail of a painted relief of Anubis in the tomb of Haremheb. The transition between the human body and the animal head (an unidentified, stylized type of dog, often drawn as a jackal) is camouflaged by the blue divine wig and broad collar. The armlets on the upper arms are worn more often by the king.*

35. *Anubis with the mummy, whose face is protected by a gilded mask with the divine beard. Isis, kneeling on the left, and Nephthys, on the right, refer to the lamentation of Osiris. Before each of them is a* shen *ring, which has a protective function. The recumbent Anubis in animal form is below, a scepter of rulership and a flail on his back. This scene is from spell 151 of the Book of the Dead, in the second corridor of the tomb of Siptah.*

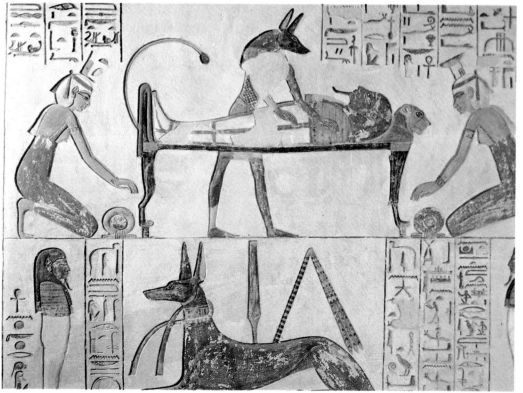

36. *King Haremheb offering round wine jars to Hathor as goddess of the West in the antechamber of the tomb of Haremheb. Hathor wears the hieroglyph for "west" on her black wig.*

37. *Maat, with her feather hieroglyph on her black wig, in the doorway between the ante-chamber and the burial chamber of the tomb of Haremheb. She says, ''I come, so that I may be with you''; this assures that in the Beyond the king is also safe in* maat, *the correct order of the world. In the background Haremheb offers wine jars to Osiris.*

38. *The falcon-headed moon god Khonsu-Neferhotep in the tomb of Ramesses IX. He wears both a full and a crescent moon on his head, from which hangs a uraeus snake with cow horns and sun disk, an allusion to the goddess Hathor as uraeus and eye of the sun god.*

39. *Nefertum, the god of ointments and pleas-ing scents, in the tomb of Haremheb. He wears the curved divine beard, broad collar, and arm-bands. With the lotus blossom on his wig he manifests himself as ''lotus to the nose of Re.''*

37

38

39

40. *Haremheb, with the royal pleated headcloth and uraeus, approaches Isis, who wears a throne hieroglyph on her black wig. The goddess holds an ankh (sign of life) in her right hand and a was (scepter of dominion) in her left. Her titles proclaim her mother of the gods and goddess of the West.*

41. *The ibis-headed god, Thoth, the ruler of Hermopolis, from a pillar in the tomb of Ramesses VI. Above is a procession of gods, which is a complete representation of the throne name of Ramesses VI.*

42. *Hathor, ''mistress of the West,'' in the tomb of Ramesses III, in a relatively rare representation with the head of a cow and two tall ostrich feathers, along with the cow horns and sun disk more usual to this goddess. In the background is the monkey-headed son of Horus, Hapy.*

40

41

42

THE PREDOMINANT THEME:
CHAPTER 5   THE JOURNEY OF THE SUN GOD

The tomb of Tuthmosis I is the oldest in the Valley and also the first whose walls bore the Amduat, originally entitled "The Book of the Hidden Chamber." Tuthmosis III and the vizier User had complete copies of the Amduat drawn on the walls of their burial chambers. The text is written cursively on a yellow background, making it appear as if an ancient papyrus were itself glued to the wall. Up to the reign of Haremheb the decoration of the royal tombs was restricted to this one book, along with scenes of the kings in the company of divinities and parts of the Litany of Re on the pillars in the tomb of Tuthmosis III. In the elaborately decorated tomb of Sety I, the first three divisions of the Amduat surrounded the royal sarcophagus in the lower pillared hall; and there was even a special summary version, excerpting the most important names and concepts from the Amduat, without the illustrations.

The Egyptians must have been particularly attached to this "Book of the Hidden Chamber," for it was the source of the most important decoration in the royal tombs for centuries. It also became the model for other illustrated texts designed along the same lines, and thus the spark generating a whole literary genre, which the Egyptians then subsumed under the heading Amduat, or "The Books of That Which Is in [am] the Netherworld [dat or duat]." This is also the principle behind the modern name Books of the Netherworld, which replaces the earlier name, "Guides to the Beyond."

Descriptions of particular regions and conditions of the Beyond had played a part in earlier ancient Egyptian funerary texts. The Book of Two Ways painted on Dynasty 12 coffins provided the occupant with an annotated map of the Beyond, identifying both recommended and undesirable routes. It was, however, completely new to attempt to describe all the aspects—promising and terrifying—of the secret confines of the Beyond, and to record them in pictures as well. This was the ambitious goal of the Amduat, and its form was adapted to the purpose; it was divided into twelve parts, corresponding to the twelve hours of the night, and thus encompassed the entire journey of the sun below the two earthly horizons.

It is here that we find a response to the ancient questions concerning the course of the sun after it disappeared in the evening and the reason for its return each morning. Visualizing the depths into which the sun dropped and following the events of the Beyond hour by hour, while reconstructing the circumstances and processes in a world beyond the limits of creation, demanded extraordinary efforts of imagination and design. It was only in the New Kingdom that this task was accomplished, when the chaos of countless historical dates was likewise reduced to a simple historical system, and similar efforts were made in other academic domains. This was the age of the onomastica; scholars systematically organized all the known facts of the world into inventories. Knowledge was based on lists, and the Amduat reveals its origins in this age with its lengthy lists of divinities and their

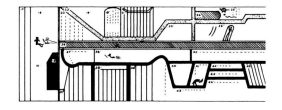

The Book of Two Ways on the bottom of a sarcophagus of Dynasty 12.

functions, which are occasionally quite tiresome for the modern reader. Similarly, another Dynasty 18 Book of the Netherworld (later incorporated as spell 168 in the Book of the Dead) lists the gods of the twelve vaults of the Netherworld, along with their functions.

The Book of Gates was also created in the Eighteenth Dynasty, shortly before the reign of Akhenaton. It arrived in the Valley only after the collapse of his revolution, when Haremheb used it in the decoration of his tomb. Here, the countless denizens of the Beyond are organized into clearly conceived groups, as a step toward ordering the chaos of the Beyond. Short notes on the material support of the dead separate the individual scenes of this pictorial composition, including—surely by design—precisely 100 scenes. This, like the Amduat, is a further contribution to the science of the Beyond, although it is a creation with poetic license, using simple descriptive passages beside poignantly symbolic images.

Like the Amduat, the Book of Gates employs the twelve-unit division for the sun's nightly journey. The title of the Amduat assured the user that he would learn "the march of the hours," with each hour suitably separated from the following by columns of text. In the Book of Gates these hourly divisions are actually given the form of gates with defensive crenellations, each guarded by a serpent that releases the bolt only for the solar bark, so that the doors remain fastened in the face of unfriendly powers.

As the hours determine the temporal progress of the sun, the gates frame its spatial course, and here again the new composition builds on older ideas. The heavens, the earth, and the Netherworld meet at the threshold of the depths, and it is here that ancient traditions placed the majestic Gate of the Horizon, through which the sun passed each morning. In the Old Kingdom Pyramid Texts it was the "Gate of the Primeval Waters," since the descent into the abyss was understood to be a bath in the primordial waters of Nun, whence the Creation originally emerged. Strong arms lifted the sun out of this abyss each morning, as dramatically depicted in the closing scene of the Book of Gates, thus splashing the Gate of the Horizon with the primeval waters encircling the world. The dead needed to cross this gate if they were to enter the realm of the departed.

The Book of the Dead also deals with the Gates of the Beyond leading into the realm of Osiris, the lord of this Netherworld. According to spell 144, the difficult path is blocked by seven gates, while spell 145 gives the threefold sum of twenty-one; twelve gates in the Book of Gates are merely the result of systematization, as they are in the Book of the Night, one of the later Books of the Heavens. While the number itself is not important, the nature of the route is, with its terrors for the uninvited and its reception for the select. Each gate is a danger, a challenge, an obstacle. In the tombs of Queens Nofretari and Tausert the guardians of the Gates are named: "the barker," "the raging one with the hippopotamus face," "he who devours the filth from his hind parts," and in a clear reference to the glowing fire of the serpent guardians:

> With hot flames, quenching not that which they burn,
> With quick killing, glowing embers, posing no questions,
> Whom no one wishes to pass, in terror of torment.

In the Book of Gates the guardians also bear threatening names and attributes: "with sharp fire," "the unapproachable," "blood-sucker," "he whose eyes spew

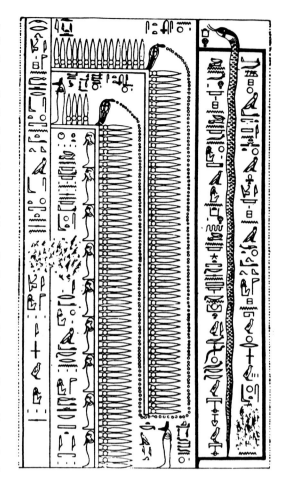

Door from the Book of Gates in the tomb of Sety I, showing serpent guardians amid dagger-shaped crenellations.

The deceased opens the door of Eternity, placed between horizontal hieroglyphic signs for "sky" and "horizon," in the Book of the Dead of Neferrenpet.

fire." The Litany of Re describes menacing doorkeepers of the Beyond, "who devour the souls and shadows of those destined to die." It is thus hardly surprising that crossing these well-guarded gates uninjured and unthreatened was a particularly important concern of the texts.

Having passed through the first gate, one arrives in a buffer region. (The Amduat relates that the first hour's travel covered 120 Egyptian, or 700 English, miles; the Book of Gates likewise emphasized the unique character of this hour.) It is only then that the first real gate of the Netherworld is reached, expressively called "The All-Devouring" or "Shroud of the Netherworld." Here, in the region of the second hour of the night, the sun god finally reaches the realm of the denizens of the Netherworld. The mountains and waters of the realm of the dead formed a perfect mirror image of the Nile Valley, with fertile green fields flanked by range after range of red desert mountains.

Beyond the edges of the luxuriant fields of the blessed dead however, there was an unfamiliar, trackless void untouched by the sun's rays: the horrifying home of the damned. The river of this realm is not the Nile but Nun, the chaos before the Creation. The descent of the sun god into this chaotic and terrifying place is a descent into the world before the Creation. "I enter a world from which I came; I alight at the place of my first birth," cries the sun in the later Book of Caverns, as he enters the realm of the dead.

As the reminder of the world before the Creation, the Netherworld is completely different, unknown, and mysterious. The deceased entered "another house—West is its name—unknown to all on earth" (as expressed on the coffin of the divine consort of Amun Ankhnesneferibre from the sixth century B.C.). In the Ramesside period, the Dat "conceals every secret: what enters does not depart." "Concealed" and "mysterious" are used in the Books of the Netherworld to describe this world: even the burial of a corpse is a "concealment" in the earth, the residents of the

Menacing guardians of the gates brandishing knives, from one of the shrines of Tutankhamun. (See plates 30–32.)

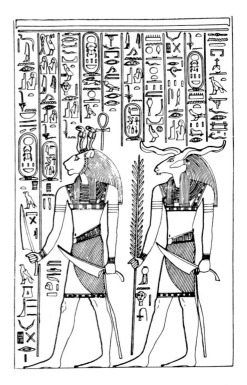

Beyond live in "mysterious caves," and the thirty-first address of the sun god in the Litany of Re is "he who sinks into the mysterious." Even the very words for "west"—the western desert as the Realm of the Dead—and "concealed" were pronounced the same (*imenet*) in Egyptian, and were not always written differently.

Darkness is the one prevailing aspect of this hidden and unknown land, joining it once again with the world before the Creation. It was called the unified or absolute darkness since the time of the Coffin Texts of the Middle Kingdom, which likewise refer to the "painful darkness of the westerners," for whom Osiris is the sovereign of darkness. The nightly sun does indeed bring light to the dim depths, but that sun is diminished, being "the dark-faced one" with a head wrapped in black in this context. This light is subdued, illuminating only a slice of the Netherworld at a time, and in no way impinging on the statement that for the living it is still "most deep, most dark, most infinite" (Book of the Dead, spell 175). In the rites of mourning, it is the "realm of endlessness and darkness, without light," where the dead "lie in darkness forever." These and similar phrases do not make this world more familiar, stressing rather the menacingly alien nature of the realm of the dead, where the bright familiar world of daily life is literally set on its head.

The Beyond is also a distorted mirror image of the here and now. Everything there is larger than life; measurements are made with "divine cubits" far larger than the earthly royal ones, and the grain grows far better than here, being reaped by the "enlightened," themselves real giants of 7 or even 9 cubits (over 12 and 15 feet, respectively). The dimensions of the Beyond given in the Amduat overshadow any earthly measures. The length of the mere buffer zone leading to the real Netherworld is greater than the entire length of the Nile Valley to a point below the second cataract, and the length of the region passed in the second hour is almost three times as great, 309 Egyptian miles, being exceeded only by the expanses of the "offering fields" in the Coffin Texts, which measured 1,000 Egyptian miles across and the same in length. The Coffin Texts note also that the "Water of the White Hippopotamus" was likewise 1,000 miles long, corresponding to the length of the heavens, "the expanse of which cannot be told."

The Egyptians suspected that the sun covered "millions of miles" on its daily journey through the heavens and the Netherworld. Thus we learn that even time had other dimensions in the Beyond, an hour of the nightly voyage corresponding to an entire life on earth. And these modifications forebode the suspension of fixed directions in time and space, as the framework itself became superfluous in the Beyond. In fact the sun travels in reverse in order to return to the eastern horizon, and thus all beings pass through the giant serpent of rebirth in reverse, from tail to mouth, transforming themselves from "elders" to "small children." The suspension of the cardinal directions is mentioned in the Dynasty 19 Book of Nut, a description of the heavens:

> The distant regions of heaven lie in perpetual darkness,
> Their borders unknown to the south, north, west, and east.
> These directions are exhausted in the primeval waters,
> Where the rays of the *ba* [of the sun god] do not pierce,
> Neither gods nor the enlightened knowing his realm to the
>   south, north, west, and east,
> Where there is no light.

These tired and suspended cardinal directions are probably the four "weary ones" in the second hour of the Book of Gates, lying before the god Atum and gazing in various directions.

The Beyond is thus a world of confusion, where up and down, right and left, before and after are all reversed; a world without straight lines, outside the bounds of time. Even the earliest funerary texts revealed the fear that one must walk "on one's head" or consume one's own excrement, as the digestive processes were also reversed. Even the goddess of heaven became one of "counterheaven," Nenet, standing on her head, and the dead thus real antipodes.

After the Old Kingdom, the Beyond of the heavens had gradually slipped into the Netherworld, and the crooked corridors of the Middle Kingdom pyramids reflect the twisted routes of the Beyond, as mapped in the roughly contemporary Book of Two Ways for private individuals. In the New Kingdom the fourth and fifth hours of the Amduat stress the zigzag course of the paths in the desert of Sokar, and the final hour reveals the edge of the Netherworld to have been a bent oval, often seen in the depictions of the sun's path as well. This is obviously the reason for the absence of axial principles in the Valley of the Kings before Akhenaton, and likewise the concept behind the oval burial chambers in the tombs in the earlier part of Dynasty 18. The architecture of the tomb is thus conditioned by the topography of the Beyond, while the texts and representations frequently take up the theme of the "bent" or "winding" waters in the landscape of the realm of the dead.

The suspension or reversal of all earthly measures affects the most elementary things, such as the normal direction of the hieroglyphic script; whole passages of the Books of the Netherworld must be read "backward." And the significance of the shawabtys, destined to carry out any work assigned to the deceased, suggests that the social hierarchy is reversed in the Beyond as well.

The clear and obligatory order of the Creation is continually thrown into doubt in the Beyond. On the other hand it appears that only these bottomless and confusingly peculiar depths are capable of renewing the Creation, which is the real purpose of the sun god's nightly "descent into hell." Virtually everything known about Egyptian conceptions of the Creation has been drawn from the funerary texts; no creation myths have been preserved.

At the beginning of the Amduat, the bark follows the goddess Maat, doubled as the "two Maats," indicating that correct and valid order incarnate descends to the dead with the sun. A breeze of creative breath goes with the solar bark, and as far as the light pierces and the magical words of creation reach, there the dead reawaken from their deathly repose. Hidden things are suddenly visible, doors open abruptly, rigid snake-heads begin to move, spewing forth fire from their lips. Everything is in motion as the crippling spell of darkness is banished.

Jubilation resounds as the sun god appears; only the damned wail at the resumption of their torments. In the Amduat, baboons acclaim the sun god in the name of all the creatures of the Beyond, making music and dancing before him, and in the scenes of the sun's path, the exultant apes represent all creation. "The gates of the great city are opened for you," they sing while pushing open the Gate of the Netherworld, that the solar bark may enter the Great or Eternal City, the Realm of the Dead with its millions. In a fraction of a second, the god has crossed the threshold and turns to the guardians, that the door be bolted fast once again. Passing into the depths of the darkness he senses the presence of his serpent-headed eternal enemy, Apophis, who may block his way even here. The frontispiece of the Litany of Re at the entrance of the Ramesside royal tombs displays the inevitable flight of the sun's dark foes when his triumphant light drives away the darkness: the snake, crocodile, and desert antelope flee the sun disk as it confidently descends into the depths.

But the universal rejoicing becomes a wail as the luminous bark moves on, passing through another well-guarded gate. Darkness drops over the region and the doors clang to a last wail before all the creatures resume the sleep of the dead. The jubilation and a dialogue with the god are followed by silence, another symbol of the Realm of the Dead and its divine Ennead, ''with heavy silence in the west.'' Deathly silence, the silence of the beginning, is that once broken by the cry of the first bird, the ''great cackler.''

Where this silence is broken, it is by meaningless sounds, themselves distorted like the space and time of the Beyond. In the eighth hour of the Amduat the sun god sails past caves in which the departed are enclosed. At his word the doors spring open and the darkness is expelled, that the sleeping dead may be seen straightening themselves and joyously responding to his reassuring pronouncements. But their answering voices do not match those of humans; they are instead the humming of bees or a wail of mourning, the bellowing of a bull or the breath of the wind, the call of a cat or a falcon, the murmur of a crowd or the splash of water. It is only in the ear of the sun god that the sounds are restored to their real values.

The god crosses the immeasurable distances of eternity in his ship, the familiar waterways of the Nile and the canals having been transferred to the Beyond. In the heavens every star and planet requires a bark; an etching on a comb of the early third millennium B.C. already sets the heavenly falcon in its own bark. The vessel of the sun is the ''Bark of Millions,'' for the god is accompanied not just by a large divine entourage but also by the blessed dead who aspire to board the sun bark—as described in the titles of numerous spells in the Book of the Dead (100, 102, 136)— and to remain forever in the company of the sun and share in the offerings. This is another way of entering the solar orbit and thus taking part in the miracle of the sun's rebirth at dawn.

In the tomb of the vizier User, the official himself can be seen at the rudder of the solar bark, where he replaces the divine pilot-coxswain Horus. The ferrying of the dead is otherwise not frequently depicted, although texts often refer to it. The

Frontispiece of the Litany of Re. A serpent above and a crocodile below take flight before the triumphant sun god, who is shown in his morning (beetle) and nocturnal (ram-headed) forms together in the solar disk. (See plate 57.)

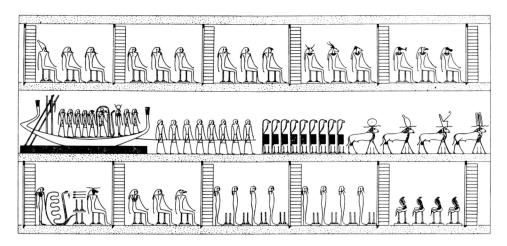

Diagram of the eighth hour of the Amduat in the tomb of Sety I. The solar bark is preceded by the four rams of the god Tatenen, embodiment of the depths of the earth. Above and below are ten caves behind wooden doors, which are inhabited by the divine beings acclaiming Re. The text says that only Re is able to understand their voices, which resemble not human speech but rather the bellowing of bulls, the crying of cats, the humming of bees, the blowing of the wind. (See plate 51.)

Egyptians believed that the souls of the dead accompanied the sun on its journey and descended into the Netherworld, where they were united with their former bodies, only to resume the voyage with the sun god, standing ram-headed in a shrine, protected by the wriggling Mehen serpent.

In the Book of Gates, the god's herald is Sia, standing at the bow and giving instructions, and opening the various doors separating one hour from the next. In the region of each hour, four humans pull on the bark's tow rope for all humanity, and aid where the oars are of no avail. In the Ramesside Books of the Heavens, jackals are harnessed before the vessel, and in the Dynasty 20 Book of the Earth, the solar bark is even drawn by human-headed uraeus serpents. The usual form depicts the goddess of the hour among those towing, and sometimes even the twelve hourly goddesses together grasp the tow rope, bringing the sun itself into the warp of time. Otherwise, it is the oarsmen who ensure that the ship glides along, simultaneously dipping their oars into the waters to the beat of a song. They are never shown in the vessel, but always in front of it. Even then, the thought was that the celestial army, the imperishable, unwearying stars themselves, were the sun god's oarsmen.

The fourth and fifth hours of the Amduat take the sun into a peculiar landscape. The realm of the god Sokar is a pure desert guarded by hordes of serpents, some of them winged. In order to move on without the necessary waterway, the sun bark turns itself into a snake, to slide over the hot sand more easily. Both the bow and stern are snake-headed, and the text describes how they spew bright fire before them, piercing the impenetrable, all-enveloping darkness. The voice of the sun god lights snakes as living torches, but the nature of this realm remains invisible even to him, only voices reaching him. During the fifth hour, he is towed past a giant oval, the secret cave of Sokar, a secluded spot guarded by the earth god Aker in the form of a double sphinx. Ominous thunder issues from within, the last remnant of a chaotic world avoided by the sun god. The gods, the blessed dead, and the damned do not wander on the paths of this region, filled with the fire that Isis spews forth. At its heart lies the Lake of Fire, whose red waves portend one of the most refined places of punishment reserved for those condemned at the Judgment of the Dead.

The solar bark with its crew and those who pull it forms the central element of each nightly hour in the two earliest Books of the Netherworld, the Amduat and the Book of Gates. The Dynasty 19 Book of Caverns and the later tracts, on the other hand, use this motif sparingly, indicating Re's presence in the Netherworld with a ram-headed deity or a simple solar disk, which is omitted entirely in those scenes showing the damned, who are visibly deprived of the sun's light. The division of the night into twelve hours is likewise absent in these later compositions: the Book of Caverns consists of two halves of three parts each, while the order of the registers is repeatedly disturbed by the insertion of particularly important pictures. The Book of Caverns is a modern appellation based on the text's division of the Realm of the Dead into a series of "caves" or "vaults" with countless strikingly placed ovals: sarcophagi of the divinities and blessed dead await the reawakening light and creative voice of the sun god.

In these Ramesside texts, the gods of the depths of the earth—Aker, Geb, and Tatenen—come to the forefront. The double sphinx Aker guards the Gates of the Netherworld in the third division of the Book of Caverns, lying above the body of Osiris; in the Book of the Earth he bears the solar bark on his back—yet another

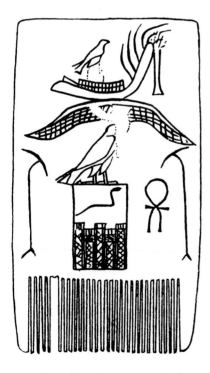

Ivory comb with the name King Djet ("Snake") of Dynasty 1; the notion of the sun god's traveling in a boat is already indicated by the sky falcon in his boat above the sky sign.

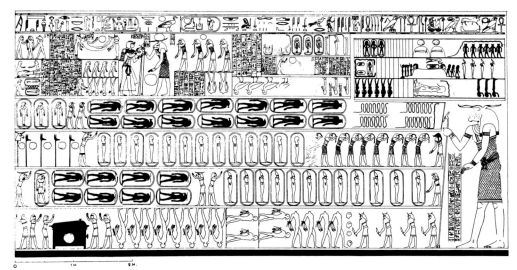

variation on the theme of the nightly journey through the depths of the earth. Countering the terror of dropping into these depths again, myriad arms propel the sun into the sky in the Book of the Earth adorning the walls of the burial chamber of Ramesses VI.

Parallel to the vision of a nightly journey through the earth just summarized is a complementary variant according to which the evening sun is swallowed by Nut, the goddess of the heavens; the sun moves through Nut's body in the night in order to pass forth newborn from her womb each morning. The god thus crosses the heavenly Beyond in this version, recalling the star-covered ceilings of the pyramidal burial chambers at the end of the Old Kingdom. A blue or black heaven sprinkled with yellow stars covers the ceilings of the shaft and antechamber of Dynasty 18 royal rock tombs, a feature that remained a royal privilege (private tombs show only ornamental ceiling decoration). The vaulted ''astronomical'' ceiling above the burial chamber of Sety I emphasizes this with pictures of the most important constellations, the decans, and the imperishable circumpolar stars of the northern sky. Further, his cenotaph at Abydos has the oldest preserved version of the Book of Nut in which a description of the Heavens is united with a table of decans. The vaulted ''astronomical'' ceiling in his tomb is found also in every later Dynasty 19 royal tomb, including that of Queen Tausert.

In Dynasty 20, the representations of the constellations are replaced with the Books of the Heavens. These deal systematically with the sun's voyage through the body of the goddess of the heavens and frequently revive motifs used in the earlier Books of the Netherworld. The interior of the divine body is divided into hours with their own gates. The corridor ceilings of these late tombs—until that of Ramesses IX—still retained constellations as monumental ''star clocks,'' which were, however, centuries out of date; their purpose was not so much to provide the correct time during the darker part of the day as to underline the analogous destiny of the dead who vanish and return. Popular belief held that their souls were incarnate in the stars themselves.

The Book of the Night deals only with the heavenly journey, adopting the traditional division of the earlier Books of the Netherworld into twelve nightly hours, just as the Book of the Day treats the daily voyage of the sun. On the ceiling of the burial chamber of Ramesses VI, the double, extended body of Nut—floating in the waves of the primordial waters—frames these two books which together cover the whole path of the sun and provide a cosmography of the heavenly regions. Familiar pictures from the sun's voyage in the Beyond and the reawakening of the dead, as well as of the punishment of the damned, reappear here.

The depths of the world are to be found in all directions: at the shores of the primeval waters, in the midst of the heavens, or in an abyss of the earth itself. Why does the sun god seek out this ''internal space'' at the close of each daily voyage, descending into the earth and the ocean, vanishing into the goddess's body? The Amduat states that the object is ''to behold [his] corpse, to examine [his] image that is in the Netherworld.'' In the Book of Caverns the god calls to the denizens of the Beyond:

> Guide me on the paths of the west,
> That I may reawaken the corpses that are there,
> That the souls may take their places and breathe,
> That I may brighten their darkness.

The Book of Gates informs us that Re ''created the Netherworld for his body.''

The goal of this ''descent into hell'' is that Re may be reunited with his corpse, and that the souls of the blessed dead may do the same. Re must perish in the depths, like all other creatures, in order to regenerate. In the Amduat the voyage of the fourth and fifth hours takes him to the dangerous and inaccessible region of the ''water hole of the Netherworld,'' and—at the lowest point of the nightly voyage— to his own corpse, indicated in several images: in normal human form rather than as a mummy, or as ''flesh'' surrounded by the ''many-faced'' serpent, an ancestor of the ouroboros. Immediately above this the sixth hour has a veritable solar cemetery, where each part of Re's body is individually buried: head, wings, and the

An abbreviated version of the Books of the Heavens on the ceiling of the sarcophagus chamber of Ramesses IX. (See plate 68.)

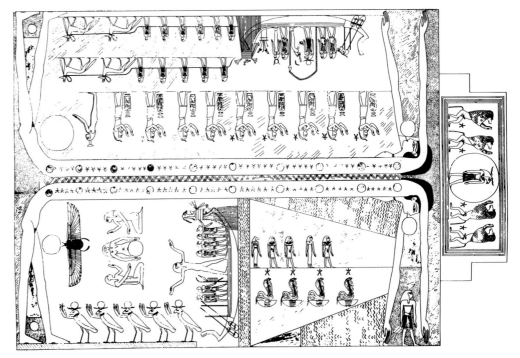

beetle's hind parts, each guarded by a fire-breathing serpent ("who is on her belly"). A new entity emerges from the division of the body. And in the seventh hour, beyond the dangerous "sandbank" of Apophis, four box-shaped tombs contain the four "images," or most important aspects, of the sun god, including Osiris, Atum, Re, and Khepri.

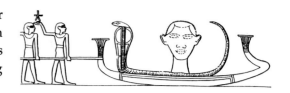

The face of the sun in the tomb of Ramesses VI.

The Book of Gates refers to the "corpse of this god" in the sixth hour, at the lowest point along the trajectory (scene 38). It is the "great mystery," invisibly carried by gods with "bent arms" calling to him, that his soul belongs to heaven and his body to the earth, and that he breathes as soon as he "assumes his body." This moment of the reunification of soul and body brings about the god's regeneration, the "kindling" of rejuvenated life. Still growing in the hidden depths, the sun follows its mounting path toward the dawn, the moment of rebirth when it becomes visible on the horizon for all creation. The sun god nevertheless spends an entire "lifetime" in each hour, deciding on the fate of the blessed and the damned. His presence awakens the departed from their deathly sleep, and as souls join bodies, life blooms everywhere.

The life-bringing presence of the sun in the realm of the dead is demonstrated in a particularly powerful way in the next-to-last hour of the Book of Gates (scene 73). Star-bearing gods tow a bark with the "face" of the sun god protected by a serpent, and the accompanying text notes: "This is the face of Re, which traverses the earth. Those who are in the Netherworld acclaim it" (with their stars, the hieroglyph for "praise"). As the "open-eyed" face is turned frontally to the beholder and thus the dead, it can unleash all its power, as the Egyptians understood it. The brilliance and the voice go forth achieving the miracle of bringing life out of death. The Litany of Re interprets the rays of the sun as the seed creating new life even in the Realm of the Dead. Viewing the face of the sun each night and enjoying its power means that one will not perish, and Re's nightly descent to the dead is a reassuring sign of the never-ending miracle of rejuvenation.

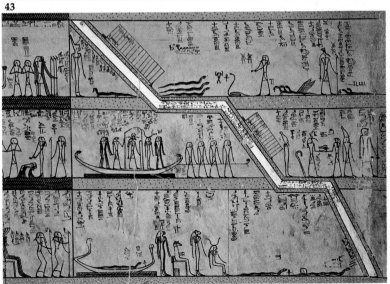

43. *The second hour of the Amduat, in the tomb of Amenophis II. In the middle register the solar bark moves past the fertile fields of the Netherworld accompanied by additional vessels, one with large ears of corn, one with a crocodile, one with the emblem of Hathor, and one with the sign of the moon. Below, gods present plants to Re and his followers.*

44. *The fourth hour of the Amduat in the tomb of Tuthmosis III. The scene is characterized by a zigzag sand road blocked by doors, which interrupts the water channel. The sun bark changes itself into a snake to make better headway.*

45

46

47

45. *Detail from the fifth hour of the Amduat in the tomb of Tuthmosis III. The sun god crosses "over the secret cave of Sokar," which is "sealed" with the head of Isis above. In this perilous cave, the falcon-headed Sokar holds a winged multiheaded serpent, a bit of the original Chaos. The oval cave is guarded by the earth god Aker as a double sphinx.*

46. *The second hour of the Book of Gates in the tomb of Haremheb. Above, the sun bark with the towing crew; below, Atum with the "exhausted ones," probably the four cardinal points which are unnecessary in the Beyond.*

47. *The three divine graves of the sixth hour of the Amduat in the tomb of Sety I. In the upper register the hieroglyphs for the head, wing, and hindquarters of the sun scarab are buried, each tomb guarded by a fire-spewing snake. Below, ringed by a five-headed snake, the sun's body assumes another form as "flesh of Khepri."*

48. *The sky goddess, Nut, in the Book of Caverns in the tomb of Ramesses VI. The sun god travels on the hands of the goddess, as both disk and ram-headed god. Between Nut's body and the two human-headed snakes are images referring to the course of the sun: the four crocodiles, the enemies of Re, are each associated with a different form of the sun.*

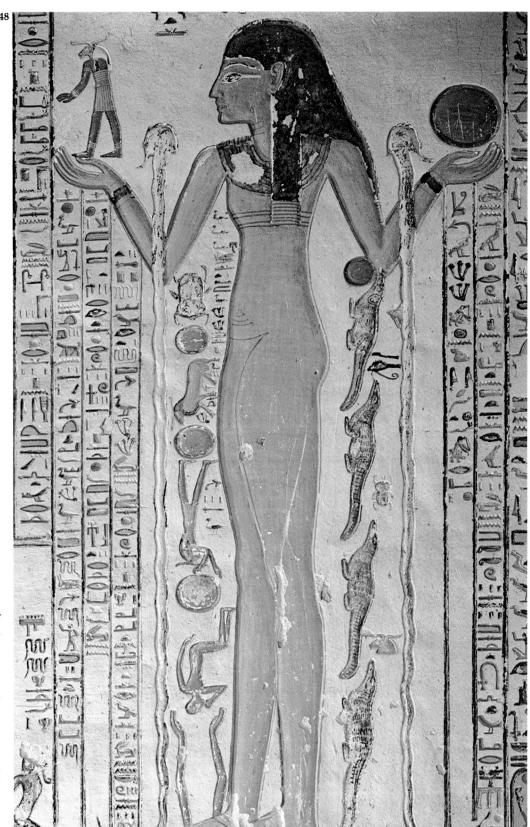

49

50

51

49. *The fourth hour of the Book of Gates in the tomb of Ramesses I. Above, mummies lie in dark coffins, not yet awakened from the sleep of death by the sun god. Below, the endlessly wound snake represents the infinity of time; each coil forms an hour that slips away devoured and then is re-formed. The goddesses who stand ''on their sea'' (indicated partly with waves and partly with black) personify the twelve hours of the night.*

50. *Middle register of the third hour of the Amduat in the sarcophagus chamber of Sety I. The bark of the goddess Pachet, with lion heads on bow and stern, and the baboon bark, ape heads on its bow and stern, ferry their divine crews. In each bark is an erect snake: the left is called ''he who spits fire with his eye,'' the right, ''he who sets fire with his face.''*

51. *Detail from the eighth hour of the Amduat in the tomb of Sety I. In the upper register the sun bark ferries the ram-headed god, protectively ringed by the* mehen *snake. Below is one of the ten caverns, sealed by red doors, from which is heard the strangely distant call of the dead identified as ''the scream of the tomcat.'' The ram-headed god (below right) rests on the hieroglyph for ''cloth,'' which signifies the supply of clothes for the dead.*

52. *Detail from the Book of the Earth in the sarcophagus chamber of Ramesses VI. The nocturnal voyage of the sun through the depths of the earth is indicated at the bottom by Aker as the double lion. The sun bark on the right is received by Tatenen, the god of the depths of the earth, and the bark on the left by Nun, the god of the primeval water. The arms of Nun lift the sun disk from the depths of the earth, the ascent repeated by the arms in the upper right.*

53. *Another detail from the Book of the Earth in the sarcophagus chamber of Ramesses VI. In the upper register the sun bark with the ram-headed god, his bird-shaped* ba, *and his manifestation as scarab beetle is accompanied by ram-headed gods who turn toward the vessel. Below, ''he who conceals the hours'' appears as procreative god, his phallus bound to the goddesses of the hours by dotted lines which go forth from him to father the sun anew, held by them as small red disks. The child and fire signs beneath the god's phallus refer also to the rejuvenated sun.*

52

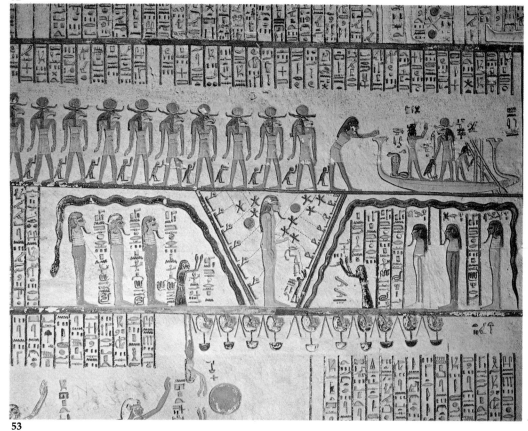

53

54

55

54/55. *The left (54) and right (55) walls of the sarcophagus chamber of Ramesses VI, with scenes and texts from the Book of the Earth. On the ceiling the duplicated image of the sky goddess Nut; at the bottom of the wall is a frieze of kneeling bound and headless "enemies," painted alternately black and red. (See plates 52–53.)*

FURTHER OBSERVATIONS ON THE JOURNEY OF THE SUN GOD

CHAPTER 6

At the entrance of the tomb of Sety I, immediately to the left stands the pharaoh himself in the rich dress of the Ramesside period, raising his hand in adoration to a falcon-headed divinity identified by the legend and the red disk on his head as Harakhty, "Horus of the Horizon," the sun god par excellence, to whom the pharaoh pays homage when entering the realm of the Beyond.

Pharaoh and sun god: this complex and wide-ranging theme dominates the decoration of this tomb's first corridor. The scene at the entrance is followed by the title and frontispiece of a religious text, the Book of the Adoration of Re in the West, usually called the Litany of Re. This text was composed at the beginning of the New Kingdom, at the same time as the Amduat. The content corresponds precisely to the title: a long litany of seventy-five addresses devoted to praising the various forms and functions of the sun god in the west, the Realm of the Dead. The first part of this book is pure adulation, but the second serves to demonstrate the dead pharaoh's complete identity with the sun god, which is on three levels: Pharaoh is Re; the ba of the god is his *ba*; and his path through the heavens and the Netherworld is that of the sun.

> I am you, and you are I,
> Your ba is my *ba*.
> Where you go in the Netherworld, there go I as well. . . .
> As you are, so am I. . . .
> Where you pass, there also I pass,
> Your travels are my own.
> My route is your route, Re,
> My travels are your very own. . . .
> I go the route of those of the horizon,
> I travel the travels of Re.

The stress of the Litany of Re, that the dead pharaoh follow in the wake of Re, takes us to the very heart of the Egyptian belief in the Beyond: the desire to take part in the celestial revolutions and to overcome death by this cosmic course. The orientation of the Old Kingdom pyramids served the same purpose for the kings; the entrances faced the northern pole of the heavens so that the soul of the deceased would climb into the region of the "imperishables," the circumpolar stars, which never drop below the horizon and are thus never obliged to descend into the terrifying depths.

Cosmic orbits were also the aspiration of the pharaohs of the Middle Kingdom, when the ecliptic decan stars came to the fore: the "untiring ones," which traverse both realms of the Beyond, the heavens and the Netherworld. Their return out of the depths of death is reassuring, as it guarantees that existence does not end there, that the dead need not descend to the depths forever.

The falcon-headed sun god Re wearing the sun disk.

Even more important and convincing as a symbol of rebirth is the simple course of the sun, the brightest and most powerful of the celestial bodies. The miracle of the sun's appearance and departure, of descent into the depths and triumphant return in rejuvenated form repeats itself daily before our very eyes. If the deceased can succeed in clambering aboard that magnificent vessel which carries the sun "millions of miles" through the space of the Beyond virtually instantaneously, if he can remain in the company of the sun forever, then he can be certain that all the terrors of death will be overcome.

The Litany of Re reveals the omnipresence and omnipotence of the sun god by means of a long row of inscribed figures, displaying in word and image the functions of this deity in the realm of the dead. The figures illustrate his seventy-five different forms of address and are simultaneously Re's various manifestations, which themselves become individual divine guardians of the deceased. They are worshipped in the temple of Ramesses II in Abydos, where they offer the pharaoh their benefaction and award him a long life and the power of life and death over his enemies, as well as freedom of movement in the Beyond, resurrection, and logistic support for all eternity. These guardians also allow the king to "rejuvenate like the moon" and put "longing for him into the hearts of all beautiful women."

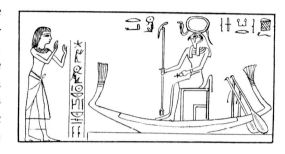

The deceased worships Re in his shrine carried by the sun bark, in the Book of the Dead of Nebseny.

In the Litany of Re the names of the various aspects of the sun god indicate the nature of the aid given Pharaoh: Shelter of *Bas*; He Who Gives the *Bas* Air; Corpse Illuminator; Creator of Breath; The Shining One; True Guide on the Ways of the Netherworld; Creator of Corpses; Rectifier of the World. Other names concern the punishment of the damned, the elimination of all "enemies" of the Creation. In this capacity the sun god is The Fetterer; The Hot One; or He of the Kettle. Beside the familiar manifestations of the god as daily-reborn child, ram, scarab beetle, "great tomcat" (his punishing form), and sacred eye, we also find unusual names, playing on the theme of death, which even Re must undergo. The god's descent into the Netherworld makes him not only Tomb Dweller, like other mortals, but also He of the Netherworld; The Secret One; The Concealed One; The Dark One or The Dark-Faced One; The Mourner or The Weeper; The Rotting One; He of the Sarcophagus. Here his destiny and being coincide with those of Osiris, so that many of the names and figures are also those of the sovereign of the dead. In shining images the Books of the Netherworld and the Litany of Re relate the nocturnal encounter of the two great gods, and their fusion into a single form, the "Joint God" with whom the parade begins. The union of Re and Osiris was conceived as temporary rather than eternal however. Re continually takes up new forms: Khepri's beetle in the morning, Harakhty's falcon at midday, Atum's ram in the evening, and the form of Osiris in the deepest night. He thus achieves sovereignty in the realm of the dead, and the deceased pharaoh may partake thereof, in his role as son of Re and heir of Osiris.

Re's activities are found also in the sun hymns contained within the Book of the Dead. Complex depictions of the sun's path show the sun's nocturnal form as Osiris (*djed* pillar), the dawning reanimation of life (ankh), and the evening's retreat into the open arms of the goddess of the West. This repeated, regular path of light opens all the paths of the Beyond for the deceased, for whom the sun god "leads the way in the Netherworld, opening the roads of the Beyond." The gates of the Beyond cannot withstand this luminous assault; "every path is open through your appearance," as Akhenaton sang to his god of light, Aton.

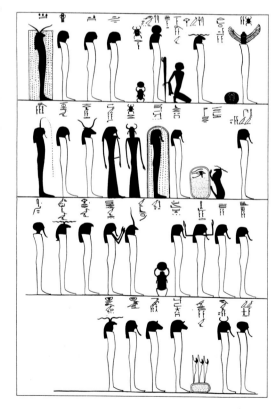

Litany of Re on a pillar in the sarcophagus chamber of Tuthmosis III. (Plate 62.)

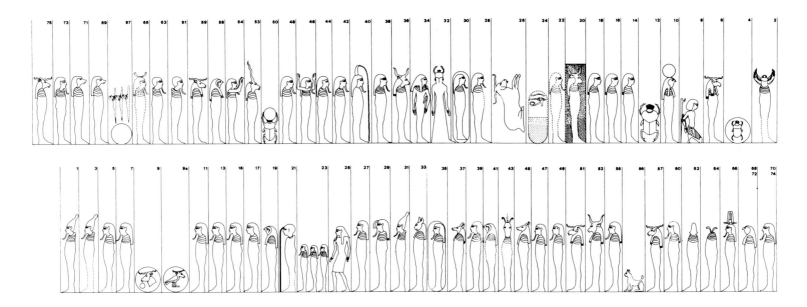

Litany of Re in the second corridor of Sety I: right wall above, left wall below. (Plates 58–61.)

The sun's course in a Theban private tomb. Below, Osiris as djed _pillar; an_ ankh _sign in the middle lifts the sun disk upward; the arms of the anonymous goddess in the Western Mountain reach for the disk from above. The scene is framed by worshipping baboons, Isis, Nephthys, and_ ba _birds._

Re is embraced by the two regions of the Beyond, day and night, which are incarnate in the goddess of the West and the goddess of the heavens, Nut. Both goddesses hold the sun god in a motherly way and transforms the tired old man into the small child who is born again each morning. "My birth is the birth of Re in the west," is the wishful expression in the Litany of Re. A few verses later, the deceased is the child of Re, Atum, and Khepri, the three manifestations of the sun god. His nurse is Nut: "she nurtures me, like the _ba_ of Re, which is in her"—this refers to the sun itself, which passes through her body. Bold images show the heavenly goddess with the sun child in her womb, signifying the mystery of the daily rebirth; the erect phallus of the precocious boy hints that this rebirth is the result of his begetting himself.

These daily and nightly courses of the sun are shown on the ceilings of late Ramesside royal tombs in a series of images, usually called the Books of the Heavens, analogous to the Books of the Netherworld, as the same motifs frequently appear in both. The pictorial cycles are framed by the overlong naked body of the heavenly goddess on the ceiling, her mouth swallowing the sun in the evening, that it may reemerge from between her thighs in the morning. Ancient hopes are expressed here, as the pharaohs wished in the Pyramid Texts to be numbered among the stars on the body of Nut, to join the certain and inalterable paths of the stars. In the New Kingdom and later, this goddess covers the sarcophagus lid, directly above the body of the deceased, receiving and bearing him again, like the sun. His wish is to lie in her arms, "that he not die forever."

As we have seen in the previous chapter, the Egyptian believed that the Beyond not only was in the abyss of the Netherworld but also was a part of the heavens, the very body of the goddess Nut. During the day the sun would glide along her body, to sink in the evening into the depths of the heavens, bordering on the infinite, "unknown to gods and spirits alike." It was here that the mysterious regeneration of the stars, and of the dead, took place. From this corner came the migratory birds whose departure and return served as a parable of death and rebirth. The bird form is used also for the depiction of human _ba_s, which move freely between the heavens and the Netherworld.

The *ba* of the sun god also appears as a ram-headed bird in the solar disk. The sun itself is a migratory bird of the Netherworld, which it seeks out each night. As the hieroglyphs allow that the word ba (usually depicted as a bird) could also be written with the homophonic symbol of the ram, the ram-headed manifestation of the sun god on his nocturnal voyage through the Netherworld suggests that he descends into the Netherworld as a *ba*, seeking his ponderous body, which lies in the depths. The Egyptian script displays once again its marvelous adaptability here, unifying thoughts and images. In a Ramesside private tomb at Deir el-Medina, a craftsman depicted the typical scene of Anubis with the mummy on its bier, with a fish for the mummy, as the word for "body" or "corpse" is written with a fish sign, indicating that the birdlike souls thus belong in the heavens, while the corpses remain in the watery abyss as fish.

These depths were regarded mostly as lying within the earth and were often represented in the Books of the Netherworld by the god Ptah-Tatenen. But the depths could also be those of the primeval ocean, Nun, or even those of the heavens, in the body of Nut. In the Book of Gates, Re's solar bark is raised out of the primeval waters by the hands of Nun. In the Books of the Heavens, the primeval waters splash the body of the heavenly goddess, and the nightly journey of the sun can be set into the body of a crocodile, revered by the Egyptians as the most powerful of the riverine creatures. The nightly voyage is thus always a journey in the depths, where the powers of fertility and regeneration are concealed. At the close of the day's long and tiring journey, the bent and aged sun god is swallowed by the depths, to reemerge the next morning as an infant or a scarab beetle, which comes out of the dung ball by itself.

All the images and texts discussed above show that the mysterious, daily miracle of the sun's transformation and rejuvenation is the central theme of the texts and images on the walls of the tombs in the Valley of the Kings. Each dawn signified a general renewal of all creation, and the Egyptian perceived an analogy in the daily transformation and rejuvenation of the dead. The importance of this process is clear from the manifold possibilities of describing it. As a child, or in the morning manifestation of a scarab beetle, the sun god emerges from between the thighs of the heavenly goddess, or rises out of the primeval waters. The "great flood" raises him as the celestial cow, and he shines out of the gates of the horizon. The most extreme simplification—almost reduced to a single hieroglyph—is in scenes of the solar cycle showing only a solar disk and a pair of arms rising out of the depths. Occasionally a bit of the Western Mountain is added, out of which emerges a pair of arms with feminine breasts drawing the sun to itself, while more detailed versions add a second pair of arms, with the sun disk being passed between them. The numinous power of the depths, pushing the sun upward, is masculine. The sun appears not always as a mere disk (although a disk rises out of a god's mouth in one illustration), but also as a ram's head, a ram's head enclosed in a solar disk, a scarab beetle, or a child; or the entire solar bark can be raised out of the depths, as at the close of the Book of Gates. This is the simplest form, hinting at the hidden powers of the depths, which embrace the sun in the evening and return it rejuvenated each morning, that it may traverse the heavens and the Netherworld, circumscribing the universe.

As we saw in the previous chapter, the Amduat sets the nocturnal rejuvenation of the sun in the body of a giant serpent, the "World Encircler," encountered in the

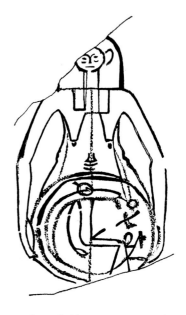

The sun god as child in the womb of the pregnant sky goddess, on a New Kingdom ostracon.

The naked sky goddess with sun, moon, and stars on her body, from the interior of a Late Period sarcophagus lid.

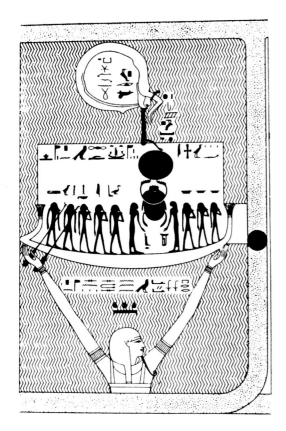

Final scene of the Book of Gates on the alabaster sarcophagus of Sety I. The solar bark is lifted from the watery abyss of Nun by Nun himself. The solar disk is carried by the sacred beetle and received by Nut standing on the head of Osiris, whose body encircles the Netherworld. (See plate 94.)

eleventh hour of the night. The idea draws on the thought of the ouroboros, the serpent that devours its own tail, a visible symbol of endlessness as the final border of the cosmos. In the twelfth hour of the night, immediately before dawn, the solar bark with all its gods and an incredible number of the blessed dead enters into the serpent's tail. The text notes that they all enter as ''honored ones,'' and the legends identifying the gods leave no doubt about the significance of this: ''old one,'' ''dotard,'' ''senile old man,'' ''gray-beard'' and so on. Weary, aged, and weakened, the sun god and his entourage enter the serpent, travel along its backbone, and step forth from its mouth as small children. The inverse route, traveling from the tip of the tail to the mouth, plays on the marvelous reversal of time, which is possible only in the Beyond—from old man to child, from death to birth. Beyond the regenerating serpent, the sun climbs up to heaven as a scarab beetle, firmly supported by the arms of Shu, the support of the heavens, who separates the gods of the earth from the gods of the heavens, and is therefore well placed to raise the sun out of the depths.

The Book of Gates also contains motifs of renewal, traversing, and ascending. In the third nightly hour the tow rope of the solar bark disappears into a long object with a bull's head at each end. This is ''the earth bark,'' ''the vessel of the gods [i.e., the dead],'' ''the ship of the Netherworld,'' apparently a picture of the earth as the Netherworld and nocturnal space of the solar voyage. The scene of the Book of Gates with the earth bark compresses the entire voyage through the Netherworld into a single image with a few bold strokes and simple allusions. It is only in the final hour of the night that the book deals with the rejuvenation and rebirth of the sun. Here, four baboons open the eastern gate of the heavens, proclaiming to a cheering world the appearance of the shining star. The rising sun joins the Netherworld to the heavens, accompanied by a chorus of eight goddesses astride serpents, and carrying stars in their hands.

This book, like the Amduat, transforms the sun god into a child. He opens the Netherworld to the heavens and moves upward while still on the arms of the god Nun, incarnate symbol of the primeval waters, whose arms raise the sun out of the depths. The solar bark with the dawn form of the beetle, provided with a divine crew, is raised in Nun's arms and grasped from above by Nut. The goddess of the heavens herself stands on the head of Osiris, whose legs are bent back ''encircling the Netherworld.'' The final goal of the new journey is shown here: the sun must return to the depths, the realm of Osiris, that the never-ending journey may commence again.

The closing scene in each of the later Books of the Netherworld varies from tomb to tomb, as new insights were taken into consideration. Merneptah put a version of the closing scene of the Book of Caverns in a prominent position on the right-hand wall of his burial chamber, and Queen Tausert did the same shortly after him. The relations are changed here, as the anonymous pairs of arms come not from the depths but from above, apparently pushing the solar disk, the sun child, and the ram-headed beetle downward. The real intention was merely to emphasize that the two pairs of arms pass the sun in its various manifestations between them, keeping it in perpetual motion. Merneptah even added his royal name to the solar manifestations, ensuring that he would join the sun's path, as in the Litany of Re.

This scene is framed by adoring creatures, the souls in bird form and their ''shadows'' as ostrich-feather fans. They lean in prayer before the sun god, whose nightly path takes him through regions of eternal darkness where obscurity is only partially pierced by the stars, and through the endless expanse of the primeval blue waters, pictured in the singular triangles that strike the visitor entering the burial chamber. The human face in the two black hills is that of the sun god in his "vault," where he is rejuvenated each night. This is the "great mystery" to which the texts refer, the eternal promise for the dead pharaoh, whose mummy lay in this room, that he would have a "life like the sun." Beneath this illustration is the ram-headed vulture which combines the day and night forms of the sun god and whose wings cover the whole width of the wall.

The opposite wall takes up the same central concern, showing the reawakening of Osiris through the light of the sun. A variation of this scene is incorporated into the Book of the Earth, which also has the motif of the earth bark from the Book of Gates. In place of a double steer is a double lion, guarding the entrance to and exit from the earth's depths and representing the god Tatenen, who at the right receives the solar bark, released by Nun on the left. In the middle of the picture is a hieroglyph-like version of the sun's path with only arms and solar disk; these are the arms of Nun propelling the star from the invisible precipices into the heavens. The depths of the earth and the primeval waters are united in a single regenerating element, in which the sun's youth is revived. In the ovals on the breast of the double lion is Shu, who separates heaven and earth and carries the sun into the heavens at the close of the Amduat.

The final gate of the Netherworld in the Amduat "raises the gods": all the other gods and blessed dead are lifted from the dark depths of water and earth along with the sun god, and the sleeping likewise emerge from the world of dreams, which the Egyptians locate in Nun, and return to the sensible light of consciousness. The world is as young as at the Creation, when everything was first allowed to rise out of the dark watery abyss of the sluggish Nun. The Egyptian was thoroughly convinced that the Creation could be repeated, that the "first time"—as he called the emergence of time—was in fact repeated every morning with the dawn, which returned youthful freshness to the world. As life emerged from moisture, it required the primeval waters for its renewal. It is with Nun that the deceased identifies himself in the Litany of Re, before moving on to equality with the sun and Osiris.

Once in the hands of the invisible powers that lift the sun out of its nightly bath of renewal and propel it through the universe, the deceased is certain he is not lost. The other possibility was that of merging with the sun and joining the path of the stars, which is never interrupted despite the perpetual threat of the Apophis serpent.

The pictures and texts on the walls of the Ramesside royal tombs bring the solar cycle into the tomb, letting the mightiest star pass through its corridors and chambers. The deceased pharaoh accompanies the sun on its journey. The representation at the tomb's entrance shows the pharaoh worshipping the sun god. Then the Litany of Re in the first corridor confirms the pharaoh's identification with the sun, from the first corridor to the very last wall of the burial chamber as we see in the tomb of Ramesses VI. Nun's arms lift the solar bark aloft. The very names of the corridors refer to this; "the first divine passage of Re, which is on the path of light," and similar appellations maintain the theme. The significance of these solar

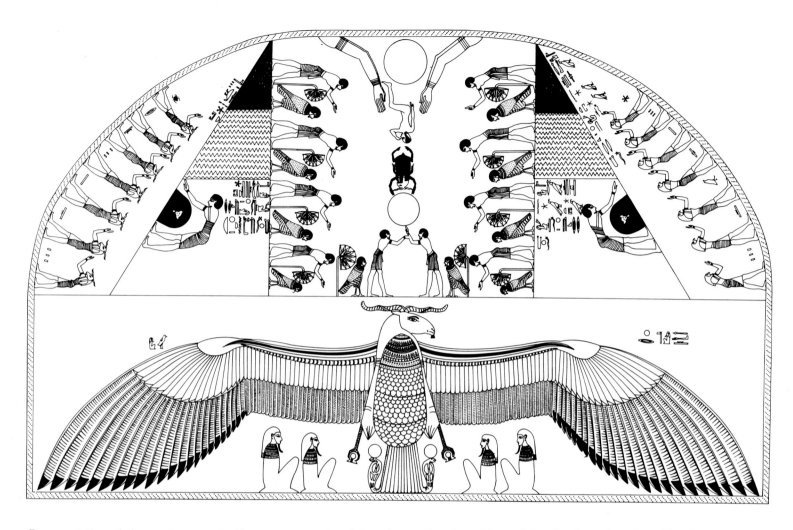

Representation of the sun's course in the sarcophagus chamber of Tausert. (Plate 64.)

aspects of the decoration is evidenced in the fact that Sety II, after regaining Thebes, had the Litany of Re carefully obliterated in the tomb of the usurper Amenmesse.

A variation on the theme of the identification of pharaoh with the sun, lost today but copied by Champollion, was placed in the tomb of Ramesses III on the right-hand wall of the burial chamber, where Merneptah and Tausert had placed their summary versions of the solar cycle. It showed a double ouroboros encircling the solar disk in the middle of which stood the pharaoh's name: ''Ramesses, Ruler of Heliopolis.'' The twelve goddesses worshipping the solar disk, and thus Ramesses as well, symbolize the twelve hours of the nightly voyage, as do the stars and disks in the outer circle. The artist exhausted all the possibilities that the form and significance of the royal name allowed him. Literally Ramesses's name means ''It is Re who bore him,'' but it is written in such a way as to permit a second reading: ''It is Re who continuously bears him,'' where Pharaoh's otherworldly existence is the object, and the sign for ''to give birth'' is precisely in the middle of the entire composition, forming its conceptual and real center. Even the title ''Ruler of Heliopolis'' receives a new meaning: Heliopolis is the ancient solar city of Egypt, to which a counterpart in the Beyond may be imagined.

The ruler who inscribes his name in the solar disk and identifies himself with the perpetual rebirth of the sun in the Beyond forms a pictorial complement to the text of the Litany of Re, proclaimed hundreds of years earlier, providing the basis for the expression of the pharaoh's most profound hope: "I am Re."

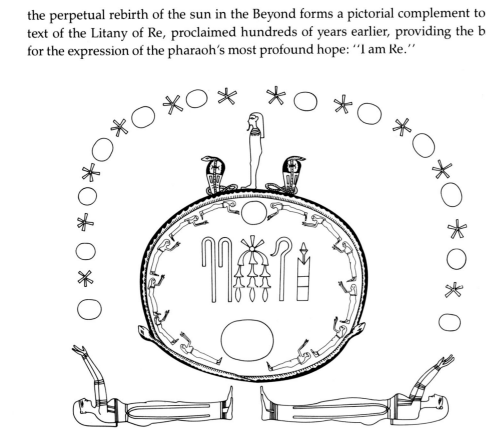

The name Ramesses "Ruler of Heliopolis," in the sun disk, in the sarcophagus chamber of Ramesses III.

56

57

56. *Entry scene in the tomb of Merneptah. The king, wearing the elaborate garments of the Ramesside Period including the* atef *crown with protective uraei, stands before the falcon-headed sun god Re-Harakhty.*

57. *Continuation of the previous scene: title, tripartite image, and beginning text of the Litany of Re in the first corridor of Merneptah's tomb. In the center of the image, the flattened sun disk with scarab and ram-headed god; above and below, enemy creatures escaping from it.*

58/59. *Figures describing the nature of the sun god, in the Litany of Re on the left wall of the second corridor of the tomb of Sety I.*

60/61. *Litany of Re on the right wall of the second corridor of the tomb of Sety I.*

62/63. *Litany of Re on the pillars of the sar-cophagus chamber of the pre-Ramesside tomb of Tuthmosis III.*

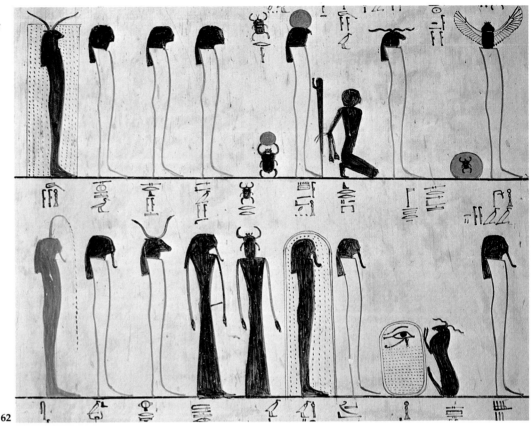

62

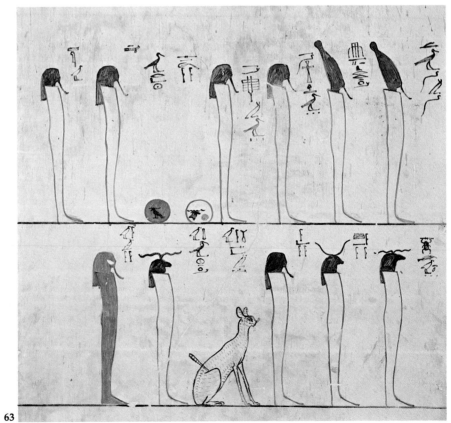

63

64/65. *Two representations of the final scene in the Book of Caverns, which recapitulates the nightly course of the sun (Tausert, 64; Merneptah, 65). The sun, moved by two pairs of arms, appears in three forms, as child, ram-headed beetle, and disk. Its course leads through a black eclipse and blue streams (the triangular shapes on either side). The deceased with their* bas *(birds) and shadows (fans), worship the sun. The ram-headed winged creature spans the entire breadth of the wall. In plate 64, lower left, are the sun bark and the earth god Aker as a double sphinx; that in the lowest register are depictions of the burial gifts.*

66. *The* ba *of the sun god as a bird with a ram's head, standing in the red sun disk and flanked by Isis (left) and Nephthys (right) as mourners. The scene, from a text in the Litany of Re, is on the starry ceiling in the second corridor of the tomb of Siptah.*

67. *Above the entrance to the tomb of Merneptah, and in all Ramesside tombs, the sun god appears in his two major forms: as scarab (morning sun) and ram-headed god (nighttime sun). The flanking figures of Isis and Nephthys, who are associated with Osiris, indicate the sun god's unification with Osiris. The sun disk is painted yellow rather than red only on this exterior scene.*

64

65

98

66

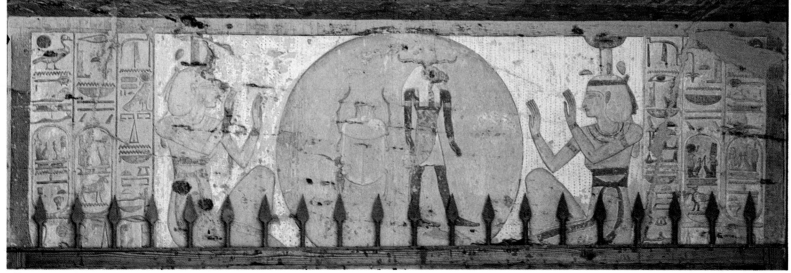

67

68

69

68. *The Book of Day and the Book of Night framed by the double form of the sky goddess, Nut. The scene is on the ceiling of the sarcophagus chamber of Ramesses VI. (See plate 54.)*

69. *The nocturnal trip of the sun through the body of a crocodile, in the sarcophagus chamber of Ramesses IX. The sun emerges in the morning with the head of a ram.*

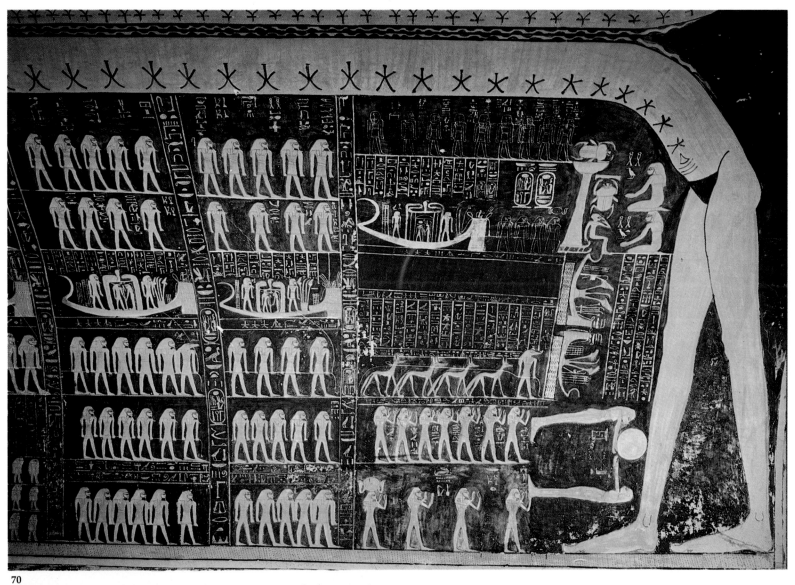

70

71

70. *The final part of the Book of the Night, in the sarcophagus chamber of Ramesses VI. The scene ends with the new birth of the sun from the sky goddess. Directly before the vulva, the ancient gods Huh and Hauhet assist in the birth of the sun child, who appears also as a scarab. Below, Isis and Nephthys carry the sun disk. (See plate 55.)*

71. *Symbolic representation of the continual ''birth'' of the hours through the god who conceals them, in the sarcophagus chamber of Tausert. The hours are indicated on both sides by goddesses and stars. The whole is surrounded by the body of the Great Snake.*

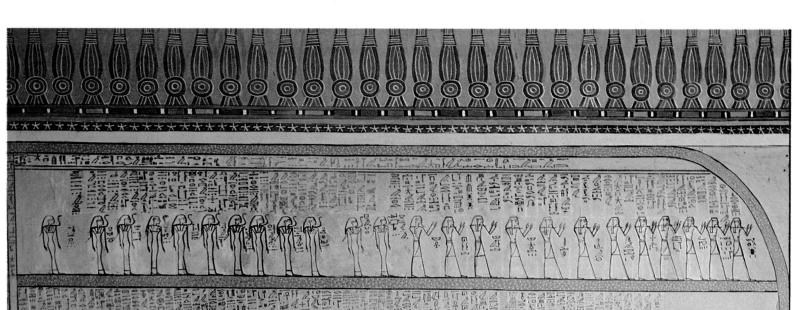

72

73

74

THE TRIUMPH OF MAGIC:
THE SUN GOD'S VICTORY
CHAPTER 7 OVER APOPHIS

Atum with Apophis from scene 13 of the Book of Gates. (See plate 95.)

72. *The twelfth hour of the Amduat in the burial chamber of Amenophis II. In the middle register the sun god in his bark rejuvenates himself together with his entourage, as he enters the body of a traveling snake, and then climbs, as a scarab, on the arms of Shu to the sky.*

73. *The concluding scene of the Book of Caverns in the upper pillared hall of the tomb of Ramesses VI. As the sun disk breaks through the boundary of the underworld on the left, he is rejuvenated as a child and a scarab.*

74. *The reawakening of Osiris through sunlight, in the burial chamber of Merneptah. The mummy is surrounded by a semicircle of stars and sun disks, concentrated especially around his face.*

The seventh hour of the Amduat describes the dramatic encounter of the sun god with his archenemy, Apophis. Every conceivable menace to the daily course of the sun has contributed to the growth of this serpent, which has "neither hands nor feet," some sources even remarking that it lacked any sensory organ. It symbolized everything chaotic and formless that seeps out of the depths of the earth, throwing the world of the Creation into doubt. Apophis is dedicated to stranding the solar bark and thus bringing the sun to a halt, which would mean the end of time and space, and hence all existence.

It is significant that the name and idea of this serpentine enemy of the Creation were unknown in the Old Kingdom. In the first prosperous period of Egyptian history the divine order was never exposed to doubt: the eternal and unavoidable menace was never clearly understood. It is, however, possible that a tradition existed relating to an earthly being that threatened the sun, as the first reference to Apophis seems to date before 2100 B.C. in the tomb of a local ruler at provincial Mo'alla. Texts in the main religious centers mention a turtle of the watery abyss as an enemy of the sun, a theological motif unknown in other contemporary religious centers.

It is surely no accident that Apophis appears only after the collapse of the Old Kingdom, when hopeless chaos overtook the seemingly well-founded trust in the worldly order of the Pyramid Age. This must have awakened the speculation that Re, the god of creation, had a hidden enemy constantly threatening him and his creation. The intellectual discussions of the collapse of order stimulated a literary awakening during the First Intermediate Period (ca. 2100–2050 B.C.). Poets relate all the horrors of the age in stylized complaints attempting to explain the sources of this incomprehensible chaos. The world "spins like a potter's wheel" and nothing can stand still, traditional values being thrown to the wind. "The royal storehouse is open to one and all. The entire palace is without its revenues." This collapse was neither the work of foreign foes nor a violent revolution, and thus it defied explanation in hitherto comprehensible terms. The king and his bureaucracy proved themselves manifestly incapable of maintaining order, with the result that the human heart revealed its propensity for evil when left to itself. But contemporary Egyptians were conscious of something concealed behind the mere human failure. They realized that powers predating the Creation contend with powers that maintain and cleanse Creation: unstable and destructive forces are an inherent part of the Creation from its inception. The figure of Apophis is thus a part of the human reaction to the challenge brought about by the First Intermediate Period.

The first references are to the "sandbank of Apophis," the most important symbol of the sun god's challenge. Apophis fills his monstrous body with river water, stranding the solar bark. Should he succeed with this project, the sun would come to a halt, and the world to an end. This cannot be permitted, and Apophis is finally defeated. But he does force the sun god to face him and his threat, even while Re attempts ''to swerve away from Apophis's path,'' seeking to pass between the distant sandbanks. While the Egyptian texts do not explicitly assert that the Creation was generated by a struggle with a chaotic monster, the Egyptian god of creation had to fend off the daily attack of this threat to his work, contending every day with the possibility of the complete negation of his creation.

Spell 414 of the Middle Kingdom Coffin Texts, entitled ''Driving Apophis from the Solar Bark,'' has practical notes on how to overcome the ''robber'' who aims to steal the *udjat* eye (actually the solar disk itself here) as the symbol of the constantly healed and renewed order of the world. Fire drops from heaven into his ''cave,'' and Apophis is bound, charmed, and dismembered—all motifs that live on in the New Kingdom Book of the Dead. In that text are a number of spells intended to avoid Apophis, as he threatens the deceased directly, depriving him of sunlight and water. Spell 108, the most detailed of these, deals with the mountain of the eastern sunrise, and continues:

> A serpent lies upon the crest of that mountain,
> Thirty cubits long . . .
> Consuming Fire is his name.
> After a while, however,
> His eye is turned against Re:
> And the bark halted,
> The rowers dumbfounded,
> For he gorges one cubit and three palms of the Great Water.

The situation is in fact grave, for the serpent has taken in well over two feet of water and rowing is no longer possible. Seth proves himself equal to the menace by uttering a spell and pressing his metal spear into the serpent's body, forcing it to disgorge all that it has swallowed, so that the solar bark may proceed on its way. Other sources record that two fish report the presence of Apophis and swim on to find another channel.

But the most important delineation of the myth of Re's encounter with Apophis are the texts and pictures in the Valley of the Kings: the New Kingdom Books of the Netherworld. These provide many details and a whole series of contemptuous names for the enemy of the sun: Raw Face, Evil Lizard, Bad, Sneaky, Rebel, Enemy. And Apophis is not alone: a whole gang, ''the offspring of the weak,'' aids his attack on the solar vessel.

This combat repeats itself in the course of the sun's journey. In the heavens, in the mountains of the horizon, and in the Netherworld, the foe is all-present, emerging out of the dark depths to menace the radiant disk, the eye of the sun. His empire is that of the world before the Creation: darkness and the watery abyss. The Book of the Day on the ceiling of the tomb of Ramesses VI shows Apophis swimming in the primeval waters, across which the solar bark passes far above. In other passages he lies on a sandbank that he created as an obstacle for the solar vessel. Five different passages in the Book of Gates describe the dramatic event, although it is the subject of only a single episode in the Amduat and the Book of Caverns.

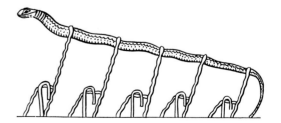

Apophis in bandages from scene 89 of the Book of Gates.

The magic nets from the Book of Gates in the tomb of Ramesses VI. (See plate 80.)

While the Books of the Netherworld do not provide one continuous account of the story, the most significant incidents and their order can be reconstructed. The serpentine body of Apophis blocks the path of the solar bark, and his withering glance (as this version does not hold him to be blind) brings the journey to a halt. The subsequent episodes take place in darkness, since the sun god is obliged to conceal his radiant eye in order to protect it. Later versions have Apophis actually swallowing the eye and being forced to return it when conquered. The darkness is broken only by the odd fire-breathing serpent, and the roar of Apophis, whose "thunderous voice" echoes through the Netherworld, terrifying the sun god and his entourage.

But before the stranded vessel is taken by the enemy, the goddess Isis at the boat's prow reaches out and throws the most powerful weapon known to god and man at the monster—magic. Isis is a powerful magician and only magic can save the Creation from the most terrible threat, just as magic made the Creation possible. It was only with the active energy of magic that the spoken word of the creator, and his specific conception of its meaning, could take form. Afterward magic served the gods to master unusual situations when more ordinary means were of no avail. From the gods, magic came to men, to be employed not merely as a means of defense but also for egotistical and aggressive purposes, such as in love potions or spells for damaging one's enemies. The Egyptians understood magic as active energy that could be used for diverse ends, both good and ill. It was personified by the god Heka, who was always in the company of the sun on his journey, ensuring that Re was never without his real creative power.

The magic with which Isis disables Apophis is boldly depicted in the tenth hour of the Book of Gates (scene 66). Thirteen divinities—some in monkey form—charm the foe with ''that which is in [their] hands.'' Each of them has a net drawn taut, a visible field of force containing and projecting their energy. Apophis is caught and bound by this force: the ''radiant'' magic strikes his head. He is neither destroyed nor killed, merely disabled, deprived of strength and his sense of orientation ''so that he cannot find himself,'' like someone who has been affected by the magic of love.

The enemy is thus subdued and the defenders of order throw cords about his body. In the eleventh hour of the Book of Gates, the scorpion goddess Selket ''lassos him when the bark of this great god is swamped,'' enabling Re to continue. The rope is held in the firm grip of the mysterious fist of a hidden god while the earth god Geb and the ''children of Horus'' also grasp it. The sun god learns of the triumph: ''Apophis is in his bonds.'' He has been rendered helpless with magic.

The danger has passed, but the solar bark is still in the dry riverbed, requiring a final effort of magic, usually accomplished by Seth. In the Book of Gates, three armed figures stand beside the gods with nets; they spear the monster's body, forcing it to expel the water it has swallowed. The water pours back into the channel, and the stranded vessel and its crew and passengers can resume the voyage. The crippled enemy remains behind, his body cut into pieces, the head detached, each coil carefully sliced. The flame of the eye of Horus burns him, and exposed to the unbearable heat of the Netherworld, he is reduced to ashes and ceases to exist.

It might appear that the triumph of order is final. But the struggle is renewed, and Apophis reappears. The threat to the Creation has been overcome only temporarily. In the temples of the Late Period, a ritual book against the solar enemy and his gang was read daily, to save the world from paralysis and catastrophe, thus

Re as ''the great tomcat'' cuts up Apophis by the isched *tree, from spell 17 of the Book of the Dead.*

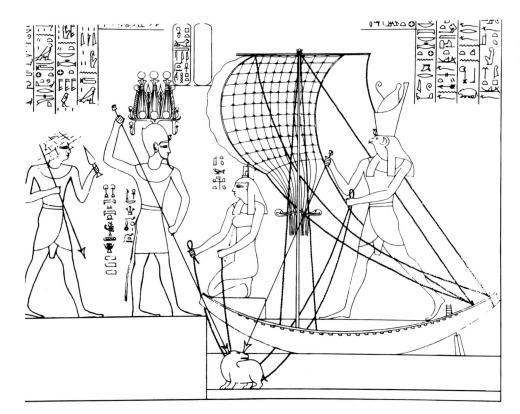

Horus, accompanied by Isis, harpoons Seth as a hippopotamus, in the Ptolemaic temple of Horus at Edfu.

striking at all of the enemies of the Creation as well as the archenemy. The ritual included a wax imitation of the serpentine fiend, which was to be dismembered and burned in place of Apophis.

Seth, the murderer of Osiris, was destroyed in a ritual similar to that for Apophis. Horus, Osiris's posthumous son and heir, assumes the role of conqueror and dragon killer, and in the temple of Edfu harpoons his enemy in the form of a hippopotamus, a plump creature with some of Seth's power. According to the original version of this myth, Seth himself overcomes the serpentine monster Apophis, thus using his incredible strength in the service of the Creation; but he also disturbs and threatens it with the murder of Osiris, his own brother.

Apophis appears to share some of this ambiguity with Seth. Apophis is not simply the principle of evil; the Egyptians always suspected that the complex interwoven structures of the world could not be reduced to the dualistic system of good and evil. The chaotic and shapeless nothing from which Apophis emerges, and into which he always returns, threatens the order of the Creation. But it includes all the elements that Creation requires for its own perpetuation and regeneration.

The reverse of the serpent's mortal menace is the reassurance incorporated unexpectedly in the snake as a symbol of rebirth in the Amduat. This paradox is subsequently summarized in a simple but brilliant image with the sun child in an ouroboros, the serpent that bites its own tail. The serpent's threatening and protective form encircles the god of creation, who returns to his childhood within the circle. In the final division of the Book of Caverns, the creature around the rejuvenated sun beetle is called simply "the great serpent." It is charmed and dismembered, and thus can be identified as Apophis, but the encircling of the sun god can refer only to the ouroboros. Serpent of Rebirth, World Encircler, Tail in Mouth, Apophis, and Great Serpent are all different names and forms of the same giant monster that daily swallows everything in order to disgorge it, rejuvenated and renewed. The miracle of the perpetual regeneration of the Creation is accomplished only with the aid of this equivocal creature.

This challenge of renewal stresses the already dangerous points of the nightly voyage. The most elaborate description in the Amduat places the episode in the immediate vicinity of the solar corpse, with which the sun god is united at the lowest point of his nightly orbit. In the sixth hour of the Amduat, this corpse is guarded by an encircling serpent, Many-Faces, clearly an ancestor of the ouroboros. In the seventh hour, four divine tombs just behind the sandbank of Apophis house the "images" of the sun god's four main forms (Atum, Khepri, Re, Osiris), and a hedge of knives protects them from the menacing closeness of the monster. The houses are separated from the bark by the enormous snake, and the sun god must overcome this horrifying obstacle to the union of ba soul and body, which is the desire of all the dead. The moment of the reawakening to life is simultaneously the moment of the greatest danger.

The menace arises once more before the sun god can repeat the primeval creation with the dawn, bringing the world into motion once again. In the last hour of the Amduat, twelve goddesses with uraei on their shoulders accompany the god, that the fiery breath of the serpents fend off Apophis at the eastern gate of the horizon, through which the god leaves the depths and climbs into the heavens. Once past the "secret sandbank of heaven" and thus out of danger, the goddesses

The sun child encircled by the never-ending ouroboros, carried by the celestial cow and the lions of the horizon. Papyrus of Herweben.

return to the Netherworld and resume their places. The dead rejoice at the sight of the living torches, the fiery snakes on the shoulders of these goddesses. Until the return of the sun, these are the only sources of light in the terrifying darkness of the Realm of the Dead.

The sun is not alone. All the dead are conscious of the threat of Apophis, and desire to aid in his eradication. In the Amduat, the whole crew of the solar bark takes an active part in the defense, and the Book of the Dead offers a number of efficacious spells for dealing with Apophis. He is only one of the dangers facing the dead, and many spells are required for their defense against countless snakes crawling about the deserts of the Netherworld, or against dangerous crocodiles. Spell 32 is intended to ''repel the four crocodiles who approach in order to take away a man's magic in the Realm of the Dead.'' Arriving from the four cardinal directions, the crocodiles, ''who eat the dead and live from magic,'' fall on the deceased, who repel them with gestures while repeating, ''Get back, you croco-dile. . . . Your abomination is in my belly.'' Even apparently innocuous creatures must be kept off: insects, or seductive women seeking to mislead the dead in the manner of the Sirens necessitate magical energy and the proper spells which have been used ''a million times.''

In this world and the next, the human race is expected to aid the gods in the defense of the Creation. This effort is mostly on behalf of the sun god and is practically a condition for a blessed life in the Beyond. But the texts of the royal tombs show that the sun god himself was threatened by the men he had created, in a tale analogous to that of the Flood in which the annihilation of rebellious humans was attempted by fire rather than water (water was always a blessing for the Egyptians, even after the worst inundation). This tale, the Destruction of Mankind, is one of the few full-length mythological texts from pharaonic Egypt preserved in its entirety. It appeared after the Amarna Period when Akhenaton undertook a very

The twelfth and last hour of the Amduat. (Plate 72.)

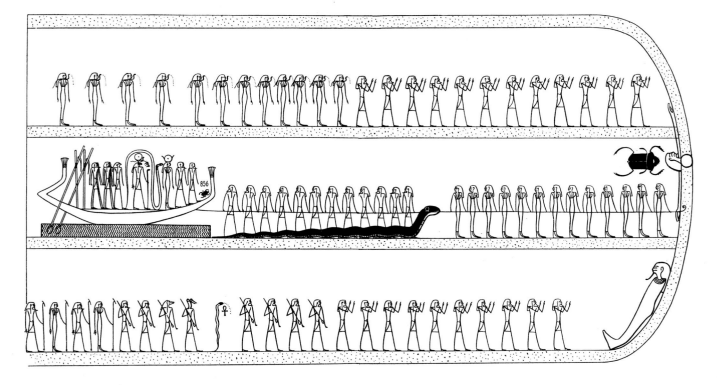

The subjugation of the enemy crocodile from spell 31 of the Book of the Dead. Papyrus of Cha.

real rebellion against the gods. The story is written in the tombs of Sety I, Ramesses II, and Ramesses III. The continuation of the story, the Book of the Celestial Cow, is preserved on the outermost gold shrine of Tutankhamun.

The text begins with a description of how men conspire against the aging sun god's kingship. After learning of the danger, the sun god calls for a divine assembly, where he pays particular attention to the advice of the primeval god Nun. Succor can be had only from the "eye," the brilliant star itself, which assumes the form of Hathor, here a goddess of vengeance. According to other mythological traditions, mankind was born from the tears of the eye of the god of creation.

After the close of the divine assembly, the text continues laconically, omitting the actual punishment of the rebels:

> The goddess then returned
> After killing the humans in the desert.

But as in the story of the Flood, humankind has not been completely annihilated, and Re decides to save the few miserable survivors from the goddess's bloodbath. He is, however, obliged to resort to deception rather than magic. Seven thousand jars of beer are dyed blood-red with ocher and poured into the fields. The goddess admires her reflection in the "blood," which she lustily laps up; soon she is drunk, "unable to recognize mankind," and gives up the pursuit.

Neither punishment nor gentleness solves the problem of men versus the rule of the sun god however, and mankind continuously rebels against the accepted order. The sun god senses the limitations of his power and, being "tired," desires to avoid another confrontation. He resigns, renouncing his sovereignty on earth, and climbs into heaven on the back of the celestial cow, from which he continues to reign undisturbed. Amazed, the eyes of mankind are directed toward the heavens. After the long day of his perpetual presence on earth, it becomes dark, for night now follows day. Men have lost their sense of orientation and clash against one another, so that the common rebellion against the sun god leads to war and conflict between men, the unavoidable consequence of every revolution.

The text then records the new decrees of the sun god, and these determine the present state of the world. An enormous picture of the celestial cow accompanies this part of the text and curiously, the text provides precise instructions about the execution of this picture. Stars in their own barks cross the belly of the cow, itself an ancient Egyptian image of the heavens, and an army of gods support the cow from below because of its remarkable height. The text goes on to describe the new arrangements for the rest of the heavens and its serpents, with Geb and Osiris being honored with the Realm of the Depths.

The sun god's retreat from the responsibilities of earthly rule parallels the course of the pharaoh after his death. He likewise departs from his earthly province, climbing into the heavens to be united with the solar disk. This is doubtless the reason for the presence of this myth in the royal tombs, preceding as it does the Ramesside Books of the Heavens, where the complete voyage of the sun is assimilated with the body of the heavenly goddess Nut.

But neither sun god nor deceased pharaoh spends the rest of eternity on the wobbly back of the celestial cow; both are obliged to descend into the dark abyss where Osiris rules. The tension between Re in the heavens and Osiris in the depths is present in the pharaoh, who is the son of both and who must merge into both

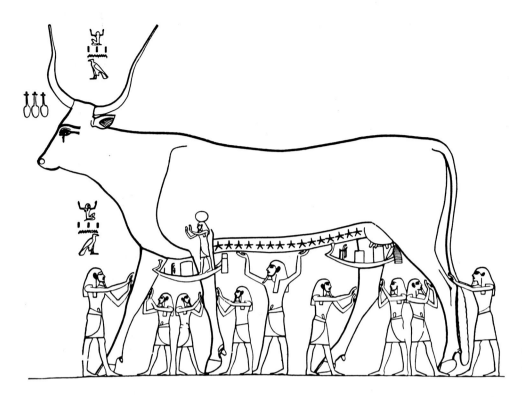

The Celestial Cow on the outermost shrine of Tutankhamun. (See plates 81–82.)

after he leaves this world. Having followed Re as the sun, he must now turn to the sovereign of the gloomy depths of the Realm of the Dead.

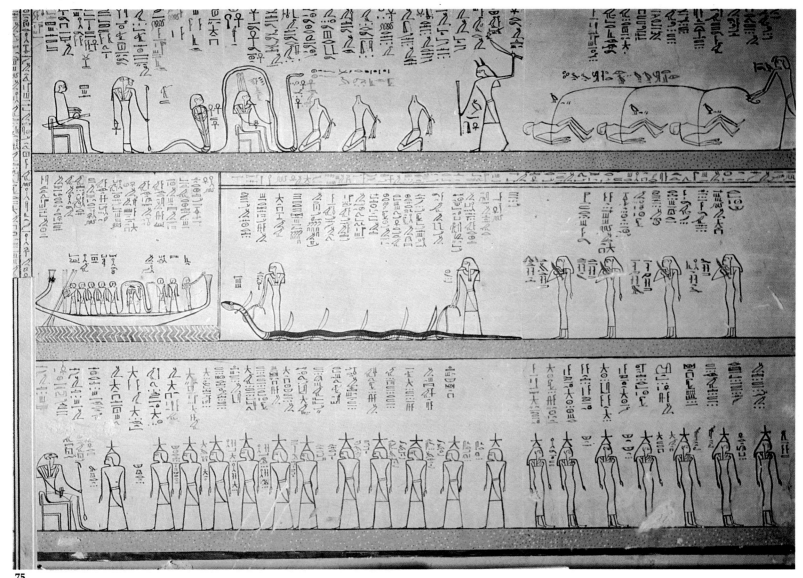

75

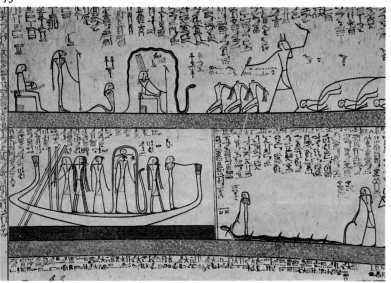

76

75/76. *The seventh hour of the Amduat in the tombs of Amenophis II (above) and his predecessor Tuthmosis III (below). The upper register shows Osiris, enthroned and ringed by the* mehen *snake, overseeing the punishment of enemies by a god with cat ears. Isis stands in the bow of the sun bark below, her exorcising hand stretched toward the approaching Apophis snake. The snake blocks the course of the sun, but he has already been rendered harmless by knives and ropes.*

77

78

77. *The Book of Day on the ceiling of the fourth corridor of the tomb of Ramesses VI. Apophis as a water snake behind the sun bark is attacked with a dagger and a spear. (See plate 68.)*

78. *The sixth hour of the Book of Gates in the upper pillared hall of the tomb of Sety I. The text describes how Apophis, '' the swallower,'' must give up the heads he has swallowed; the heads in turn swallow the snake.*

79

80

79. *The eleventh hour of the Book of Gates in the tomb of Ramesses VI. The fist of an invisible being grasps the rope to which Apophis and his helpers are tied. Geb on the left and three of the sons of Horus above also hold the rope.*

80. *The tenth hour of the Book of Gates in the tomb of Ramesses VI. Apophis as a many-coiled snake is assaulted by armed beings and gods with magic nets. Directly in front of Apophis is ''the aged one,'' half lying and pulling on a rope. (See plate 100.)*

81

81. *The Celestial Cow in the tomb of Sety I, in its present condition. The cow supported by Shu and other gods; stars along its belly travel within its body.*

82. *The Celestial Cow in the tomb of Sety I, in a watercolor by Robert Hay from after 1824.*

82

114

THE KINGDOM OF OSIRIS:

CHAPTER 8

THE NETHERWORLD

It was evident to the Egyptians that even the gods were mortal, and the Osiris myth conveys the inevitability of this fate in a particularly brutal and dramatic way. Osiris is not only murdered by his brother Seth, but actually dismembered, the pieces of his body thrown helter-skelter into the Nile and consigned to oblivion. The worst kind of death has overtaken him before he has been able to beget an heir who will ensure the continuity of his kingship, which Seth naturally wishes to seize for himself; mummification or ritual burial of Osiris is completely out of the question. Therefore the Osiris myth offers comfort to those who die without hope of funerary rites and assures them that even then life follows death.

Loyalty beyond death achieves the miracle. Isis, the wife-sister of Osiris, gathers the various parts of his body with help from her friends, and supplies the missing phallus to assure her husband a posthumous child by conceiving Horus from Osiris's dead body. Seth's scheme is thwarted: Horus's presence guarantees the victory of right and parentage, the transmission of the inheritance from father to son, which cannot be interrupted even by violence. Horus must still prove his mettle, but he triumphs in the end, using deceit and Isis's magical powers to overcome Seth's reliance on unrefined violence. Ceremoniously, the divine magistrates at Heliopolis decide the matter: Osiris is given the sovereignty of the depths into which he descended, and Horus is made king on earth, to be personified by the ruling pharaoh. Another version records a conciliatory conclusion in which Seth is awarded dominion over his own proper region, the barren deserts and the foreign countries beyond the limits of the Creation, where he can range freely.

In the Old Kingdom Pyramid Texts the king aspires to heavenly rule after death, Osiris and his Realm of the Dead being a doubtful region better avoided. But the fact of death makes the king himself an "Osiris"; he bears this name as a title of honor. And after the Old Kingdom, the rest of the dead gradually usurp the title for themselves; ultimately, everyone in the Realm of the Dead becomes an "Osiris so-and-so," assuming the name and taking up the role as well.

The Book of the Dead contains a last remnant of these ancient prejudices against the Realm of the Depths, the deceased wishing to "escape this evil land where the stars fall upside down on their faces and know not how to raise themselves up" (Book of the Dead, spell 99B). The noteworthy "Discussion of the Beyond" between Atum and Osiris in spell 175 also reflects this aversion to the Beyond. Surveying his new realm, Osiris remarks that it is a place dominated by negatives: a waterless desert without wind and the joys of love: in short, the "deepest, darkest, emptiest" place imaginable. He also finds it difficult to accept the fact that he is the only god excluded from taking part in the voyage on the Bark of Millions, as he cannot leave his throne. Atum attempts to console him with abstract assurances, patiently explaining that water, air, and desire are replaced by enlightenment, and bread and beer by absolute peace of heart. This is followed by the decisive advan-

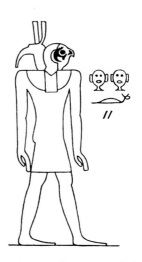

Horus and Seth united in a single being, the god "with the two faces," from the Amduat.

tage that Osiris' enemy Seth cannot approach him in the depths, and his son Horus has inherited his kingship on earth. Osiris in any case regularly sees the sun god and continues to exist with him millions of years after the rest of the universe is long gone.

During Dynasty 12, the living of the Realm of the Dead were shifted from the heavens into the Netherworld; this threw Osiris and his mythical fate into a more agreeable light. Distrust in the gloomy depths is gradually replaced by a general acceptance of the necessity of perpetual regeneration, which is possible there alone. The Osiris myth conjures up the terrors of death only to conjure them away; the worst forms of decay, "after all the worms have finished their work" (Book of the Dead, spell 154), become an essential condition for resurrection. Spell 154 was inscribed on the shroud of Tuthmosis III and describes the indelicate putrefaction of the body after death; it is in the end "a stinking mess," literally transformed into "a lot of worms." The spell states, however, that it is intended to "prevent a man's corpse from perishing" and includes an address to the father Osiris:

> Your members shall continue to be,
> You do not decay, you do not rot,
> You are not turned to dust,
> You do not stink, and are not corrupt.
> You shall not become worms.

When the late books concerning the Netherworld deal with the decay and putrefaction of Osiris, referring to him as "corrupt, the lord of stench," this is understood in a positive fashion, and the oozing secretions of the corpse are assumed to be particularly powerful. The residents of the western Realm of the Dead "live from the stench of his decay" (Book of Caverns), and according to spell 94 of the Book of the Dead, the dead scribe can use Osiris's secretions as ink, taking advantage of their powers for himself. Thus, even the sun god who descends into the Netherworld becomes "the putrid" (Litany of Re, address 22), although his life-giving word and his living light guarantee that Osiris and all the dead will rise from decay and putrefaction, throwing aside all traces of it.

The corpse of Osiris at the center of these miraculous events is itself veiled in mystery. It lies at the most secret place in the whole Netherworld, known only to Osiris and his most loyal associates. Isis and Nephthys guard it eternally, lest Seth find it and repeat his sacrilege. In the Book of the Earth, Anubis and a mysterious "god of the concealed chamber" extend their arms over a mysterious box containing what remains of Osiris. The corporeally intact god stands above, his soul rejoicing before him, the earth god Geb behind. Three menacing serpents stretch themselves around the shrine, and the fate of his foes is graphically depicted: bound and beheaded, they kneel around the shrine, their blood pouring into a fiery kettle held high by demonic tormentors.

"You breathe when you hear my voice" is the awakening call of Re as the rays of sunlight enter the shrine and coffin of the sovereign of the dead. The same shining disk appears in another scene from the Book of the Earth, where Osiris, supported by his "two sisters," has just begun to rise, and Horus, offspring of a conception on the other side of death, is coming forth from his father's body. "Horus came from the seed of his father when he was already putrid" (Book of the Dead, spell 78).

This procreative power, unbroken even in death, is portrayed in the Book of

The "hidden space" of the Beyond, from the Book of the Earth in the tomb of Ramesses VI. (Plate 54, upper right.)

Horus emerging from the corpse of Osiris, the sun disk behind him, in the burial chamber of Ramesses VI. (Plate 54, upper right.)

Osiris rises upward, while his enemies below plunge downward; from the sixth part of the Book of Caverns.

Caverns by placing Osiris's mummy with its erect phallus in the deepest part of the Netherworld, even below the earth god Aker. A serpent "with terrifying mien" protectively encircles the body, "that the dead not come too close." The divine corpse in the deepest darkness is again surrounded by suffering enemies: damned by Re in the name of Osiris to the annihilation center, where they are rendered harmless. The blessed dead inhale the fragrant odors of the veiled putrefaction of the divine corpse so that they may live. In another passage of the final division of the Book of Caverns, Osiris is entrusted to "the Great Serpent," which is at once the ouroboros and Apophis, while his enemies fall into the abyss from which he is emerging, his legs still beneath the horizon.

Being dead, Osiris is always in danger and requires the aid of the sun god on his nightly voyage. Re thus fulfills the role of the loyal son Horus, forcing his way against all odds to his father in the Netherworld, and the texts of the Beyond frequently identify him as "Horus of the Netherworld." The Book of Gates (scene 22) describes this forcefully, as Osiris calls to his son from the midst of the entourage protectively surrounding his shrine: "Come to me, my son Horus, so that you may protect me from those who acted against me." Horus then replaces Osiris's "bandages," symbolizing his own uninjured state. In the Book of the Night, Horus attends to Osiris, "that he not be alone."

Spell 78 of the Book of the Dead develops a theme present in spell 312 of the earlier Coffin Texts, intended to aid the dead "in assuming the form of a falcon." It begins, likewise, with Osiris calling for his son's aid, that he come and support him against Seth,

> That he not come who caused me hurt,
> Beholding me in the house of darkness,
> And uncover my weakness that is hidden.

The gods encourage Horus to obey the summons, but he is more interested in defending his earthly inheritance, begging support from the "lords of all" on the "edge of heaven," than in seeking out his father in the darkness of the Netherworld. Instead, he lends his falcon form to a messenger whom he dispatches to his father: a spark from the solar disk who introduces himself to the guardians of the Realm of the Dead as an ancient being, older even than Isis, who bore Horus. This is insufficient, however, and the paths to the Beyond remain closed while the messenger is grilled like the dead and forced to provide himself with signs of power, which are initially lacking. He is eventually given leave to proceed, "to behold the birth of the great gods," the mystery of daily regeneration. In the end, the terrible deities of the Netherworld lie prostrate before him and he arrives at "Osiris's house," where the guards respectfully let him pass on. Having reached his goal despite the obstacles, Osiris is then told that, as Bull of the West, he will continue to rule over the Realm of the Dead, while Horus has ascended to his earthly throne and "is served and feared by millions."

Osiris is thus the lord of his own house in the Netherworld, bearing the ancient royal title of "bull"; the Book of Caverns depicts him and his entire entourage with bull heads. As the ruler of the Beyond, he is all-present in both private and royal New Kingdom funerary texts, and in crucial scenes of tomb decoration as well. In the divine scenes of the royal tombs, he greets the "justified" dead. On the rear wall of the shaft he sits enthroned with Anubis and Horus-the-son-of-Isis behind him. On the rear wall of the upper pillared hall, Horus himself leads the king, who is also the loyal son born to Isis, to Osiris's throne. Osiris usually appears tightly wrapped in bright white raiment representing the limbless unarticulated divine body, mummiform although without any initial reference to mummification. His crossed hands hold the royal insignia, flagellum, and crook; his head bears the tall white crown to which the New Kingdom usually added an ostrich feather on each side, as well as other elements. In the royal tombs his hands and face—the only visible parts of his body—are often green, demonstrating his "greening," the fresh and prosperous state of having overcome death. Other scenes give him a black skin, recalling his dark realm of death.

In the tomb of Sety I we encounter a very special manifestation of Osiris as a personified *djed* pillar. The pillar is wrapped in a garment, and crossed arms hold the royal insignia, while eyes peer out of the crown. This is the logical extension of the thought that the *djed* was Osiris's backbone. Originally, the columns must have been a kind of bound sheaf of the first grain of the harvest. A popular amulet, the *djed* promised stability and continuity, drawing on Osiris's own survival. The nightly unification of the sun god with Osiris led to the frequent appearance of the sign in scenes of the voyage of the sun.

Like all the important gods of the Egyptian pantheon, Osiris has many names, referring to his important roles and character. Funerary texts frequently use Wennefer (related to the Greek Onnophris, and surviving in the modern name Onofrio) and Khentyimentiu. Wennefer, "the Perfect One," is inspired by the god's return to life. Khentyimentiu, "Foremost of the Westerners," refers to his role as sovereign; "bull" of the Realm of the Dead is a reference to his role as king of the living and king of eternity.

According to the Amduat, Osiris is the "most distinguished" and "august" of all the dead. He offers sweet air and food in his deep realm, because he partakes of the creative words of the sun god and continues to rule the secrets of the plants, which reappear year after year. Scene 46 of the Book of Gates visualized the ancient thought that Osiris was incorporated simultaneously in dying and reviving plants, which awakened to new life, blossoming at the rays of the sun.

> Thriving are the fields of the Netherworld,
> As Re shines over the body of Osiris.
> At your rising the plants appear.

These verses are well illustrated on a painted coffin of Dynasty 21 showing ears of grain ripening out of Osiris's body below a solar disk embraced by a pair of arms. Above this are Aker's double sphinx and the solar bark, the whole composition recalling scenes from the Book of Caverns and the Book of the Earth, which place the divine corpse in the deepest recess of the earth below Aker. Further references to Osiris's vegetative power are found in the "Osiris beds" of royal and private burials in the Valley of the Kings. These consisted of a wooden base in the form of the god's silhouette covered with fertile soil and sown with grain, the green shoots bringing to life the mythical revival of the lord of the Beyond, and vicariously that of the deceased himself.

Spell 69 of the Book of the Dead lets the deceased speak for Osiris: "I am Osiris . . . the eldest of the gods, heir of my father Geb." However, the deceased must then request that the doorkeepers announce him to Osiris, that he may receive his

Osiris as djed *pillar in the tomb of Nofretari. (See plates 91–92.)*

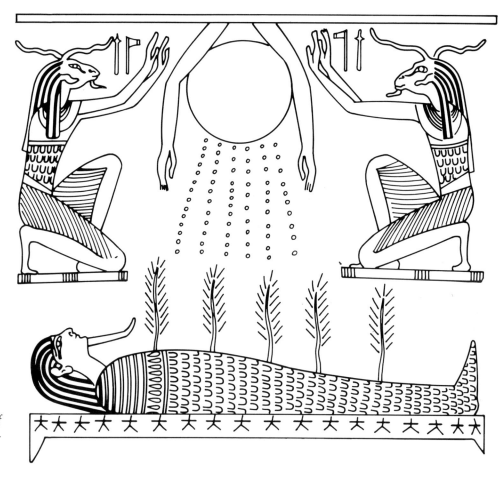

Plants sprout from a mummy, under the rays of the sun. From a coffin in the Fitzwilliam Museum, Cambridge.

"quantities of breads and beer" together with him. Another passage stresses that the deceased is a "vassal" of the god. The Egyptians were not shy of apparent contradictions in letting the dead become an "Osiris," but it was clear that this "Osiris" was a mere subject of the sovereign of the Realm of the Dead, that is, the god Osiris. Just as the deceased strives to join in the celestial revolutions inevitably leading to perpetual rejuvenation and rebirth, so he desires to enter into the nature and destiny of Osiris, following a path leading just as inevitably to sovereignty and triumph, according to the exemplary analogy of the myth. Consistency in contradiction even caused the Egyptians to unite Re and Osiris, the celestial sun god and the lord of the depths, into a single form. This was the logical consequence of the effort to grasp the many facets of the relationship between the two gods and make them visually perceptible.

At the beginning of the Book of Caverns, ram-headed Re steps down into the Netherworld, stretching his arms out in the expectation that he will be led on the paths of that world. It is a constant theme of the texts that Re desires to behold Osiris, awakening and reviving him and all the blessed dead with his light. And since the time of Merneptah, this theme of the awakening of Osiris is prominently displayed in the royal burial chamber opposite the scene of the solar path. A semicircle of stars and solar disks protects the divine mummy "in its vault" flanked by two pairs of Osiris figures. This mummy logically incorporates the sun god and Osiris, but also that of the deceased pharaoh. And in fact the royal mummy lay

The resurrection of Osiris and the voyage through Aker, from the Book of the Earth. (Plate 55, top center.)

within its stone sarcophagus precisely between this scene of awakening and the scene of the solar path.

Ramesses VI's burial chamber had this very image, slightly modified, set into the Book of the Earth. At the zenith just above the mummy, the celestial arc is broken with a large disk from which emerges the god's falcon head, his form during the day, sending forth a life-giving ray to the mummy. The text notes that this is "the secret corpse, Aker's great secret," and as in the Book of Caverns and on the coffin, it is beneath Aker's double sphinx, which supports the god's vessel on its nightly journey through the depths. The text also refers to the corpse of "him of the horizon" (Akhty) and identifies it as "the corpse in which Re is," since the sun god enters this body, which is at once his own and that of Osiris. Literally, "light enters his body as an utterance coming forth from the solar disk." Light and the life-giving world are joined to attain resurrection, and the sweet breath of air brings life, with Osiris's body "breathing through the solar disk," according to the Book of Caverns.

The whole conceptual range of life and resurrection is caught in this one image, appearing in modified form on the mythological papyri and painted coffins of Dynasty 21, often with the falcon's head peering directly out of the heavens and sending forth streams of light to the mummy. Usually Re traverses the heavens in his vessel, but one papyrus replaces this motif with Osiris's *djed* pillar, flanked by the worshipping sisters Isis and Nephthys, who mourn the mummy below. Laments for the lifeless god and acclaim for the resurrected one in the form of the djed are united into a single picture. Another version gives the mummy an ointment cone and removes the divine beard, identifying the mummy as the body of the deceased and revealing the real purpose of these images: the desire of the dead to be awakened by the sunlight each night, to arise from the sleep of death, like Osiris.

We have already observed that the earlier texts deliberately avoided identifying

Additional scenes of resurrection from papyri of Dynasty 21.

the mummy as that of either Re or Osiris. The texts of the sixth hour of the Amduat are equally ambiguous about the corpse of the sun. The birdlike, divine soul of Re, which swoops out of the heavens and into the Netherworld, is at once the *ba* of Re and of Osiris. But the two gods are by no means identical, despite this ambiguity. They are joined in a specific manner, which gave the theologians of the New Kingdom considerable food for thought. The definition of this relationship did not rely on syncretism, the creation of a hyphenated god like Amun-Re or Ptah-Sokar-Osiris; there is no Re-Osiris emerging triumphant at the close of the New Kingdom. Instead, as early as the Middle Kingdom Coffin Texts it is remarked that one god ''appears'' as the other, and the New Kingdom considered that the union of their souls begat the ''united *ba*,'' which speaks with ''a single mouth,'' according to the Abydos stela of Ramesses IV.

The concept of ''unification'' can be traced back to the Litany of Re and the early New Kingdom, where the deceased pharaoh aspired to be identified as Re and Osiris. The union of these two gods is simply formulated:

> A shout of joy is in the Realm of the Dead:
> ''Re it is, who has gone into Osiris,
> Osiris reposes in Re.''

The last two verses were taken up in the Book of the Dead, and they appear as a note accompanying a figure in the tombs of Queen Nofretari and some Ramesside officials in which the mutual encompassing of the two gods in a single body is boldly and simply presented. This united god has Osiris's limbless mummy form with the ram's head and solar disk belonging to the nightly manifestation of the sun god. Isis and Nephthys, who grasp this powerful being, actually belong to the realm of Osiris, accompanying Re only secondarily as a result of Re's role as Osiris. The ram's head suggests the *ba* soul (which need not always be depicted in bird form) as well. Egyptian theologians seem to have understood the mysterious event of unification as taking place each night when the solar *ba* joined Osiris's corpse, and believed that this body was actually his own corpse, visited in the depths of the Netherworld. This inspired the hope that the souls of all the blessed dead would unite with their bodies, as required for revival and rejuvenation in the Beyond. On one of his golden shrines, Nephthys reassures the youthful Tutankhamun:

The bas *of Re and Osiris meet one another in Mendes, in Ani's Book of the Dead.*

> Your ba shall belong to heaven before Re,
> Your body to earth with Osiris,
> And your ba shall spend every day on your body.

Encompassing the two gods in the nature and appearance of each other, creating this new mysterious divine form uniting heaven and earth—this is the great mystery of the Netherworld. The poets of the royal funerary texts veil the process in secretive allusions. In the seventh address of the Litany of Re, the dead are summoned to a stair, the ancient image of the first hill, which bore the Creation and gave its shape to the Step Pyramid. In the mythological papyri and painted coffins of Dynasty 21, this stair is shown with the body of Osiris. There it is the "secret shrine . . . guarded by the two women," namely, Isis and Nephthys. The "hidden form" is foreign to the blessed and the damned alike, familiar only to Re and Osiris, whose common body it is. As a special honor the dead pharaoh is permitted to approach it, and by means of the subsequent "member divinization" he becomes completely godlike in nature. After declaring his identity with the sun god, the deceased cries: "I am Osiris, my strength is that of Osiris, my power is that of Osiris," but he bids Re to "open the earth for my *ba*!"

When the sun god departs from the Netherworld in the morning, climbing up into the heavens, the body remains in the darkness below. It is "the image of Osiris who is in the darkness," as the Amduat puts it in a note beside the visible shell of the mummy at the close of the twelfth hour. In the same scene, Osiris's entourage surrounds him, comforting him with a hymn in which the word *ankh* ("life") is constantly repeated. Osiris remains a "lord of life," even when Re has departed; he retains his sovereignty over the depths of the abyss, its mysterious powers, its horrors and promises. He awaits the return of the sun god amid the bizarre creatures who surround and protect him. And the god does return from the dazzling heavens, seeking renewal in the depths.

Rosetau is the blessed place where the dead desire to share the lively and happy company of Osiris. In the Beyond, it is the sister city of Abydos, the goal of earthly pilgrims, where the living erected tombs, chapels, or small stelae in the vicinity of Osiris's temples, in order to be present at the god's Mysteries, the yearly festival at which mythical events were recounted, reenacting the death and revival. In spell 138 of the Book of the Dead, the deceased arrives at an otherworldly Abydos, where the gods greet him with acclaim as son of Osiris, but he is in general more concerned with attaining access to Rosetau (spells 117–119), where the enlightened receive their bread and beer in the company of Osiris. There they find themselves in the familiar landscape of the stream of the Netherworld, and everything necessary is at hand. In the fields of Rosetau, the deceased calls to the Sovereign of the Dead:

> Hail to you, Osiris . . .
> Raise yourself.
> Yours is the might in Rosetau,
> Yours the power in Abydos.
> Crossing the heavens, sailing with Re,
> You behold your people.

The final verse may surprise us, as Osiris is doomed to remain in the Netherworld. But the god who emerges triumphantly before our eyes from the gates of the

On a pillar in the room adjoining the burial chamber of Sety I, Osiris is named in the hieroglyphs above as Khentyimentiu "Foremost of the Westerners," Wennefer "the Perfect One," and he who dwells in Igaret "the necropolis."

eastern horizon is in fact the *ba* of Osiris, which traverses the arc of the heavens with Re, and with Re the souls of the deceased remain eternally in the light of the sun. And thus Osiris is included in the celestial orbit—not only as a *djed* pillar from which the sun begins its ascent, but in many other forms as well. Like Osiris himself, the Osiris-Re motif was constantly revived and renewed. One bold and original version shows the united god as the combination of mummy and ram, set in the solar bark and guarded by Isis and Nephthys, whose *djed* and *ankh* amulets guarantee him endurance and life. The god is surrounded by the hieroglyph for fire signifying the wall of fire protecting the sun, and all hostile powers are kept away. The text notes that ''the great god, the lord of the heavens'' is constantly on the move with his vessel, from the Netherworld (the desert) to the starry heavens, and back to the depths. The meeting place of the two spheres is indicated by the pair of arms embracing the solar disk, symbolizing the anonymous powers that keep it and the whole world in motion. This power propels the sun from horizon to horizon, the nightly embrace permitting Osiris and Re to become one, returning the Creation to its youth.

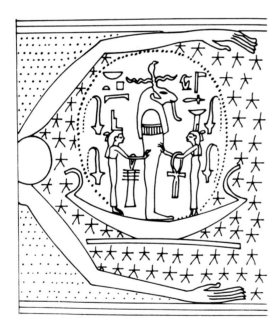

The voyage of Re-Osiris; Papyrus of Tentamun.

View from the burial chamber of Sety I back into the antechamber. On the pillar Osiris, holding a crook and flail, receives the king; on the wall above is part of the Amduat.

Osiris with Hathor receives the king guided by Horus in the upper pillared hall of the tomb of Sety I. (Plate 83.)

83. *James Burton's copy of the scene with the enthroned Osiris on the rear wall of the upper pillared hall in the tomb of Sety I. The pharaoh stands before the sovereign of the Realm of the Dead. Sety I is accompanied by falcon-headed Horus wearing the double crown. Behind Osiris stands Hathor as goddess of the West. Both Sety and Osiris hold the shepherd's crook and flail as symbols of rulership, while the deities flanking them hold the* ankh, *the symbol for life. The* ankh *also appears on the base of the throne, alternating with the signs for stability (djed) and well-being (was). The symbol of the unification of the two lands is placed on the throne. Above Osiris is a winged sun disk and a cavetto cornice surmounted by a frieze of uraeus snakes wearing sun disks.*

84

85

84. *Antechamber in the tomb of Haremheb. Haremheb offers Osiris, "Lord of the West and Lord of Eternity," two jars of wine. The green-skinned god wears a white crown with ostrich feathers and holds the attributes of his dominion over the Realm of the Dead.*

85. *The composite Re and Osiris, cared for by Isis (right) and Nephthys (left), from the Litany of Re in the tomb of Nofretari.*

86. *One of the four pillars in the burial chamber of Nofretari, showing the representations of the djed pillars on the inner faces, surrounded by the titles and names of the Great Royal Wife. The pillar faces in the tomb of the queen's husband, Ramesses II, must have been similarly decorated.*

86

87. *Tomb of Tausert. Osiris, enthroned in a shrine, wears the* atef *crown from which are suspended protective uraeus snakes carrying sun disks. In addition to his normal white garment, he wears a red cape and a jeweled collar. His skin color is the usual green. Before Osiris stand the four sons of Horus on a lotus blossom; behind him on the adjacent wall is Isis, followed by Nephthys. The shrine is surmounted by the hieroglyph for "west," which holds two scepters and is flanked by recumbent Anubis jackals.*

87

88. *Tomb of Tausert. The god Ptah wears a close-fitting cap and a pectoral over a collar. He stands in a shrine, enveloped by the wings of Maat, ''daughter of Re.''*

89

89. *A shrine in the tomb of Tausert with Horus, son of Osiris (left), and Anubis (right) before Osiris. Osiris is named Lady of the Sky since the queen (originally represented worshipping outside the shrine) has joined the essence of the god. Osiris has green skin and holds his attributes; Horus wears the double crown of the king. The shrine is crowned with a frieze of protective uraeus snakes.*

90

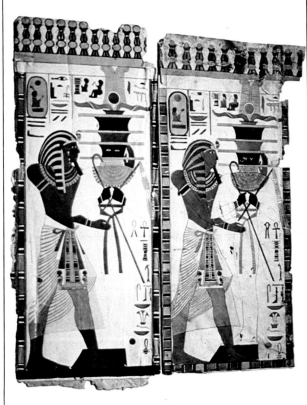

91

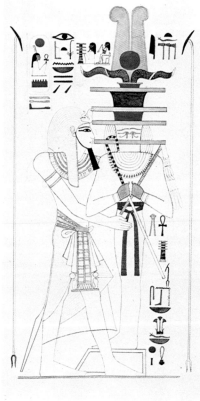

92

90. *The four sides of a pillar in the burial chamber of Sety I in a watercolor by Belzoni. The gods represented here are, from left to right, Osiris, Anubis (ram-headed), Khepri, and one of the acclaiming "souls of Hieraconpolis."*

91. *Pillar face in the side room of the burial chamber of Sety I in a watercolor by Belzoni. The pharaoh embraces Osiris personified as a djed pillar.*

92. *The same scene as plate 91 in an unfinished watercolor by J. Burton.*

93

93. *Another watercolor by Hay from the tomb of Ramesses III. The pharaoh (right) pours purified water and offers incense before a deity identified by the inscription as Ptah-Sokar-Osiris. Behind the deity stands the "mother of the gods," Isis, wearing Hathor's headdress of cow horns, within which is a sun disk. Isis's winged arms protect the god, while her hands hold the symbols for life and well-being. The pharaoh wears a broad collar above his thin linen garments and a wig with a protecting uraeus serpent on his forehead.*

THE JUST REWARDED WITH LIFE FROM DEATH

CHAPTER 9

Anubis attends to the mummy in its coffin while the deceased's ba *bird extends "life" and "breath" to him. The scene takes place in a tomb crowned by a small pyramid.*

The deceased burns incense and pours a libation for his ka, *which is placed on a divine standard in a vignette, from spell 105 of the Book of the Dead.*

In the hope of eventually reaching the Realm of the Blessed, both kings and commoners were conveyed after death to the Hall of Mummification to begin their journey to the Beyond. There, at the hands of specially educated funerary priests, the physical remains of the body were prepared for the long and dangerous journey into the Beyond; the Egyptians considered their bodies essential for the life in the Beyond. The internal organs most susceptible to decay were removed, to be wrapped carefully and placed individually in four canopic jars set in the tomb with the coffin. The divine guardian of this activity was the jackal-headed Anubis, who was the last to put his hand on the mummy as it lay on the bier, illustrated by a popular vignette used in the Valley of the Kings since the end of Dynasty 19.

Those parts of the human being not constrained by material existence parted from the body at death, only to rejoin it in the fields of the Beyond, renewing the living entity. The Egyptians did not simply conceive of a spiritual "soul" as the counterpart of the physical body; they realized the human being was far more complicated than that. One of these nonmaterial elements was the *ka*, representing restless power rather than a tranquil soul, potential energy that could be increased with material attentions. "For your *ka*" is the blessing accompanying every presentation of food or drink, while everything of a displeasing nature is "an abomination for the *ka*." It determines the moods of a person, while the actual deeds are guided by the heart. The dead "go to their *ka*" in the Beyond. But the *ka* does not play a particularly important role in the Books of the Netherworld or the Book of the Dead, perhaps because the sun god's care for the material welfare of the dead essentially takes over its role.

The *ba*, however, is very important in the texts of the Beyond. This is the unconstrained, freely moving element of every being, which passes undisturbed through space and time. While the body remains bound to the earth, the *ba* belongs to the heavens, and is thus frequently seen among the stars, the "thousand *bas*" of the goddess of the heavens. The usual form is that of a bird (a stork, and in the New Kingdom commonly a human-headed bird), symbolizing mobility and freedom; the unification of the *ba* and the body, which even the sun god experiences every night, is the decisive event bringing the dead back to life. Coffins of the Late Period prominently display this meeting, adapted from spell 89 of the Book of the Dead, showing the *ba* bird fluttering above the mummy.

Another active part of the human is the shadow, which the Egyptians understood to be more than just the visible shadow, but not comparable with that part of the soul usually called "shadow" in Jungian psychology. Like the *ka*, it is a source of power; the shadow of a divinity can bestow power on humans, or even take a visible form. Like the *ba*, it moves with mysterious swiftness and enters the Netherworld, bringing life to the motionless corpse. An ostrich-feather fan, which gives shade, is the usual sign for the shadow, but it can also be depicted as a silhouette of a human body.

Among the other parts of the human being having their own independent existence, the name and the heart deserve attention. Creation came about by naming names, and thus every object has its proper name, without which it vanishes into nonexistence: hence the practice of effacing names of undesirable gods or kings. The visible and audible survival of a name after death is a symbol of immortality, and a passage in the Coffin Texts calls upon the deceased to assert: "I live the life, I will not perish, my name will never perish in this land for all time."

The ba *and shadow of the deceased next to his tomb, from spell 92 in the Book of the Dead of Neferubenef.*

As for the heart, the Egyptians regarded it as the central human organ of volition and desire, the "free will" carrying the responsibility for improper behavior as well. The human heart is constantly devising evil plans contrary to the divine plan of creation. In the Judgment of the Dead the deceased must be assured that his heart will conceal incorrect behavior, as this could lead to his being damned to eternal punishment. The imploring entreaties of spells 26 through 30 of the Book of the Dead are designed to prevent the heart from being taken away or permitted to oppose him:

> This my heart shall not rise against me.
> Obey me, my heart,
> I am your owner.
> As you are in my body, you will not harm me.
> . . .
> Rise not as a witness,
> Accuse me not before the Lord of All.

The deceased with his heart, from the Book of the Dead of Nachtamun.

The process of mummification took seventy days, a period not determined by technical necessity, but rather chosen for its cosmic suitability; the seventy days correspond to the period during which each of the decans remains invisible before reappearing above the horizon to be observed again. Every ten days, one of the thirty-six decans "dies," to be replaced by another "living" in its place. The drop below the horizon is interpreted as a descent into the Netherworld, where the body spends seventy days in the house of Geb the earth god. The Book of Nut refers to this as the time in which the stars purify themselves and are regenerated, preparing for a new life, as is hoped for the deceased as well.

After these seventy days in the Hall of Mummification the body was conveyed to the tomb in a solemn funeral procession. The coffin crosses the desert sands on an ox-drawn sled, although high officials of the land replace the beasts in royal funerals, as revealed in a mural in the tomb of Tutankhamun: twelve royal companions and counselors drag the coffin in a shrine. The successor, as a loyal son, performs various funerary rituals. The most important consists in opening the mouths of the mummy and the statue of the deceased. At the same time, wildly gesticulating mourning women with unbound hair raise their voices in a piercing wail.

Protected by cloth wrappings, amulets, magical spells, and other measures, the deceased is prepared to start on the long and dangerous journey into the Realm of the Dead, following the path of the sun into the West. Before him await Osiris and the Judgment of the Dead. If the scales balance and the sum total of his deeds matches the divine order of *maat*, Osiris, the king of the living, will accept him in the Beyond, where life is perpetually renewed.

At the Judgment of the Dead the deceased is pictured no longer as a mummy but in a form that must correspond to his ideal appearance on earth, and it is thus that we encounter him in his life and work in the Beyond. In the Books of the Netherworld the dead are depicted as mummies only in connection with the funeral or in order to stress the lifelessness of the dead before the arrival of the sun god. The mummy serves merely as a protective cover for the sleep of death, and the deceased has no intention of retaining this constraining form associated with so much unpleasantness: the body is bound by cloth and unable to move; bodily functions are inhibited, while essential organs, such as the eyes, are lacking and must be "reopened."

In scene 40 of the Book of Gates, the sun god addresses the deceased lying as mummies on a serpent-formed bier:

> Your flesh shall rise up for you,
> Your bones shall fuse themselves for you,
> Your members shall collect themselves for you,
> Your flesh shall reassemble for you!
> Sweet be the breath for your noses,
> Unraveled be your mummy cloths,
> Unveiled be your mummy masks!
> Sunlight for your divine eyes,
> That with them you shall see the Light!
> Lift yourselves from your weariness,
> That you may receive your fields!

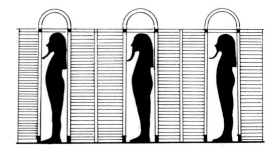

Mummies in their cases lying in shrines, in a detail from the ninth scene of the Book of Gates.

This stretching and reawakening of the body, inspired by the divine word, requires several phases until all restrictions are removed. Initially, the mummies lie rigid on their biers or stand stiffly in shrines whose doors are released at the call of the sun god, that his light may enter and drive away the darkness. In the next stage the mummies raise their heads, and lie sphinxlike on their biers. In another stage they are almost half erect, appearing to be seated or engaged in gymnastic exercises. Paintings on the ceilings of the tombs of Ramesses VI and Ramesses IX show various stages of the process, adumbrating Christian scenes of the resurrection.

The mummy wrappings are unbound and removed: the face is rid of the protective mask and the extremities are free to move. The legs spring apart and the erect phallus demonstrates returning virility. All bodily functions recover, and an "enlightened" body of the Beyond emerges from the bandaged mummy; the other elements of the human being, primarily the soul and the shadow, join the newly risen body, to worship joyfully the sun god who has awakened it from the sleep of death.

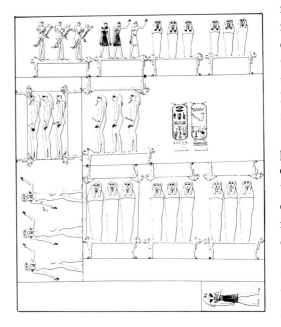

Various stages of resurrection, on the painted ceiling in the tomb of Ramesses IX. (See plate 102.)

The flesh of this new body is "firm"; the eyes, ears, and heart have been "returned" to the deceased, that they may perform their respective functions. Uniting with the *ba* brings life, breath, and movement. The deceased is now an *akh*, an enlightened spirit with incredibly heightened bodily capabilities to whom the entire universe is open and accessible. Whatever problems the deceased faced on earth are now gone. What was lacking is now supplied, and—in what the Egyptians

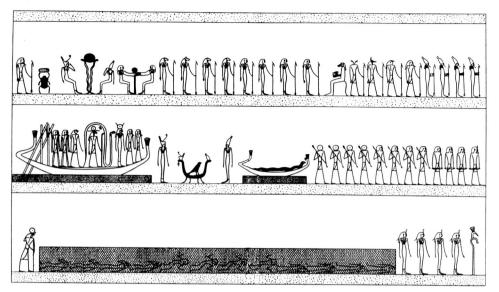

Scheme of the tenth hour of the Amduat, with the apotheosis by drowning in the lower register. The text of this scene states that those who drowned had direct access to the Netherworld. Horus, leaning on a staff, helps them find their way to the Fields of the Blessed and become united again with their bas. (Plate 98.)

considered to be the greatest magical accomplishment on earth—even a lost head can now be replaced.

A special problem was posed by people who drowned in the Nile and were devoured by crocodiles. In such cases, probably not very rare, the body was lost and could not be mummified; the deceased was deprived of the protective mummy form. Several passages in the Books of the Netherworld show that the drowned reached the shores of the Beyond directly from the Nile, arriving from the primeval waters and thus into the depths of the world. In Roman Egypt the drowned were revered and considered especially blessed, and here the analogy to Osiris, who was thrown into the water, played an important role. Parts of the tenth hour of the Amduat and the ninth hour of the Book of Gates resemble one another in their detailed treatment of this theme. In a large rectangular pool—representing the primeval water, Nun—swim several groups of naked drowned, in quite different positions: some on their backs, others on their bellies, still others on their sides. In the Amduat, Horus calls to them from the riverbank, while in the Book of Gates it is the passing sun god himself who promises that they will be able to breathe in the water and that their bodies will not decompose: "Your members are not putrefied, your flesh is not decomposed!" Their souls are also provided for, and their bodies can land uninjured on the shores of the Netherworld, where they may benefit from all the Beyond has to offer, even without the ritual burial ceremonies.

Despite the Egyptian custom of mummification, the disintegration of the body appears in some Egyptian funerary texts as positive and desirable; "ponderousness" or "weariness" becomes a prerequisite for regeneration. The decay of the old substance is necessary in order to permit the new to arise from it: absolute decay must precede absolute renewal, out of the amorphous deceased rises his rejuvenated and perfect form. This is another aspect of death, only apparently contradicting the orderly attempt to retain bodily integrity against all threats. The Egyptian did not hesitate to set contradictions side by side. Preserved mummies reveal just how roughly funerary priests plied their craft. A truly ancient practice known from the earliest tombs comes to the fore here: deliberate mutilations were carried out to prevent the body from leaving the tomb and returning. Later, division and decay were considered to be necessary for a complete renewal, as illustrated by the myth of Osiris, and even the corpse of the solar beetle was buried in three separate parts in the Amduat.

Once awakened by the sun god, the deceased can step forth, free and unconstrained, into the familiar landscape of the blessed in which he finds himself. Everything necessary for his welfare prospers here, and the god even compounds this by offering all that is needed from his bark as he sails past. After all, the "enlightened" body and the *ba* of the deceased both require material nourishment. Even the earliest tomb reliefs show the departed before an enormous heap of offerings on a table, a never-ending repast replete with dainties. In the New Kingdom the delightful vision of the goddess of the tree provides the deceased not only with shade but also water and food: the *ba* as well receives a trickle of cool water, and it partakes of the pools of the Beyond before flying off into the endless universe.

The Egyptians did not conceive of these activities as a purely passive consumption of offerings by which they had merely to wait for a fried dove to fly into their mouths: the deceased reaches out for the dove himself, and plows his own field, numbering himself among the farmers of the Wernes fields, or the workers of the "rush fields"; even the pharaoh works in the funerary temple of Ramesses III. The less exciting labor—such as unceasingly maintaining the irrigation canals, fertilizing the fields, or even freeing them from wind-blown sand—was, however, not among the tasks to which the deceased aspired. In the Old Kingdom, statuettes of servants and craftsmen were placed in the tomb to do these chores; these were later followed by models of whole household units, and after the late Middle Kingdom shawabtys belonged to the essentials of every burial. The dead merely had to plow, sow, and reap in the fields assigned to them. In the Book of Gates there are gods with a measuring cord "dividing fields for the blessed" to whom the sun god calls out: "Just are you to those who are, unjust to those who are not!"—these latter being the damned. "Shining" grain grows in these otherworldly fields: its brightness is compared with that of the sun and it grows to a suitably extraordinary height, corresponding to the incredible dimensions of the Realm of the Dead.

The deceased pharaoh aspires to sovereignty over the whole of the Beyond, as was awarded to Osiris. In the commoners' Book of the Dead, the departed must content themselves with a bit of land or an honored place in the solar bark, as the available space must be shared with the millions of dead who preceded them. That all nations, including even the ancient foes of Egypt, are present in the Beyond is shown in scene 30 of the Book of Gates with the "four races of man." There, four Egyptians—the "cattle of Re"—are accompanied by four Asiatics, Nubians, and Libyans in their respective costumes. They also are attended to and provided for, receiving places in the Realm of the Dead. The beginning of the same work stresses that all beings must go away to the "hidden place": men and gods must share it with "all beasts and crawling creatures."

The scene with the races of men belongs to the cosmopolitan period at the end of Dynasty 18 and the beginning of Dynasty 19, when the royal family made diplomatic marriages with the ruling houses of Egypt's traditional enemies. Arrogance and the normal disdain for foreigners resumed after this brief interlude, and again the Egyptians found themselves alone in the Beyond. The Beyond is an Egyptian landscape. Completely surrounded by the desert are luxuriant fields

Plowing and harvesting in the Fields of the Blessed, from spell 110 of the Book of the Dead.

Egyptians, Asiatics, Nubians, and Libyans, from the Book of Gates. (See plates 105, 107– 109.)

along a river cut by canals and streams which are constant obstacles for the dead, and as in the Beyond, the only useful vehicle is a boat. Present in even the earliest funerary texts is the ferryman. The departed depend on him and expect an intense grilling. The conversation with the ferryman was incorporated into the New Kingdom Book of the Dead in spell 99, "For Obtaining a Ferryboat in the Realm of the Dead" (which includes also a lengthy catalogue of boat parts). Once awakened, the ferryman plies the dead with irksome questions, and his assistant has the rather discouraging name "He Who Turns Back." The deceased is thus well advised to make himself a boat in the "yards of the gods" (spell 136A). No longer requiring the ferryman's vessel, he need not cry out, "Help me, leave me not without a boat!" But he will also miss the comforting response, "Come with me, enlightened one, and sail to a familiar place!"

In the royal Books of the Netherworld, the ferryboat has no role, as Pharaoh is assured that he will be among the select in the entourage of Re, or indeed become Re himself, free to sail across the heavens in a vessel that overcomes all obstacles and finds all gates magically opened, happily sailing by the menacing guardians. He must know these guardians, however, as "whoever knows them passes them in peace" (Amduat). The Book of the Dead provides commoners with spells enabling them to "board the bark of Re with those who are in his entourage" and thus with the divine crew, as stated in spell 100; even a picture of the vessel was to be placed on the chest of the deceased, to assure him that he will be able to board and debark without complications.

The solar vessel carries not only the blessed dead, but also all the offerings they require. Bread and beer are the most elementary provisions offered by the pharaoh to his servants on earth, and in the Beyond these supplies are carried on the solar bark. Almost every scene of the Book of Gates closes with a variation on this theme:

> Their offerings are bread,
> Their beer is a sacred draft,
> Their refreshment is water.

or
> They are those who give fields and offerings
> To the gods and the blessed dead in the West.
> Their offerings are in the rush fields,
> Their offerings are what comes forth from them.

As a special honor for those who act justly, "their beer is wine" (scene 43). The water constantly mentioned in these texts is the primeval water copiously flowing through the Netherworld. In the Amduat the oarsmen splash it on the blessed dead, for whom even the water of the Lake of Fire is a cool refreshment.

Greens supplement the basics, but meat and fowl—which are always heaped on the offering tables of the dead—are not mentioned in the texts concerned with food in the Beyond. Also important in the Beyond was the provision of clothing for the dead, a procedure that becomes important in the eighth and ninth hours of Amduat. The beings encountered are literally seated on their clothes, or at least on the hieroglyph for "cloth." The enlightened body must be properly clothed; the Egyptians did not know of any "heavenly nakedness," as nudity was the symbol of helplessness, something one would wish on one's foes. Even the goddess Ishtar in the Near East laid aside her divine power with her clothing as she descended into

The serpent, a personification of Time in the eleventh hour of the Amduat, swallows the stars, the already expended hours of the night.

the Netherworld. Bright white linen raiment is the prerogative of the blessed dead, contrasting starkly with the black mummiform coffins and demonstrating the return to life in familiar garb.

The most important offering of all, however, was the sun's light, cutting the bonds of darkness. The constantly recurring motif of the liberating effect of light is depicted by the rays of a radiant sun crossing rigid mummies which are then awakened and given the breath of life. The miracle is repeated each hour of the night: the luminous rays breaking the constraints of death call life forth from the protective but restrictive mummy form. Doors open, light pierces the darkest pits, the dead stretch their heads out of coffins, serpents breathe fire, mysterious creatures step out of their hidden abodes, and the entire Netherworld resounds with jubilant worship of the god who has freed them from the bonds of darkness and death.

As the sun god moves into the region of the next hour, the fairy tale is reversed: just when the dead have been awakened to life, doors close, pits and coffins are sealed, darkness descends, and the wailing dead resume their sleep of death in mummy form. Their bodies remain hidden from those on earth, concealed in the depths of the earth: only their *ba*s and shadows follow the light and the sun god, to be seen as migratory birds or stars in this world. All paths are open for them, and for them is the cry of joy: ''Open are the Gates of the Netherworld, open are the earth and its pits.'' Their bodies bring forth one last wail before their coffins are sealed in darkness.

> They shout to Re, wailing to the great god
> After he has passed them.
> When he is gone, darkness envelops them,
> And their pits are sealed above them.

Bearers of the ''lifetime'' snake, from the Book of Gates in the upper pillared hall in the tomb of Sety I. These gods measure out lifetime to each of the souls in the West.

This is the eternal cycle of the Egyptian, with life always leading to death, and death to life. The awakening to rejuvenated life never lasts more than an hour, after which life and light pass on with the sun god, even though an hour of the Beyond is adjusted to that world's monstrous dimensions and corresponds to an entire lifetime here on earth.

The Egyptians' concept of time is revealed by the poetic philosophers of the Books of the Netherworld. Whence come the mysterious hours, and where do they go? In the Amduat, the hours emerge from the mouth of a serpent which itself embodies time. When an hour has passed, it is "swallowed" or "taken away." Other passages depict the hours not as stars, but as women, goddesses who guide the sun god, whose "faces belong to darkness, their backs to the light," each hour possessing a dark and light side. And thus scene 20 in the Book of Gates depicts the twelve goddesses of the hours on either side of a serpent with endless coils: this is Time, from whose body the hours are born as small snakes, emerging one after another, only to be swallowed by the goddesses. In the Book of the Earth is a scene of the procreation preceding this birth; a giant divine figure with an erect phallus is surrounded by stars, solar disks, and the twelve goddesses of the hours, all joined to one another by dotted lines.

Even the "lifetimes" of those in the Realm of the Dead are from the infinite reserves of a monstrous serpent's body held by twelve gods who measure and determine their length. Two other scenes of the same book show the continuum of time as an endless rope emerging from a god's mouth. Each coil of the doubly twisted cord is an hour of the Beyond, and thus an entire lifetime on earth. In a wealth of motifs almost as inexhaustible as time itself, it is demonstrated that the blessed dead are guaranteed millions of years and more, in hourlong units for as long as the world endures.

Furthermore, this is not empty time but a fulfilling and heightened existence. The Egyptians did not look forward to a pale shadowy Beyond, but rather to an existence full of life, with constant change and development, unconstrained by all the sorrows and troubles of this world. It is repeatedly stressed that the blessed dead are content, and that they have attained a "peace of heart," more important than the bread and beer originally presented by Atum to Osiris, sovereign of the Netherworld (Book of the Dead, spell 175).

This peace exists wherever *maat*, the normal, commonsense order of existence, prevails. In the seventh hour of the Book of Gates the blessed are called to the temple of the god "who lives from *maat*," and they bear this *maat*, whose symbol is an ostrich feather, on their heads. Those who have complied in all their affairs with the just order here on earth and have consequently been "justified" in the Judgment of the Dead are now promised "an existence until the end, under *maat*." This assures them that the living order of the Creation will carry them through all eternity, until the end of time itself. But woe unto those of the dead who do not bear *maat*, who have departed from the established order here on earth, and who disregard the basic rules of human life! For them the world gapes open, and they are swallowed up in the depths of the earth, never to be released again, rejuvenation eternally withheld from them.

94. *The final scene of the Book of Gates in the upper pillared hall of the tomb of Ramesses VI. Nun lifts the sun bark out of the depths of the primeval water into the heavens. A tiny figure of the sky goddess, Nut, reaches down to the sun disk (now destroyed); above is Osiris, "who encircles the underworld," bending backward.*

95. *The beginning of the third hour of the Book of Gates in the sarcophagus chamber of Sety I. Re passes a row of shrines containing erect mummies. Their upright rather than horizontal position is the result of Re's command; his rays penetrate the shrines and grant the mummies new life. The solar bark is ringed by the protective* mehen *snake and accompanied by the two personifications of creative power, Sia, insight/ knowledge, and Heka, magic. Below, Atum leans on a staff, banishing the many-coiled serpent Apophis from the presence of Re.*

96. *Detail of the fifth hour of the Book of Gates in the upper pillared hall of the tomb of Sety I. Gods holding a rope measure the fertile fields so that the blessed dead can plant and harvest. This hall, like the corridors, has a white background for the scenes, unlike the sarcophagus chamber with its yellow background.*

97. *One of the mummies in the "entourage of Osiris who sleeps the sleep of death," from the sixth hour of the Book of Gates in the upper pillared hall of the tomb of Sety I. The mummy lies on a snake-shaped bier from which he will rise to new life at the passing of the sun god.*

94

95

96

97

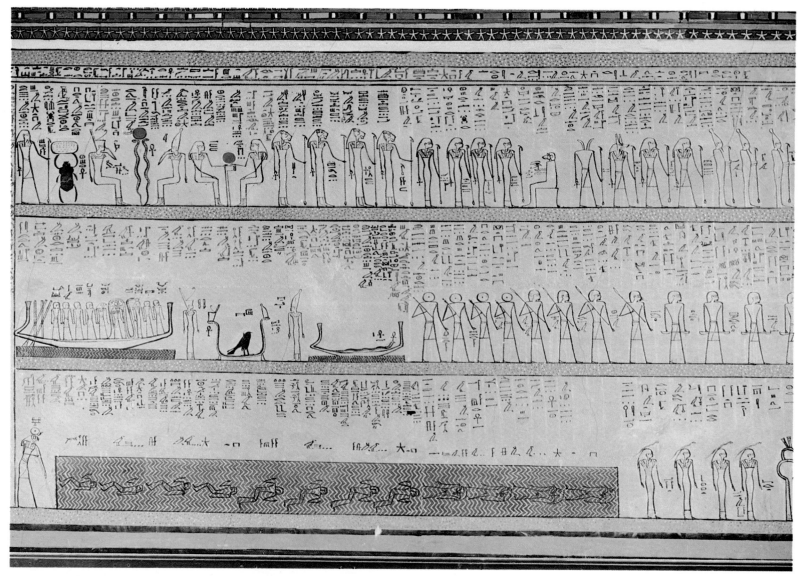

98

99

98. *The tenth hour of the Amduat in the tomb of Amenophis II, showing the deification of the drowned in the lower register. In different positions, the drowned swim in a great watery rectangle, the primeval ocean, Nun. At the command of Horus (on the left), they are brought to land, where despite their not being mummified they are granted a blessed existence. In the middle register a procession of gods armed with arrows, spears, and bows protect the sun god in the solar bark against his enemies.*

99. *Depiction of the drowned in the Book of Gates in the tomb of Tausert.*

100. *The ninth hour of the Book of Gates in the tomb of Ramesses VI contains a scene of the deification of the drowned that is similar to that in the Amduat. Above, bird-formed souls "who are in the fiery island" worship the sun god; below, a fire-spitting serpent projects its sweltering heat toward the condemned.*

101. *Depiction of the drowned in the Book of Gates in the tomb of Tausert. (See plates 99 and 33.)*

102

103

104

146

105

102. *The blessed dead raise themselves from their biers to new life on the ceiling of the third corridor of the tomb of Ramesses IX.*

103. *Stars and a list of decans on the ceiling of the second corridor of the tomb of Ramesses IX.*

104. *Stars on the ceiling of the burial chamber of Sety I.*

105. *The four races of mankind in the fifth hour of the Book of Gates in the tomb of Sety I, after a copy by Minutoli. Right to left are an Egyptian, an Asiatic (with long beard and colored kilt), a dark-skinned Nubian, and four light-skinned Libyans (tattooed, with side-locks, and feathers in the hair). The foreigners, Egypt's traditional enemies, appear nonetheless in the Beyond, assured divine protection.*

106. *A mound of food offerings for the dead, in the private Theban tomb of Sennefer.*

106

107

108

109

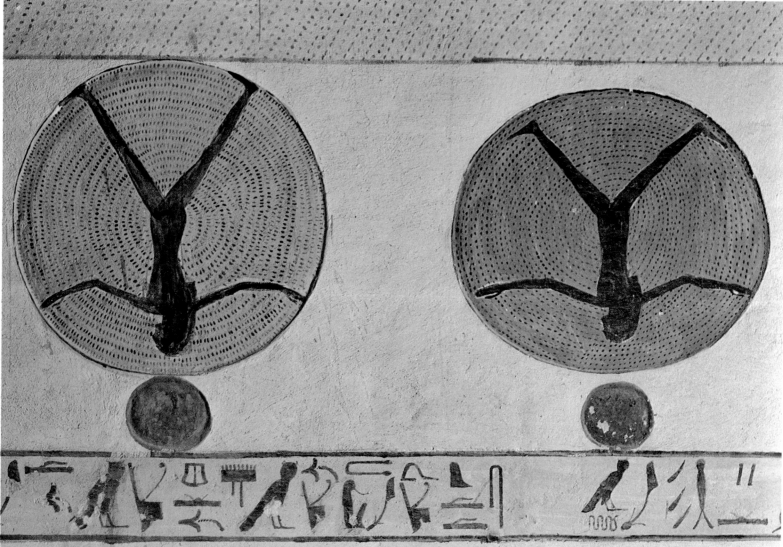

110

148

THE UNJUST DAMNED
CHAPTER 10 TO NONEXISTENCE

As Lord of the Underworld, Osiris judges the dead and separates them, according to the Amduat, into two categories, ''the prospering and the exterminated.'' In the Old Kingdom, the Court of the Dead was prepared to take testimony from geese and cattle, but the court was not perpetual, and convened ad hoc to restore the just order. It was only in the period of transition between the Old and Middle Kingdoms that the concept of a general and automatic Judgment of the Dead became firmly anchored in Egyptian thought. The Teaching of Merykare from the First Intermediate Period (ca. 2000 B.C.) is the earliest known text alluding to this:

> The Magistrates who redress wrong:
> You know that they are not kindly
> On that day of righting wrong,
> In that hour when they convene.

About 500 years later, the Judgment of the Dead took its final form in the New Kingdom Book of the Dead (spells 30 and 125), and the earliest datable pictorial

Scenes of judgment from the Book of the Dead. The upper scene shows the judgment of a private person who stands before Osiris, Isis, Nephthys, and the sons of Horus (on the lotus). The scale balances the heart of the deceased with the feather symbol of Maat.

107–109. *Asiatics (107), Nubians (108), and Libyans (109) in the fifth hour of the Book of Gates in the tomb of Ramesses III.*

110. *Detail from an otherwise unknown Book of the Netherworld in the tomb of Ramesses IX. The cross-formed figures in the yellow and red disks perhaps indicate the whirling movement of light. Below is a cryptographic inscription.*

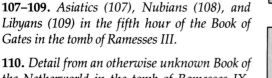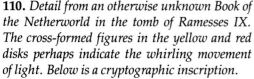

representation appeared in the Valley of the Kings. Illustrating spell 30 of the funerary papyrus in the tomb of the commoner Maiherperi is a scene with Osiris enthroned before scales on which a statuette of the deceased is weighed against his heart. The text beseeches the heart "not to oppose [the deceased] in the Realm of the Dead," appearing as neither witness nor plaintiff, remaining loyal and in harmony with him, so that the scales will appear balanced. This scene of the balance scales becomes part of the standard illustration of the Book of the Dead; although the details vary and the menacing figure of the "Devourer of the Dead" may appear, the basic motif remains the same. Anubis, who attends to the preparation of the mummy and thus has the clearest view of its innermost nature, attends also to the balance, while ibis-headed Thoth records the results. The pillow of childbirth rests at one side, promising rebirth and rejuvenation, should the examination be passed. The Devourer of the Dead, a monstrous personification of the jaws of death, awaits, should the court swing the other way.

At once demanding and imploring, the deceased makes a declaration of innocence before the tribunal and its divine advisory board:

> Behold, I have come to you,
> Bringing justice to you,
> Repelling evil for you.
> I have not done evil against men.
> I have not impoverished my associates.
> I have not acted crookedly in the Place of Justice.
>
> . . .
>
> I have not defiled a god.
> I have not worsened the lot of an orphan.
> I have not done what the gods detest.
> I have not calumniated a servant to his master.
> I have not caused either pain or hunger.
> I have not brought forth tears.
> I have not killed.
> I have not commanded to kill.
> I have not caused anyone sorrow.

And thus it continues in an almost endless litany in which every one of the forty-two advisors to the court is individually addressed by name and origin. Each denial of a specific form of injustice cleanses another layer of the earthly taint, bringing forth unblemished justice—*maat*—and ensuring the purity of the deceased, a requirement for a blessed life in the Beyond. "I am pure!" Four times this simple cry echoes through the Hall of Justice, and this is sufficient for the deceased "to be purged of all the evil he has done," as promised in spell 125. This is the power of the word. Magic is at work here: not as a substitute for ethically spotless behavior, but rather as an additional measure available to men in the most dangerous episode of human existence. The Judgment of the Dead is irreversible, threatening complete and final annihilation. The dead and all their dependents must take advantage of every possible means of warding off this fate, and magic is the weapon par excellence in this conflict.

Some scenes in the Books of the Netherworld record the results of the verdict. In the seventh hour of the Amduat, immediately above the enchantment of Apophis, a

The Hall of Judgment with the enthroned Osiris, from the Book of Gates in the burial chamber of Haremheb. (See plate 111.)

cat-headed demon—"he of the violent face"—carries out the sentence on the condemned, whose decapitated bodies kneel before Osiris as Judge of the Dead. It can be assumed that this punishing demon is in fact a manifestation of Re, also known as the "Great Cat" who destroys Apophis and other foes in one ancient myth. The condemned here are, however, "the foes of Osiris"; they have done evil against him and show that the Judgment of the Dead is not far removed from the divine Court of Heliopolis, which defended Osiris against Seth and his "gang," endeavoring to despoil Horus of his lawful inheritance. This punishment is equally a matter of firmly establishing justice beyond death, and satisfying the violently murdered Osiris in the Beyond. Osiris himself is the chief judge, in place of the earth god Geb or the sun god Re, and the guilt of the condemned at his feet is never precisely defined and must finally be ascribed to the ill deeds of Seth.

This aspect is particularly clear in the judgment scene of the Book of Gates, prominently placed on the back wall of the burial chamber in Haremheb's tomb, immediately above the royal sarcophagus and accompanied by cleverly formulated cryptographic notes. According to one of these, the scene is intended for the "protection of Osiris," as he is shown to be victorious over all his enemies: Seth assumes the form of a fleeing pig, and the damned lie at Osiris's feet, while the blessed are lined up on the steps of the dais. Osiris usually wears the double crown here, rather than his own; it symbolizes the pharaoh's role as sovereign of Upper and Lower Egypt, and Osiris also holds the royal scepter in his hands. He is king of the Realm of the Dead, ruling the blessed and the damned, "those who are and those who are not." The earthly pharaoh aspires to the same role as Osiris, judging his enemies, and this aspiration caused Merneptah to use spell 125 of the Book of the Dead in his tomb. This was the first time a spell from the Book of the Dead was used in the Valley of the Kings, although the thought that the pharaoh himself would have to account for his deeds first appeared at least a thousand years earlier in the First Intermediate Period.

With Osiris's foes "beneath his heels" and a monster waiting beside the scales, the fate of those who are condemned is merely indicated, not defined. Many scenes of the Books of the Netherworld are, however, dedicated to elaborate descriptions of their miserable lot, with unquenchable imagination attending to every detail. The sun god's nightly journey frequently leads him close to places of eternal torture, which his word unfailingly renews. In general the sun avoids such unpleasant spheres, sailing far above them, so that not even the glimmer of his rays penetrates into these recesses of the earth. Punishment is depicted in the lowest register, and the later Books of the Netherworld usually stress the god's absence by omitting the solar disk in those scenes where the damned are shown. The condemned cannot hear the god either; pushed into the bottomless darkness, they can neither hear nor see.

All benefaction is thus withheld from the enemies of divine order. And the contrast of their destiny to that of the blessed is effectively summarized in a judgment scene from the Book of the Night: "You shall not behold your God!" they are told, while the blessed learn that "Re is in your eyes, the breath of life in your noses." Life-giving light does not reach the punished, water and food are denied them, the breath of life is cut off: standing on their heads, they live from the "abomination of their hearts," their own excrement. They are not given clean clothes but are left naked and bound, completely defenseless. Certain scenes from Dynasty 20 even omit their genitalia, indicating that they are denied descendants and heirs. Their names and all memory of their very existence is to be obliterated. Even their burials are nullified, the texts relating that their mummy wrappings are torn away, their protection destroyed (calling to mind the New Testament story of Lazarus and the rich man, and the demotic Setna story, in which a rich man's luxurious burial is confiscated in the Beyond and given to the blessed poor, who had been unceremoniously thrown, wrapped in mats, into shallow pits).

The authors of the texts of the Netherworld did not, however, content themselves only with the deprivations of the damned. They went on to provide detailed descriptions of every variety of torture, unrolling an amazing catalogue of infernal punishments, the like of which is to be found only in Christian manuscripts of the late Middle Ages. The demonic torturers and executioners are described dramatically. In spell 17 of the Book of the Dead—which had parallels in the Coffin Texts—the deceased begs mercy:

> Save me from that dog-faced god
> Whose eyebrows are human,
> Who lives off the victims of war,
> Guarding the meanders of the Lake of Fire,

Swallowing corpses and dominating hearts,
Wounding without being seen . . .
Seizing souls and lapping up rot,
Living from the putrid;
The guardian of darkness in obscurity
Terrorizing the weary.
Their knives shall not pierce me
And down to their slaughterhouses I shall not go,
To their butchers' blocks
To abide their traps.
Nothing shall be prepared for me from that which the gods detest.

Similarly horrible creatures "who knock off heads and slit throats, attacking hearts to draw them forth, initiating bloodbaths" (spell 71), live in the places of punishment: according to a letter from Osiris to the other gods, his realm is "filled with savage-faced messengers fearing neither god not goddess." The third hour of the Amduat shows bellowing demons "who crush enemies" while "letting their voices echo," but he who knows them "cannot perish from their bellowing or fall into their pits." The roar of raging demons and their wailing victims forms a sharp contrast to the heavenly peace of the Realm of the Dead.

In the Litany of Re, even the pharaoh fears "those blood-smeared demons with sharp knives who rip out hearts [and carry] them off to their ovens," saying, "They shall not go to work on me!" The deceased takes every measure to avoid these dreadful fellows, whom the Litany of Re identifies as the messengers of the sun god:

O Re of the west,
Who disciplines and oversees the Netherworld,
Preserve me from your messengers
Who destroy souls and corpses,

Punishment by knives, from the Book of Caverns in the tomb of Ramesses VI. The bound enemies have already lost their heads, which lie before their feet. (Plate 117.)

The impatient hasty ones in thy slaughterhouses—
That they not seize me and grab me,
That their steps not hurry against me,
That they not turn me over to their slaughterhouses,
That they not tighten their cords about me
That I not be placed on their offering stands.
I have not disappeared in the land of extermination.
I was not punished in the west.

But there is no salvation for those foes of Osiris who defy the order of the Creation and are not separated from their sins at the Judgment of the Dead. Their actual crimes are not intrinsically important: whether killers, liars, or thieves, they are ''enemies'' and are destined for punishment, which extends from simple binding of the arms to annihilation.

Being bound places the guilty on a level with ordinary livestock led to slaughter, or with prisoners of war. Since the dawn of history, prisoners with their arms bound behind their backs symbolize the enemy. ''You are bound, you are firmly bound with cord! I commanded that you be bound, and your arms shall not open,'' cries the triumphant Atum in the second hour of the Book of Gates to the evildoers who have opposed the sun god and are now called upon, bound and bent, to await their punishment. In the ninth hour of the same work, the foes of Osiris are bound in three different ways. Horus calls to them: ''Your arms are upon your heads, you rebels! You are bound from behind, you villains, that you may be beheaded and annihilated!'' In the Book of Caverns, their arms are bent or even ''knotted,'' and in spell 17 of the Book of the Dead the god Shemesu drags them, bound, to the block.

In a few scenes of the Books of the Netherworld, the damned are even tied to the stake, and the eighth address in the Litany of Re illustrates the sun god's role as the eliminator of these enemies. In the seventh nightly hour in the Book of Gates,

The ''stakes of Geb,'' from the Book of Gates in the tomb of Ramesses VI. (See plate 112.)

The damned, turned upside down and beheaded, in the burial chamber of Ramesses VI. (Plates 54, center, and 125.)

154

The damned, with torches as heads, in the burial chamber of Ramesses VI. (Plate 54, upper left.)

the sun god arrives at the seven stakes of the earth god Geb, each of which is crowned with a jackal's head. Bound to them are the enemies of various divinities, "condemned in the west" and awaiting their final punishment. Demons with terrifying names (Rapacious, Squeezer, Brutal, Terror, Exacting, Ripper) assure that "they not come forth from your hands, that they not escape from your fingers," as commanded by Atum.

Their bondage and confinement in the deepest recesses of the earth are intended to ensure that they do not rise again and cause more trouble. The sun god binds the pharaoh's enemies "that they not leave the earth"; his role as "lord of the cords for the enemies" has a special manifestation, appearing twice in the Amduat and again in the Litany of Re. In place of a head, two black ropes emerge from the neck of this figure, identified as cords for confining the enemies.

The binding of these villains is merely a hint of what is to come. The form of address makes this relatively clear, and in the tombs of Ramesses VI and Ramesses IX, the burial chamber and corridors are decorated with whole rows of bound and beheaded enemies, color-coded alternately red (bloody) and black (nonbeing). The earlier Books of the Netherworld provide similar scenes, such as that with figures before the enthroned Osiris in the seventh hour of the Amduat. The later Book of Caverns shows the heads laid literally at the feet of the enemies (2,000 years earlier the Narmer Palette shows this same treatment of royal enemies). Elsewhere, the headless are held upside down by vengeful demons. The tearing out of the heart is referred to in numerous texts, and depicted with brutal simplicity in the Book of Caverns. The same work records that "the darkness of the annihilated consists of blood"; they swim in the darkness of their own blood, which a later text relates was distilled out of them, to flow into the red burning water of the Lake of Fire.

The Egyptians also conceived of an eternal "unquenchable fire" as belonging to the punishments of this hell. The tongues and eyes of the demonic torturers spew forth fire, as do the knives they grasp. The countless serpents crawling around the Beyond exhale a poisonous burning breath on the sinners. This is demonstrated in the ninth hour of the Book of Gates, where variously bound enemies are helplessly sprayed with bright red fire from the mouth of the "great and fiery" monstrous serpent. After delivering the sentence, the god Horus turns to the serpent, requesting of her:

> Open your mouth, expose your jaws,
> That you spit fire on the enemies of my father!
> That you burn their corpses
> And cook their souls

With the burning breath of your mouth,
With the embers in your body.

Following this is a note: "Then comes forth the fire of this serpent, and then these enemies are consumed in the fire." In the Book of Caverns, the sun god assigns three monstrous serpents to "guard the rebels" in the "place of extermination," requesting that they also slit their throats and "hack off their heads."

In some scenes the punished have burning torches where their heads should be, indicating perpetual corporal punishment. For a people prizing corporal integrity after death, consignment of the body to flames symbolized the absolute negation of existence—the hardest imaginable sentence on earth, although rarely executed. (Tomb-robbers neutralized the victims of their sacrilegious acts by setting fire to the mummies.)

The lowest register of the eleventh hour in the Amduat places the bodies and separated heads of the damned—along with their souls and shadows—in fiery pits pictorially represented as hill-like formations, the last of which contains "the upside-down ones." Each pit is assigned to a fire-breathing goddess holding a dagger. Another fire-breathing serpent "who burns millions" comes to her aid, while Horus holds court before the dead:

> The blade of vengeance is for your bodies;
> Death for your souls,
> Darkness for your shadows,
> The block for your heads.
> You never lived, you are turned about,
> And you rise not, for you stumbled into your pits,
> Whence you escape not, nor are freed.
> This serpent's flames are for you,
> And the fire of this goddess ["Who Is Above Her Cauldron"] is for you.
> . . .
> The dagger of the goddess ["With the Daggers"] is in you,
> Tearing your bodies asunder.

"Nevermore shall you behold the living on earth," are Horus's closing words, and the whole miserable company is left in dark and painful captivity for all time. In the Book of Gates (scene 22), the "chief annihilator" and four assistants guard the opening of each of four flaming traps, reminiscent of early Christian descriptions of hell. As usual, Horus encourages the torturers, calling out, "Seize these foes of my father and drag them off to your traps to account for the pain they have caused [Osiris]."

At the center of the infernal punishments is the Lake of Fire, whose very water is fire, pictured with red waves occasionally adorned with beheaded sinners swimming among them. The ancient Book of Two Ways (part of the Middle Kingdom Coffin Texts) states that "no one can pass through the flame surrounding it." The Lake of Fire, located at the very bottom of the lowest register of the Amduat's fifth hour, below the chaotic oval of Sokar, is mourned by the gods of the Netherworld. The theme is repeatedly mentioned in the Book of Gates. Once it is a circular "hole of fire," whose unapproachable flames offer Osiris cooling refreshment, while its

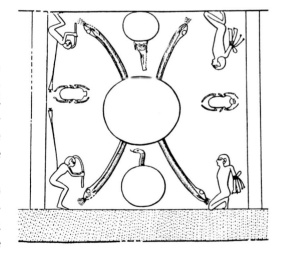

Four fire-spitting serpents shooting forth from the sun, burning the damned, in the tomb of Ramesses VI. Two of the damned are bound and two are pierced by arrows.

A caldron with (from top to bottom) shadows, souls, and flesh of the damned; from the Book of Caverns in the tomb of Ramesses VI.

consuming fire threatens his foes. This ambivalence is to be found in scene 10 of the Book of Gates as well:

> This lake is full of grain,
> The water of the lake is fiery.
> Birds fly away
> When they see its water,
> When they sense the stench of what is in it.

The grain is for the nourishment of the dead, and the flames for the damned. The condemned are shoved into this stench, while the blessed dead are wrapped in fragrant scents. In the Book of the Dead, the Lake of Fire, surrounded by acclaiming baboons and guardian cobras, is mentioned just after the spell of the Judgment of the Dead, where the fate of the damned is suggested. As fire-breathing serpents are commonplace in the Beyond, the Lake of Serpents in the Book of Gates (scene 17) may be another variation on the theme of the Lake of Fire.

With the fiery pits of the eleventh hour of the Amduat is a demon, "He Who Is Above His Cauldrons"; in the Litany of Re, "He of the Cauldron" is a manifestation of the sun god himself, "who controls the fire in his cauldrons, and beheads the annihilated," thus being another apparition of the god as a tormenting spirit beside the Fetterer. The figure associated with this, appellation 65 of the Litany, bears a cauldron on his head; but the later Books of the Netherworld do not stop at mere suggestions—they show the cauldrons in use. Heads, hearts, corpses, souls, and shadows are thrown upside down into the boiling water; serpents and other avenging demons attend to the glowing fire, spewing flames into it, while mysterious arms heave the whole out of the dark depths of the "annihilation centers" into the visible regions of the Netherworld. Schematic cross-sections of three of these cauldrons are shown in the fifth division of the Book of Caverns, and the accompanying texts record the orders of the sun god to his servants:

On the left the Judgment of the Dead; on the right the bestial "Devourer of the Dead" before a caldron containing the punished. From a Roman period tomb painting at Akhmim in Middle Egypt.

> O cobra-shaped creature above your flame,
> Spewing fire into your cauldron
> Containing the heads of Osiris's foes . . . !
> Throw your torch into your cauldron,
> Cook the foes of the sovereign of the Netherworld!
> O you two cobras, flaming and burning,
> Breathe your flames and kindle the blaze
> Below that cauldron holding the foes of Osiris.

An Egyptian tomb painting from the Roman period a thousand years later unites the scenes of the weighing of the scales from the Judgment of the Dead with scenes of the devouring monster and the boiling cauldron, indicating the multiple menace awaiting the damned. It was but a small step from such scenes to those of the infernal cauldrons of the Christian Middle Ages, where this ancient Egyptian tradition survived.

The real purpose of all these hellish horrors was neither eternal torment for its own sake nor a kind of purgatory, but the absolute elimination of everything hostile to Osiris and the divine order. The annihilation center from the Book of Caverns is a place of punishment from which "there is no escape." Everything that takes place there is in complete contrast to the fate of the blessed dead. Instead of bringing body and soul together, the characters of the damned are condemned to complete destruction, their bodies consigned to the all-consuming flames. Infernal stench replaces fragrance. Instead of rising from the depths to experience the god's light, the damned fall into darkness, into the deepest recesses of the earth. Instead of reawakening and being renewed, they are threatened with the complete, absolute, and final negation of existence: the second death, the pervading horror of the texts of the Beyond.

"I have commanded your elimination and damned you to nonexistence," are Re's comfortless words for his "foes" in the annihilation centers, those who have already lost their heads and hearts. But even Apophis, who appears as a sort of chief devil in this place of punishment, always reappears after being mutilated and destroyed. And thus the punishment of the dead must be repeated each time the god traverses the Netherworld, night after night. The nonexistence to which the punished are condemned is not nothingness but rather the denial of a blessed life in the Realm of the Dead. It is the complete absence of the sun god without any mitigating circumstances.

The Book of Caverns describes this condition with the statement that the Eye of Horus does not approach the damned. This is a message packed with meaning: the Eye of Horus signifies every positive value known to the Egyptian in the Beyond. It is the "eye" of the heavenly sun god; it is the offerings presented to the gods and the dead alike. But it is also the wounded eye of Horus that was made whole, an image of desired renewal and regeneration. If it is withheld from the corrupt, then they lack everything that makes life worth living. With a devastating refusal, the god of the Creation makes the Beyond an eternal hell.

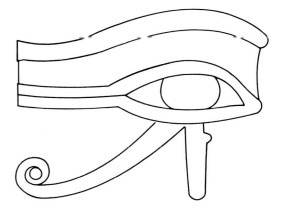

The sound eye of Horus (udjat).

111

112

111. *The Judgment Hall of the Book of Gates in the tomb of Ramesses VI. Before the enthroned Osiris are a scale and the just on the stairs. Above, a pig in a bark represents the enemy, as both Seth and Apophis. The labels for this scene are all cryptographic.*

112. *The stakes of Geb from the seventh hour of the Book of Gates in the tomb of Ramesses III. Condemned souls are bound to stakes and guarded by their torturers.*

113. *The fifth hour of the Book of Gates in the tomb of Ramesses VI. It is a counterpart to the scene with Nut in plate 48. Osiris is represented with erect phallus, united with his bird-formed* ba *on his head. The lower right shows part of a caldron containing decapitated and bound bodies. Heat for the pot is provided by fire-spitting snakes.*

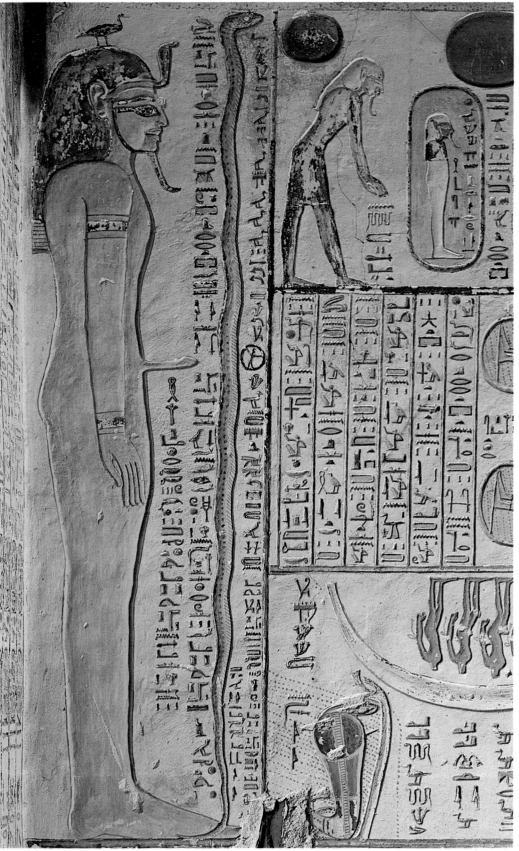

113

159

114

116

117

115

114. *The third hour of the Book of Gates in the burial chamber of the tomb of Sety I. The Lake of Fire is painted red with blue waves. It offers cool refreshment for the blessed in their white wraps, but for the damned it is fiery heat, a place of punishment.*

115. *The fourth hour of the Book of Gates in the tomb of Sety I. Two of the four fire-filled traps await those whose punishment will be renewed.*

116. *Spell 126 in the Book of the Dead in the tomb of Ramesses VI. The king prays before two representations of the Lake of Fire, which are guarded by four baboons and marked with the hieroglyph for "fire" on all four sides.*

117. *Sixth section of the Book of Caverns in the tomb of Ramesses VI. A goddess severs the heads of the condemned.*

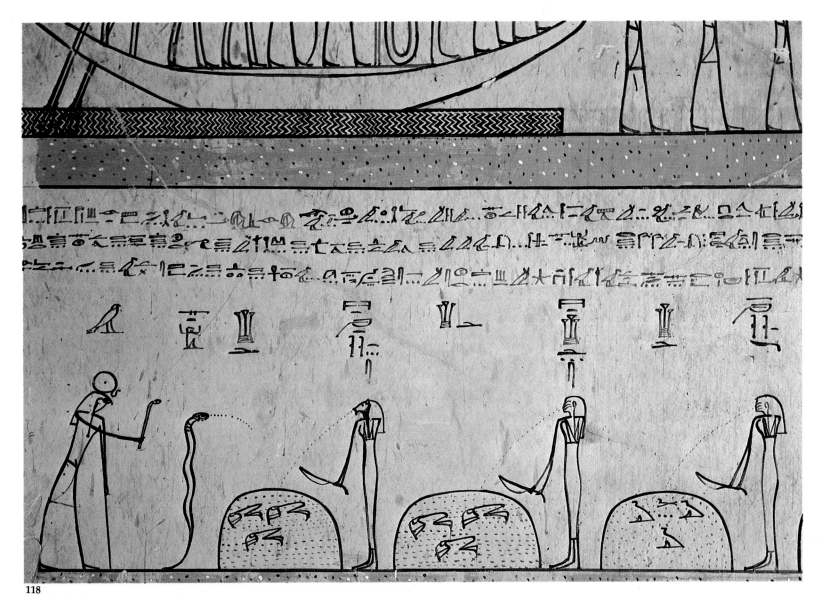

118

119

120

118. *The eleventh hour of the Amduat in the burial chamber of Tuthmosis III. The scene begins on the left: Horus, falcon-headed and wearing a sun disk, stands with the snake ''who burns millions'' before deities who spit fire into graves. The third grave contains the souls of the condemned.*

119/120. *In the tomb of Ramesses IX, bound and decapitated enemies are painted alternately red (for blood) and blue (for nonexistence). They are unclothed, and without genitalia.*

121

121. *Detail from the Book of the Earth in the burial chamber of Ramesses VI. In the lowest register are two caldrons containing the heads and body parts of enemies. A fire-spitting head heats each pot; between the caldrons two goddesses guard a heart, possibly Osiris's.*

122. *Detail from the second section of the Book of Caverns in the tomb of Ramesses VI. Naked bound enemies are depicted upended, without genitalia, and with their hearts hanging outside their bodies.*

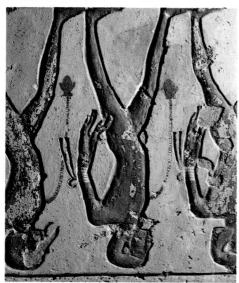

122

123. *Scene from the ninth hour of the Book of Gates in the tomb of Tausert. A serpent spews its fire at bound sinners.*

124

125

124. *The Book of Earth in the tomb of Ramesses VI. The upper register shows goddesses binding the damned, each with the hieroglyph for ''fire'' on his head. Below, ringed by the Apophis snake, whose head has been cut by a knife, Osiris stands between the ''corpse of Tatenen'' on the left and the ''corpse of Geb'' on the right. The feet of the three gods are below the surface of the earth. (See plate 54.)*

125. *The Book of Earth in the tomb of Ramesses VI. Upturned decapitated and bloody enemies are grasped by black executioners. (See plate 54.)*

CHAPTER 11 EQUIPPED FOR ETERNITY

Much of Egyptian art is a creative response to death—a desire to produce monuments and objects in this life that would continue to be useful in the eternal Realm of the Dead in the Beyond. Even before the dawn of history, perishable articles in tomb inventories gave way to objects made of enduring stone, and thus the Egyptians acquired their first experience in forcing this solid material to yield to their own wishes; they rapidly realized that even the granite and diorite with which their land was blessed could be rendered pliable.

Palettes for the preparation of cosmetics were frequently made of slate formed in the shape of animals that later appear as symbols of regeneration: fish, turtle, gazelle, and hippopotamus. Since cosmetics were intended to return youthful liveliness to the dead, it is not surprising that the Egyptians selected the shapes of animals whose characteristic life-styles tended to confirm their belief that death was merely the prelude to revival in the Beyond. The numerous bird-shaped palettes may hint at a desire for freedom of movement in the Beyond: the soul's undisturbed flight to the heavens. To the ancient Egyptians the disappearance and return of migratory birds suggested that the dead were only temporarily deprived of life, before commencing again. It is surely of significance that among both sculpted animals and theriomorphic vessels, the forms of "regenerative" animals, later associated with life in the Beyond, are already favored: frog, toad, hedgehog, and hippopotamus, as well as the lion, ibex, gazelle, which survive in the wilderness. Numerous apes (mostly baboons) also belong to this domain, and they were to develop a multifaceted relationship with the conceptual world of rejuvenation and regeneration, their green color appropriate to the "greening," prospering state of the revived dead. Whatever the case, these archaic animal figures from the birth of Egyptian art are closely related to the magnificent animal figures of the Middle Kingdom and to the animals of seal amulets. Even a plant form—the regenerative lotus blossom—was used as an early vessel shape.

In the earliest painted decoration on the pottery vessels of the Amratian and Negada periods, it would appear that the motifs are almost exclusively concerned with burial and the Beyond. A ship dominates these paintings (ships occur also in clay and stone); it carries the dead to a burial on the edge of the desert, and then on the waterways of the Beyond. "Dancers" wail in mourning in a landscape that seems to include barrows and *ba* birds, although the details are not entirely clear.

The first sculpted human figures, naked women and bearded men, are like earlier figures painted on vessels but have not yet been convincingly identified. They are certainly not divine figures, and it is possible that they are related to burial and survival in the Beyond. The preserved statues of kings and officials from the first dynasties of the historical era belong to the equipment of the tomb, erected in a separate room of a private tomb or royal funerary temple in order to assure survival in the Beyond. Even after the Old Kingdom, when statues were required also for this world, the most important task of Egyptian sculptors was still the carving of statues for the tombs.

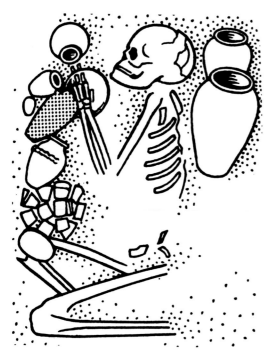

Prehistoric burial with offerings for the deceased.

The origins of sculpture and painting are thus firmly anchored in the world of death and revival, transcending the perishability of human existence. One has the impression that even in the most prosperous days of later periods, Egyptian artists and craftsmen devoted almost all their efforts to death and the Beyond, which in no way constrained the liveliness of their work. Most of what we know about the daily life of the ancient Egyptians—their farming and handiwork, parties and music, games and sport—comes from their tombs. With minor exceptions, the remains of their villages have perished, while the cemeteries have endured, even today preserving their decorative record of life on lasting walls of stone.

Painted pottery jar of the Negada II culture (ca. 3100 B.C.).

Treasure hunters robbed most tombs of their offerings many centuries ago, so that only a few fragments hint at the magnificent treasures they once contained. Intact royal burials found by archaelogists are rare: Tutankhamun's treasures in Luxor and those of some equally insignificant kings of Dynasties 21 and 22 in Tanis are supplemented only by the treasures of Cheops's mother, Queen Hetepheres, from Giza; the grave goods of some Dynasty 12 princesses from Lahun and Dahshur. Even private tombs have yielded few intact burials: the treasures of Amenophis III's in-laws, Yuya and Tuya; of their approximate contemporary the architect Kha; and of the Ramesside craftsman Sennedjem.

Thus while we have only a small selection of the portable objects, the decoration on tomb walls has withstood the test of time; from the depiction there, we are able to reconstruct a good part of the objects that have been lost forever. (As mentioned in the introduction, these pictures have suffered considerably in recent years and will themselves soon be lost if action is not taken immediately.) Since the dawn of history, grave goods were recorded in a "list of offerings" detailing the nature and quantity required or desired. Preserved in painting or relief, the power of the word guaranteed that the deceased would receive the necessary provisions. The list is frequently visible in scenes where the deceased are seated before an offering table with bread, of which they commence to partake. The list includes breads, beers, wines, grains, fruits, and meats, as well as various ointments, cosmetics, oils, incense, cloth and ready-made garments, vessels and tools: in short, an almost complete inventory of everything required for the journey to and the sojourn in the Beyond. Part of what was included in these lists was pictured in a single register among the funerary texts on coffins of the Middle Kingdom; there we also find weapons (bow and arrow, ax, dagger) and royal insignia (crown, staff, royal kilt), intended as powerful amulets for the private citizen. The New Kingdom adds a portrayal of the funeral procession to the basic repertoire of private tomb decoration, depicting additional grave goods; a sled with a coffin is followed by a line of porters who carry boxes and caskets, the contents drawn above the closed containers in the usual Egyptian manner. In the tomb of Mayor Sennefer, his servants bring cloth, kilts, sandals, a mummy mask, a winged scarab amulet, and more. His "beloved sister" provides him with additional amulets, among which we discern again a scarab beetle.

Depictions of funerary goods in the Valley of the Kings begin in the tomb of Sety I. In an ancillary room near the burial chamber, which Sety doubtless intended for his treasures, the bench along the walls reveals paintings of divine shrines and animal-headed ceremonial beds (like those preserved in the tomb of Tutankhamun). These paintings are, unfortunately, almost completely lost today, but Belzoni, who discovered the tomb, made complete copies. In the tomb of Tausert, similar representations were visible in the lower part of the burial chamber: pieces of furniture, vessels, statues, and amulets. Her husband, Sety II, had an entire room of his tomb decorated exclusively with divine and royal statuettes, which are matched by identical pieces among the treasures of Tutankhamun, among them the pharaoh on a panther and in a papyrus boat. Ramesses III had several niches of the second corridor of his tomb decorated with furniture, weapons, vessels, and other objects from his tomb equipment. After taking account of the representations and the various items recovered in different tombs, one can form a reasonably reliable idea of what a "typical" royal funerary treasure would have looked like. According to this, the treasures of Tutankhamun would have been by no means atypical, although they would have been distributed into more rooms.

The motif of the funerary procession as depicted in so many private tombs of the New Kingdom appears in only one royal tomb, that of Tutankhamun. On one wall is a double shrine with the royal mummy in a small bark, resting on a sled drawn by the highest officials of the realm rather than the traditional oxen. A short inscription, which bears no individual names and titles, is identified as: "Speech of the officials and great ones of the palace towing the Osiris Nebkheperure [Tutankhamun] into the west." They say, "O Nebkheperure, come in peace, you god! Prepare yourself, earth!" Two of these officials wear the costume of the vizier, the highest functionary of Upper and Lower Egypt. Bereft of wig and kilt, they wear only the ankle-length mantle that leaves their shoulders free. The single official behind them, just in front of the sled, is clearly their superior and can be only Haremheb, the regent of the land. Aye, the new Pharaoh, is dressed as a priest and performs the ceremony of the opening of the mouth on the Osiris-shaped mummy of his predecessor.

Elaborate versions of this ancient ritual to open the mouth of the mummy are preserved in the tombs of Sety I and Tausert. The opening of the mouth is intended

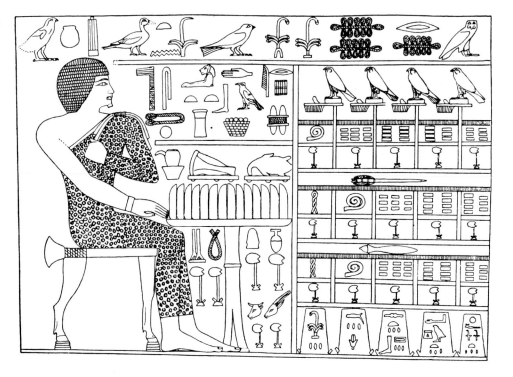

The deceased with an offering table piled with food before him and a list of cloth and grain. Slab stela from a Dynasty 4 mastaba at Giza.

not merely to prepare the mouth for receiving food and for speech, but also for awakening all the senses of the deceased. The eyes must be reopened for the reality of the Beyond, where the living gods can be seen. The opening of the mouth can be performed on statues as well as the lifeless mummy, bringing them to life as well. It is a necessary precursor to the enjoyment of the offerings. The significance of the ritual is made clear by the fact that it is the only one included in the decoration program of the royal rock tombs.

Innumerable pot sherds testify to the use of jars and bowls containing foodstuffs as accompaniment for the pharaoh on his journey into the Beyond. Other products were kept in baskets, a number of which have survived the millennia. Inscriptions from the tomb of Tutankhamun record the contents of various vessels, where even chemical analysis could offer no clues. There are wines of various dates and vintages, such as ''Year 5, wine of the domains of Aton on the western branch of the Nile. Chief vintner Any.'' Other jars contained ''honey of finest quality.'' Grapes and other fruits were in bowls, ''15 loaves'' in a basket, dried fish in boxes, ''fried goose'' in a goose-shaped box.

Smaller alabaster vessels contained ointments and eye paint; others carried combs, hairpins, and razors; all these contributed to regeneration. A polished metal mirror could reflect the deceased, and its very name, *ankh*, promises a renewal of life. Tutankhamun's mirror case has the shape of the sign of life, and other indications tie the mirror to the solar disk. One can imagine the rays of the night sun as they struck this mirror, to be bounced off to dazzle the darkness of the Netherworld. Plenty of linen was carried into every tomb, as well as garments, sandals, and occasionally wigs. These were among the basic necessities required by, and promised to, the dead in the Beyond so that they could always be arrayed in new and clean apparel.

The pharaoh could hardly be expected to crouch on the bare ground in the Beyond, and so along with the ceremonial gilded throne, Tutankhamun was equipped with armchairs, folding chairs, stools, and footstools. There were also several beds, aside from three magnificent animal-headed biers, for the relaxed moments when the sleep of death interrupted the joyous reawakening. The headrests could visibly raise the pharaoh's head; one of the headrests was supported by the arms of Shu, god of the air, elevating the dead pharaoh from the depths of the Netherworld up to heaven between the two lions of the horizon. Headrests were frequently decorated with images of the apotropaic deities Bes and Taweret, who were especially important for those who slept defenselessly. Lamps accomplished the same purpose in driving off hostile powers; they served the dead as a glowing eye of Horus when they were deprived of the light of the sun and its ''comrade,'' the moon. Spell 137 of the Book of the Dead places the four torch-bearing sons of Horus around the deceased, guarding him just as they guarded Osiris, that Seth not come and injure him again.

The pharaoh could also employ weapons of war from his treasures to defend himself, and even princesses could take at least a dagger along on the journey into the Beyond. Among the symbols of royal suzerainty are various scepters and staffs; Tutankhamun's tomb contained several with the image of an enemy on the lower end, to permit Pharaoh to shove the faces of his foes effortlessly into the dust at every step. The same principle guided the decoration of his sandals, so that the enemies were again literally ''beneath his soles.'' The most powerful and ''magi-

Funerary rituals, including wailing women and the Opening of the Mouth, from Hunefer's Book of the Dead. Below are the offerings for the deceased.

Bes gods with tambourine and knives, flanking the lion-headed Taweret. Chair of Princess Sitamun, daughter of Amenophis III.

cal'' parts of the royal costume, the assorted crowns, were missing in Tutankhamun's tomb. This can hardly be an accident of preservation. Temple scenes include the most diverse crowns at every opportunity, but in the royal tombs the dead ruler almost never wears a crown, being content with a simple royal headcloth. Since we do not find original crowns among the royal funerary treasure we must rely on wall paintings and copies.

The royal chariots represented as playing a key role in battles of the New Kingdom were intended also to bear the pharaoh in the Beyond. Complete chariots were found in the tombs of Yuya and Tutankhamun, although the proud steeds were omitted. Scenes of the hunt abound in tomb decoration, and this may have been one purpose of the chariots (Tutankhamun took seven with him). The most modern ''weapon'' of the day, the chariot was intended for use against enemies, among whom were numbered the creatures of the hunt, and was most assuredly not an everyday vehicle of transport. The boat was the vehicle par excellence on the watery ways of the Beyond, and several spells of the Book of the Dead were devoted to assuring the deceased of a boat. Entire seagoing vessels were the rule in the Old Kingdom; Tutankhamun had a wide selection of models at his disposal.

Craftsmen building a shrine and other furniture for the tomb; from private tomb no. 217 at Thebes.

In fact boats were the last remnant of the earlier wealth of models taken into the tombs of the great and mighty during the First Intermediate Period and the early Middle Kingdom: laborers, house and courtyard, ships and their crews, whole workshops were included. During the Middle Kingdom these were gradually replaced by a new type of grave good, the shawabty. The earliest specimens are simple amorphous wooden sticks, but in the New Kingdom and Dynasties 25 and 26 of the Late Period, they became finely worked human figurines made of the most diverse materials and sizes. Originally meant as mummiform substitute corpses for the deceased who could not be properly mummified during the chaos of the First Intermediate Period, shawabtys were later inscribed with names and titles. Only subsequently did the thought arise that these figures could be used as substitutes for the disagreeable tasks carried out by the servant statuettes in the Old Kingdom. Since the late Middle Kingdom, shawabtys bear an inscription identical to spell 6 of the New Kingdom Book of the Dead, intended ''to let a shawabty perform work in the Realm of the Dead'':

Isis, Nephthys, and several serpents protect the deceased pharaoh, on a sarcophagus lid in the tomb of Queen Tausert.

> O Shawabty,
> If I am summoned,
> If I am chosen to perform any work
> That is done in the Netherworld,
> If a man is compelled to works,
> You shall be chosen rather than I on every occasion,
> Preparing the fields or flooding the banks
> Or moving sand from east to west:
> ''Here I am!'' you shall say.

The deceased thus delegates the shawabty to accept every obligation to perform public works which, as in this world, might be his lot in the Beyond. This meant above all being freed from dreary tasks such as clearing canals and fields. These are not servants but substitutes, and quite a number of them were brought into the tomb, prepared to relieve the dead of any disagreeable obligations and allow him to pursue the nobler tasks, such as plowing, sowing, and reaping in the luxuriant fields of the Beyond. Tutankhamun had 413 shawabtys; the ideal number was, however, 365 (one figurine for each day of the Egyptian year), which could be supplemented with several supervisors. Hoes and baskets to carry out their drudgery were usually painted on the figures, but occasionally miniature instruments were found, as in the tomb of Tutankhamun. Shawabtys thus had quite specific tasks and did not directly guarantee the vital functions of the deceased.

Wooden and stone tomb statues were of vital importance to the dead. For millennia after the dawn of history, the Egyptians regarded a tomb statue as an essential accessory. In the Valley of the Kings, these were mostly made of wood and tarred, like those found by Belzoni in the tombs of Ramesses I and Sety I, and like the two royal ''guardians'' from the tomb of Tutankhamun. There were no stone royal statues in the Valley of the Kings, as these properly belonged to the royal funerary temple at the edge of the cultivated areas on the west bank and to the temples of the gods on the other side of the river, where they could continue to enjoy offerings long after the pharaoh's death.

It was only in these temples on both banks of the Nile that the pharaoh was worshipped after his death. After he was interred in the Valley of the Kings, the tomb was not intended to be reopened; the mummy rested in the security of a coffin made of precious metals, stone, and wood, amid abundant supplies for the long journey into the Beyond. His protection was guaranteed by weapons, tools, and powerful amulets. Among these the scarab beetle particularly draws our attention: the symbol of the rejuvenated newly arisen sun, along with the hale, uninjured eye, promised an unscathed arrival.

Together with the appropriate paintings, an arsenal of figures created an extraordinary atmosphere of divine presence. The sarcophagus grew with the overall dimensions of the tomb, providing more surface for reliefs. As for the reliefs, they originally included the divine protectors of Osiris: Isis, Nephthys, and the sons of Horus. But after the Amarna Period, winged goddesses extended their feathered limbs around the corners of the sarcophagus. This all-encompassing protection is vividly and delicately portrayed in the four gilded goddesses who generously spread their arms across all four sides of the small shrine bearing the canopic jars of Tutankhamun. In their comforting embrace, the pharaoh is secure with his numerous protective shells, certain of a life "through all eternity," while awaiting the awakening light of the sun.

Finally we must refer to the texts and the paintings in the tombs. It is not only gold that brightens the darkness of the tombs. The paintings were intended to let the sun shine in, driving forth death, darkness, and opposition. The sun's path through the Netherworld, the revival of the dead, and the union with Osiris's corpse by being depicted in the royal tomb were made real, becoming the most certain guarantee for the pharaoh's revival. From the solar disk at the entrance to the sarcophagus in the pillared hall, the route of the sun was to be that of the

Row of gods with cryptographic labels. Most of the gods show the mixed form of human body and animal head, the head indicating something about their nature. From one of the gold shrines of Tutankhamun.

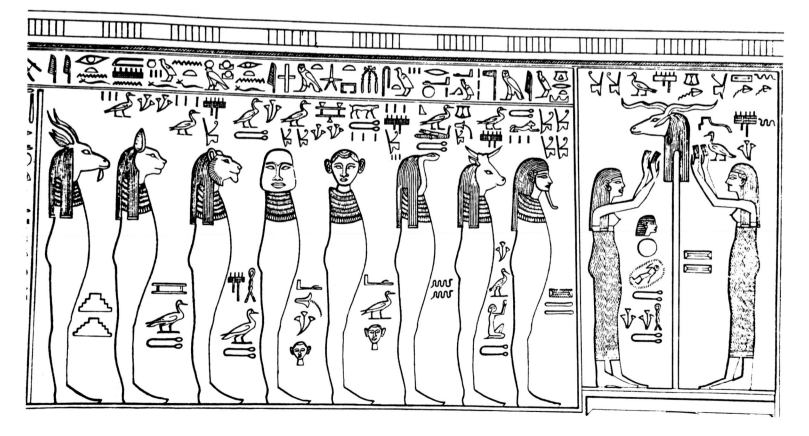

The pharaoh, Isis, and Nephthys worship the sun god above the entry to Ramesses X's tomb. The figures are framed by the sky, the Western Mountain, and according to the inscription, the east and west horizons. (See plates 66, 67.)

pharaoh's body and soul. Each night, in the mysterious depths of the tomb, the separate parts were to be brought together, and the rejuvenated body came forth from the coffin, laying the confining mummy aside to enjoy a new life. This is the goal and only purpose of all efforts. Even King Merykare, who lived in the chaotic days between the Old and Middle Kingdoms, did not forget his father's words about the Beyond:

> He who attains it having done no wrong,
> He is like unto a god there,
> Striding free like unto the lords of eternity.

The funerary banquet in the Dynasty 19 tomb of Sennedjem, a workman in the royal necropolis. To the right are seated relatives; to the left men and women carry birds, perfume, and flowers.

The Dynasty 18 tomb of the steward Djehuty. Above, Djehuty and his mother sit with offerings piled before them: a mat with jars of ointment at the top; a table loaded with bread, vegetables, fruits, and meat; at the bottom a stand holding wine bottles, and to the left a jug of beer wrapped with a lotus sending fragrance to the deceased. The scene below was repainted when the tomb was usurped in Ramesside times.

In the tomb of the Dynasty 18 vizier Ramosa, two offering bearers carry flowers, fruits, and ducks for the deceased. Only the eyes are highlighted with paint on the shallow relief.

126

127

126. *Cortege in the burial chamber of Tutankhamun. The king's mummy in its sarcophagus lies in a shrine placed within a bark, which rests in turn on a sled. Pulling the sled are the highest officials of the state, among them the two viziers, whose heads are shaved and who wear their special dress. The lone, highest-ranking official at the end can be only Haremheb, regent of the land, even though the officials are not individually named in the inscription.*

127. *Tomb of Sennefer. Servants carry various grave goods for the burial of Sennefer, mayor of Thebes. The contents of the chests are shown above each, for example, sandals, royal kilts, and a mummy mask. Below are piled loaves of bread and slaughtered beef.*

128

128. *Red granite sarcophagus of Haremheb. The winged protective goddesses Isis, Nephthys, Neith, and Selket guard it on all four corners; Anubis and the sons of Horus are represented on the long sides of the sarcophagus.*

129. *Lid of the red granite inner sarcophagus of Merneptah. Shaped as a royal cartouche, it bears a three-dimensional representation of the deceased king, encircled by the ouroboros.*

130

131

130/131. *Scenes from the ritual of the Opening of the Mouth for statues of the king in the tomb of Sety I.*

132. *The Opening of the Mouth as represented in the tomb of Tausert. The* sem *priest, standing before the royal statue, has put on a special bib for the ceremony.*

133

133–138. *Statues of gods and kings represented in the tomb of Sety II. Actual statues of this type were found in the tomb of Tutankhamun.*

134

135

136

137

138

139

140

CHAPTER 12

THE TOMBS
OF THE KING'S FAMILY
AND HIS SUBJECTS

The courtiers of the first historical pharaohs accompanied their masters into death. Pharaoh Djer, an early king of Dynasty 1, had no fewer than 318 regularly ordered subsidiary tombs around his tomb at Abydos; and analogous to the large tomb stelae of the pharaoh were ninety-seven small stelae inscribed with names and titles, identifying the occupants of these burial chambers. Seventy-six of these stelae belonged to women and two to court dwarves; on other nonroyal stelae from Abydos, funerary priests and even dogs are encountered. These people were obviously not the top officials but represented the private entourage of the pharaoh, his actual court meant to serve him in the Beyond. It has been asserted that these men, women, dwarves, and dogs were cold-bloodedly killed in order that they might accompany the king into the Beyond, and the custom was known in contemporary Mesopotamia so it is not impossible; but it cannot be proven in Egypt, and we possess absolutely no evidence for human sacrifice after Dynasty 1. Dwarves and dogs, here placed on the same level as servants, belonged to the highly esteemed members of the royal court even later. On the stela of a Dynasty 11 king (ca. 2100 B.C.) the royal hounds are depicted and named, and the Egyptian translations of their foreign names even supplied.

The administrative center of the newly unified state was most probably first established at Memphis, "the balance of the two lands," where Upper and Lower Egypt meet. Thus one could expect to find the tombs of the king's actual administrators here, and these men were in fact buried in the major Archaic cemeteries at Saqqara and Helwan, both in the immediate vicinity of Memphis. Several of these nonroyal tombs can be assigned to a single reign and far outstrip the private tombs at Abydos both in size and in wealth of offerings. Private tombs are not distinguished from royal private ones as happened in the Old Kingdom and later; but all the highest officials of the Archaic Period were chosen exclusively from the royal family and were thus closely related to the king. One difference is clear, however: only the kings and one queen had a second tomb in the holy district of Abydos.

Following the Archaic Period, the Pyramid Age created a strictly hierarchical order for tomb complexes, with the smaller pyramids for queens placed along the west side of those of the kings. The only relatively complete royal tomb treasure recovered from the Old Kingdom, however, was that of Queen Hetepheres, Cheops's mother, found in a shaft tomb beside Cheops's causeway; it may actually have been a secondary burial as a protection against robbery. The rest of the royal family was buried in tombs east of the pyramid, while the leading officials were assigned tombs in the western cemetery. All assumed the form of a mastaba: a bench-shaped superstructure—solid or equipped with small funerary chapels—which covered a tomb shaft with the burial chamber. Only the position and size of

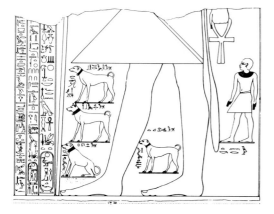

Dog stela of Antef II (2118–2069 B.C.).

139. *Representations of boxes and vessels in the burial chamber of Tausert.*

140. *A watercolor by Belzoni showing a hippopotamus-headed funerary bed, two mirrors, and a lamp in the side room of the tomb of Sety I. This scene is now almost completely destroyed.*

the tomb permitted distinction of difference in rank. The chief royal architect, for instance, reserved especially desirable places for himself and his staff. Another means of distinction in importance was a sarcophagus from the royal quarries, presented by the king. In the course of time even the free spaces between tombs were occupied by new ones; the uniform structure of the west cemetery as we know it is the result of a long development.

After the royal necropolis was removed from Giza, funerary priests and lesser officials were still buried near the pyramids there. The importance of the necropolis rapidly declined, however, and officials built their tombs in developing cemeteries in Abusir and Saqqara. As always, the highest officials sought positions as close as possible to the royal tomb and tried to keep pace with the architectural and religious development of their royal masters. And as the extent of decoration of the royal chapels and temple increased, so did that of the private tombs; the vizier Mereruka of early Dynasty 6 achieved the record of thirty-two decorated rooms.

Beside such "funerary palaces" that epitomized the principle of the tomb as the dwelling of the dead, the simple mastabas appear very unpretentious, although they were a privilege of the higher officials. Parallel with the monumental tombs were the cemeteries of ordinary people where the nonmummified corpse of the deceased was interred in a simple pit, marked by a heap of stones and sand. But even here grave goods were deposited: pottery vessels and amulets, the barest of provender and protection for the hereafter. These burials have been studied less, but their existence underlines the spectrum of possibilities available, and enables us to judge the degree to which the Egyptians assumed that a social structure existed in the Beyond.

It is certain, at least in the New Kingdom, that neither tomb nor mummification was essential; failing the examination on the Day of Judgment nullified all expenditures for the funeral, while the poor man who emerged "justified" had before him all the possibilities of eternity in the hereafter. However, despite theoretical equality among all people in the face of death, the Egyptian repeatedly attempted to protect himself with every available material and spiritual means against the threat to his existence from the powers of death and decay; and the eternity of the Beyond was sought by imitating the form and nature of the royal tomb concept as much as possible.

In the periods of political and economic weaknesses following the Old, Middle, and New Kingdoms, royalty conceded many prerogatives which were immediately adopted by private individuals, although members of royalty generally attempted to defy the tendency to democratization by creating new privileges to maintain its role at the peak of the social pyramid. An early case of the reduction of royalty's preeminent position can be followed in Dynasty 6, particularly during the long reign of Pepy II (ca. 2254–2160 B.C.). Second pyramids and royal funerary texts appeared then in the queenly tomb complexes, and the subsequent centuries saw the royal Pyramid Texts evolve into the humble Coffin Texts: these became the common property of the upper class, adorning its coffins and protecting its members.

Spatial proximity to the royal tomb also lost its significance. Ever since Dynasty 4, upper-echelon officials had built themselves tombs where they were posted in the provinces, and at the close of the Old Kingdom, provincial centers became increasingly independent, both politically and religiously. In Middle and Upper

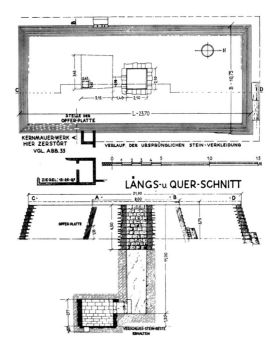

Ground plan and cross-section of a Dynasty 4 mastaba. (Plan by H. Junker.)

Reconstruction of mastabas according to Perrot-Chipiez.

(southern) Egypt, local monarchs established their own cemeteries; even in the distant Dakhla oasis, a governor's tomb dating to Dynasty 6 has recently been uncovered within an extensive cemetery. Here, far from the Nile Valley, the mastaba form was still employed, while contemporary monarchs in Middle and Upper Egypt (e.g., in Beni Hasan, north of Tell Amarna, and at Aswan) preferred rock tombs in prominent positions overlooking the river, with carved façades and constructed causeways. In Thebes both forms are present, mastabas from the early Old Kingdom and rock tombs from the end of this period, as well as the local variation of courtyard tomb combined with a broad pillared façade, which was used by the native kings of Dynasty 11. The importance of Abydos for commoners also grew during this intermediate period as the deceased identified themselves with Osiris, who had become closely associated with this cemetery toward the end of the Old Kingdom. In the Middle Kingdom Abydos became his major place of worship, and the mysteries of Osiris's death and resurrection were celebrated there annually. His tomb was revered in the precinct of the ancient royal tombs.

In the Middle Kingdom the pharaohs emphasized their humanity, reducing further the gap separating them from the rest of mankind. This era produced no specifically royal funerary texts; however, the pyramid-shaped tomb was reserved for the king and, in unusual cases, his closest relatives. Thus Princess Neferuptah, daughter of Amenemhat III, had a small pyramid in Hawara, not far from that of her father with its famous "labyrinth." Other princesses and upper-level officials used the mastaba form.

In the New Kingdom, the period of the Valley of the Kings, an apparent reversal took place in the form of private tombs. The mayor of Thebes, Ineni, first chief architect in the Valley of the Kings, had a well-placed, finely decorated tomb behind an impressive pillared façade. The contemporary high priest of Amun, Hapuseneb, adorned the front of his tomb with six freestanding pillars, while the vizier Ametju and the later architect Senenmut each allowed themselves eight. In stark contrast, the monarch Tuthmosis I received a tiny rock tomb in a hidden corner of what was to become the Valley of the Kings, with a single pillar in the unprepossessing burial chamber. Although the size of the royal tomb increased from reign to reign, it was repeatedly matched in size by the tombs of officials.

This comparison of form is but a deceptive first impression: a more thorough examination reveals that the fastidiously observed hierarchy was maintained, with the royal tomb at the top. Decisive for the rank of a tomb was its position and decoration. The Valley of the Kings was reserved for ruling kings. Hatshepsut, for instance, as a royal wife, excavated her first tomb outside the Valley, receiving a new tomb in this especially holy cemetery only after her accession to the throne. During her reign she permitted her nurse In and her architect Hapuseneb to excavate tombs for themselves in the Valley as well, but in a most limited plan: they had simple vertical shafts leading to undecorated burial chambers. Members of the royal family had slightly better tombs that included the main elements of the royal corridor tomb, but in the simplest form: stairway, sloping passage, burial chamber. Such plain, undecorated complexes were awarded to Hatshepsut's nurse, and later Yuya and Tuya, Amenophis III's in-laws, whose rich treasures were discovered by the Davis expedition in 1905. The mummy of their daughter, Queen Teye, also lay in the Valley of the Kings, although this was by no means a rule for all Dynasty 18 queens. Not one of these had a decorated tomb or stone sarcophagus; as a sub-

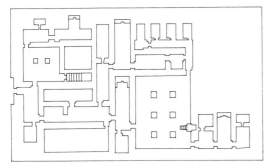

Ground plan of the expanded tomb of Mereruka from the beginning of Dynasty 6 at Saqqara.

Concealed entrance to the tomb of Tuthmosis I (on the right).

185

stitute and unusual honor several received an extremely large wooden outer coffin.

In general the abundant royal progeny of the New Kingdom was only seldom given the right to a burial in the Valley of the Kings. While many of these sons and daughters were buried in other parts of the country (Memphis, the Fayum), toward the end of Dynasty 18 a new tomb beyond the simple corridor-and-shaft variety was developed for them in the Valley. This tomb is characterized by two or more similar main burial chambers and therefore may be designated as a polytaph; all other tombs in the Valley have only one clearly defined burial chamber, easily distinguished from the many small ancillary rooms filled with treasure. Among others, the tomb of Tutankhamun belongs to this new category. Its canonic proportions confirm that it was not originally intended for a royal burial: by applying a flimsy version of the royal tomb decoration to the walls and piling the chambers with the necessary offerings, a minimal compromise with the inappropriate architecture was achieved.

Everything denied to the queens, princes, and princesses in the strict hierarchy of the Valley was conceded to them during the Ramesside Period in a neighboring valley to the south, the Valley of the Queens. Since the beginning of the New Kingdom, members of the royal family had been interred there, but its systematic use began only after the Amarna Period. Recent discoveries confirm that Haremhab's consort was buried not in Thebes but in the tomb begun by Haremheb in Saqqara while he was still a mere general; he abandoned his own part of the tomb there after his accession to the throne in order to be buried in the Valley at Thebes. The queens of his successors Ramesses I and Sety I were favored with tombs in the Valley of the Queens.

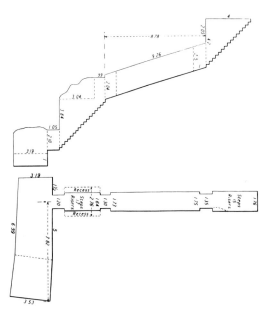

Corridor tomb of Yuya and Tuya in ground plan and cross-section.

While the royal family was normally not allowed burial in the Valley of the Kings, its tombs elsewhere did reflect royal perogatives in decoration and even form. By far the most extreme example is the magnificently decorated tomb of Queen Nofretari, consort of Ramesses II during the third decade of his reign (1279–1213 B.C.); here some of the most gifted artists were employed. The quality of the colorfully painted reliefs in her tomb is equal to that of the royal tomb of her husband, and the imagery itself is a deliberate and delicately refined echo of royal tomb decoration. However, the proportions of the corridors and chambers are distinct from those of her husband's tomb.

As a queen, Nofretari did not have the right to use royal funerary texts; she chose instead corresponding spells and vignettes from the Book of the Dead, which were available for anyone's use and were frequently drawn upon by the officials of the time. In place of the royal Book of Gates, spells from the Book of the Dead relating to the doors of the Beyond (spells 144ff) adorned the walls of her burial chamber; and in place of the book of the Celestial Cow, the well-known image of Hathor the cow in the Western Mountain is used in a subsidiary chamber. However, the famous picture of the unified form of Re and Osiris appears for the first time in this tomb, illustrating a verse of the royal Litany of Re which was here taken up in the Book of the Dead (spell 180). Two other particularly important funerary texts completed the program of image and word: spell 148 guaranteed the general material welfare of the deceased in the uncertain and dangerous world of the Beyond (seen in Nofretari's tomb in a vignette of the holy cow together with her steer, and the four oars of the heavens; the text was omitted); and the 400 verses of spell 17, the longest and best-illustrated chapter in the book, provided a condensed

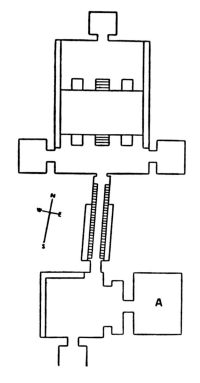

Ground plan of the tomb of Queen Nofretari.

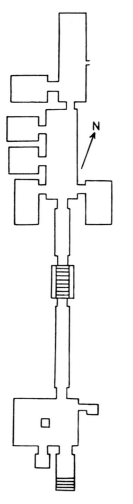

Undecorated multiple grave in the Valley of the Kings (no. 12).

version of the most important texts in the Book of the Dead, enhanced with various explanatory notes.

Other motifs in Nofretari's tomb were taken directly from the imagery of the royal tombs, projecting it far beyond the tombs of officials and princes into a class of its own. Aside from the pillars, these included the heavenly stars painted on the ceiling of the burial chamber, recalling the heavenly Beyond; flowers, symbolizing Upper and Lower Egypt, and the pharaoh's sovereignty over the "Two Lands"; Maat, the personification of justice and world order—all motifs that properly belong only in a king's tomb.

Several other elements reveal the relationship between Nofretari's tomb and that of the king. Ramesses II revived the principle of the bent axis in royal tomb architecture, which had been the convention prior to Akhenaton. This principle appears in diminished form in the plan of the queen's tomb, as well as in the Ramesseum and other constructions. The bent axis cannot be ascribed to mere accident or technical inability, but must be understood as a response to the straight axes of the Amarna Period, through which sunlight was supposed to be directed as far as possible into the Realm of the Dead; the later Ramesside kings again imitated the crookedness of the Beyond. Ramesses II also changed the role of the pillars in the burial chamber (with Nofretari following suit), so that the pillar faces in front of the sarcophagus, previously painted with scenes showing the pharaoh with a divinity, were now decorated with a *djed* pillar signifying Osiris; thus reference was made to the dead king's role as Osiris. At the same time, the *djed*, which seems to have been a kind of sheaf made of the first ears of the harvest, was an effective and powerful protective amulet for the deceased. In Ramesses's own seriously damaged burial chamber only traces of the *djed* can be recognized, but the completely preserved counterpart in the tomb of Nofretari enables us to re-create the original appearance of Ramesses II's pillar faces.

In each scene Nofretari appears before the divinities alone, without her royal husband and without any mention of his name. This is true also of the tombs of other queens; in the case of Queen Tyti and a few others, we are not even sure whose consorts they were. The opposite is true of the many sons of Ramesses III— probably all struck down by the same epidemic—who apparently could not appear alone before the gods of the Beyond, invariably following in the train of their royal father. In the corridors of these colorfully decorated tombs are the frightful door-keepers of the Beyond (from the Book of the Dead), who must be disarmed so that the deceased can stride unhindered through the Beyond. The only prince to have a decorated tomb in the Valley of the Kings is one of Ramesses IX's sons, Mon-tuherkhepeshef (KV 19). This prince apparently reached a ripe age and no longer required the aid of a royal intermediary; he faces the gods alone.

Toward the end of Dynasty 19, three tombs were simultaneously prepared in a corner of the Valley, which give further examples of the meshing of private aims and royal prerogatives. In each case the hierarchic rank was carefully observed, and thus the tombs are particularly instructive. Pharaoh Siptah (1196–1190 B.C.), who died young, received a "normal" royal tomb with the usual decoration. The relatively well-preserved first two corridors have the text and figures of the Litany of Re and the Amduat, and these are supplemented with divine scenes showing Anubis at the bier of Osiris. The third corridor with the fourth and fifth hours of the Amduat is largely destroyed, and the rest of the tomb was left unfinished.

The second tomb was for Queen Tausert, probably Siptah's stepmother and regent. She assumed the royal titles of Pharaoh after Siptah's death, as Hatshepsut had done 300 years earlier, and started a tomb a few yards away from his, the only decorated queen's tomb in this holy precinct. The previous taboo against royal scenes was only partially violated here, as the decoration in the front part of the tomb precisely corresponds to the usual scheme for a queen's tomb at the time: royal funerary texts are absent, and the divine scenes have the doorkeepers from the Book of the Dead, along with their legends. And as in the tomb of Nofretari, there are direct borrowings from the inventory of the royal tomb: the ritual of the opening of the mouth, the winged goddess Maat, Anubis at the bier of Osiris, and so on. However, the pillars of the tomb's first hall are decorated with divine scenes, the walls are covered with excerpts from various royal Books of the Netherworld, and the constellations on the vaulted "astronomical" ceiling almost give the impression of a royal tomb. On the other hand the pillars are rather slender, and the measuring tape reveals that—as in the corridors—the royal proportions have been studiously avoided. In Siptah's tomb the corridors are 5 cubits (more than 8 feet, six inches) wide, as was the rule for a royal tomb since the days of Amenophis III. Tausert kept her measurements an entire cubit below this, even in height. The difference is even clearer in the pillars. The front row consists of square pillars slightly more than 2 feet wide; those of the back row are rectangular, about 2 by 3 feet, and thus correctly maintain their distance to the canonic square royal pillars, 2 cubits (3 feet, 5 inches) across.

Notes on the walls indicate that Tausert started to extend the tomb beyond this half-canonical pillared hall in the short period of her independent reign. Her death caused work on the tomb to be suspended, and it is unclear whether she intended to continue with a canonical second pillared hall appropriate to her new role. Whatever the case, the prescribed royal measures are found in the single completed pillar, which is 2 cubits across. The unusual tomb of this unusual queen therefore reveals three separate stages of execution: a preliminary essay using nonroyal decoration and nonroyal proportions; a second version with royal decoration and nonroyal proportions; and a third form intended to be completely royal. Her successor, Sethnakht, founder of Dynasty 20, appropriated the third part of her tomb and continued it. Both corridors and the new larger pillared hall which are his contributions have exclusively royal proportions and decoration; he whitewashed the queen's figures in the first part of the tomb and replaced them with his own. He was thus able to have one of the largest tombs in the valley, despite his having one of the shortest reigns. The third tomb is that of Tausert's chancellor, Biya, who must have played a role quite similar to that of Senenmut under Hatshepsut. The measures of his tomb are clearly reduced from those of the royal tombs; and although the decoration was just begun, its existence and the form of the corridor are singular for a private tomb in the Valley of the Kings and indicate an unusual honor.

As mentioned above, Hatshepsut (1479–1457 B.C.) had previously allowed several officials to be buried in undecorated tombs in the Valley. She also started to permit officials to use royal texts, thereby beginning the modification of these texts. Her vizier, User, was the only one permitted to adorn his burial chamber in the Qurna hillside with the royal Books of the Netherworld, the Amduat and the Litany of Re; all other officials—including Senenmut—had to content themselves with

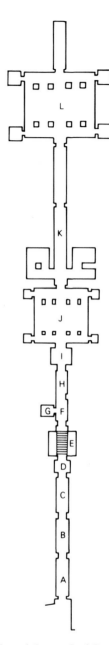

Ground plan of the tomb of Queen Tausert.

spells from the Book of the Dead and the Pyramid Texts. Indeed, User went so far as to place members of his own family among the figures of the Litany of Re and thus on the same level as other manifestations of the sun god. The influential Senenmut benefited in other ways: he built a tomb in the forecourt of Hatshepsut's royal funerary temple and decorated it with a royal "astronomical" ceiling, including the decan constellations and the planets.

Hatshepsut's coregent and successor, Tuthmosis III, apparently did not grant similar privileges. However, his son Amenophis II (1427–1401 B.C.) permitted the newly appointed vizier, Amenemope, as well as other officials, the honor of a burial in the Valley. The treasure of the "fan-bearer" Maiherperi, found in a shaft tomb in the Valley, included one of the earliest illustrated manuscripts of the Book of the Dead, which must date to the reign of Amenophis II. Previous Books of the Dead were sparsely illustrated, while later versions have a vignette for practically every spell, usually summarizing the spell with a pregnant image. The Book of the Dead was available to anyone with the necessary financial resources (an illustrated copy could cost as much as a good cow in the barter economy of ancient Egypt), but only in the most unusual circumstances did a private person have access to the royal Books of the Netherworld and other royal works dealing with the Beyond.

Another official who enjoyed a favored position under Amenophis II was Sennefer, mayor of Thebes and brother of the vizier Amenemope. He was one of the leading officials of the state, recruited from the king's friends during his youth and military career. To prevent the close relationship with the king from ending with death, Sennefer was allowed not only to place his own tomb in the Valley of the Kings but also to bury his brother there. Sennefer put his wife, Senetnay, in an unused corridor tomb; the canopic jars of this former royal nurse with special privileges were found by Carter in Tomb KV 42, originally built by Tuthmosis II but apparently never used.

Sennefer himself was at the top of the local administration, which oversaw the growing necropolis in the west; he behaved like a small king and was successful in improving his own tomb with obvious and hidden borrowings from the royal sphere. For instance, while the chapels in officials' tombs usually had pillars, Sennefer was the first official of the New Kingdom to place four decorated pillars in his burial chamber, thus reflecting the royal burial chamber. He stopped short of the royal canon and employed none of the royal funerary texts, but he compensated for this with representations of the burial procession and various rites performed for the deceased. He also used a worshipping scene with the most important gods of the dead, Osiris and Anubis, and the complete text of spell 151 of the Book of the Dead, which covers the most important elements of the burial with protection in the Beyond. The burial chamber of his tomb charms the visitor today with its vivid colors and the grapevine motifs covering the ceiling and parts of the walls, an obvious reference to the desired resurrection in the Beyond and to the enlivening and regenerating effects of wine. In one corner of the chamber, almost lost beneath the vines, the attentive visitor can glimpse a vulture spreading its protective wings; this motif is unique in a private tomb; it belongs in a royal tomb or temple. The ceilings of the first corridors of the Ramesside tombs in the Valley of the Kings display long series of such protective vultures, which occasionally have the heads of snakes or falcons; they play the same role as vultures protecting the central aisle of a temple leading into the sanctuary.

Other officials of later periods also sought the privileges of the royal sphere. Amenhotep, son of Hapu, received his own funerary temple from his king, Amenophis III. He was an extremely powerful official who would later become deified; this would otherwise have been unthinkable for a private official. Biya, Queen Tausert's chancellor, has already been mentioned; not long after him, Tjanefer, the third priest of Amun, used passages from the royal Book of Gates side by side with texts from the Book of the Dead in his tomb. All these tombs belonged to the top of the administration. The scribes and craftsmen who worked in the royal tombs and decorated their own tombs on the slopes above Deir el-Medina did not borrow from the royal repertoire with which they were in daily contact.

After the end of the New Kingdom (ca. 1070 B.C.), the long-held notions of rank and taboo were lost. The kings built their tomb complexes in the north, far from Thebes, and the tombs in the Valley of the Kings, like those in the Theban necropolis, were reused for private burials. The Theban high priests of Amun formed a new dominant class during Dynasty 21, and they established a number of mummy caches around the temples of Deir el-Bahri in which they brought together individual burials of their relatives. Some were included in the royal cache, where the mummies from the Valley of the Kings were assembled, but most of them were in a second cache in front of the temple, discovered by Georges Daressy in 1891. This subterranean complex had been filled hurriedly with coffins, canopic jars, and shawabty boxes, and it was cleared by Daressy and his helpers with equal dispatch. In no less than 153 coffins—101 of which had an outer coffin as well—were the relatives of the high priest Menkheper, who died around 990 B.C. So many individual items were recovered that the Egyptian government chose to share parts of the treasure with European and American nations. These gifts were distributed in 1893–1894, and this explains the presence of a coffin from the Deir el-Bahri cache in the town hall of Appenzell, of others in Mexico City, and of still others in Russian and Scandinavian museums.

The presence of these caches around the temple at Deir el-Bahri may very likely indicate an attempt to imitate the new form of the royal tomb, the temenos. This is clearly the case with the divine consorts of Amun, who took over the worldly and spiritual roles of the high priests after the chaos of the ninth century B.C., and became royal satraps in Upper Egypt. Like kings, they assumed praenomens, and they patterned their bureaucracy after that of the royal court, celebrating the royal jubilee festivals and establishing their tombs in the precincts of New Kingdom funerary temples, the Ramesseum, and later Medinet Habu, where superstructures between the high gate and first pylon are visible. These simple brick structures contrast starkly with the "tomb palaces" that the administrators of the divine consorts built for themselves during Dynasties 25 and 26 just at the desert beyond the cultivated areas. These giant brick superstructures cover elaborate subterranean complexes which are copiously illustrated with religious texts. Beside the Pyramid Texts and the Book of the Dead, the royal New Kingdom Books of the Netherworld were generously used one last time, in exemplary precise copies. But the older literature is only copied and no new texts were created during this period.

Motifs from the Books of the Netherworld were still being copied for tombs, coffins, and papyri in the Roman period, and even lived on to influence early Christian gnostic apocalyptic literature. But with the Persian conquest in 525 B.C., the glories of the Theban necropolis belonged to the past.

Papyrus with spell 151 from the Book of the Dead (British Museum, 10010). In the center Anubis is at the bier of the deceased. (See plate 147.)

141

142

141. *West cemetery near the pyramid of Cheops at Giza, with the carefully arranged mastabas of the officials and priests of the king.*

142. *Cliffs at Beni Hasan in Middle Egypt, with the rock tombs of the district princes of Dynasties 11 and 12.*

143. *Tomb of Queen Nofretari. The enthroned sun god Re-Harakhty is promising the queen "the lifetime of Re." Around his disk is a protective snake, and behind him is Hathor as goddess of the West; with the hieroglyph for "west" on her head, she is named "the one who is over Thebes" and "mistress of all the gods." Both thrones carry the symbol of the "unification of the two lands" on the side.*

144. *The winged goddess Maat in the tomb of Nofretari, with the hieroglyphic sign of her name (an ostrich feather) on her wig. She protectively surrounds the deceased as the daughter of Re. Above her are the sky sign, and the night sky with yellow stars.*

145. *Tomb of Sennefer. Osiris and Anubis, the most important gods of the dead, sit in a shrine surrounded by grapevines. Osiris holds the crook and flail as the insignias of his rule in the Realm of the Dead. The hieroglyphs above give him the paradoxical title Osiris, "King of the Living."*

146. *The continuation of the scene in plate 145 shows Sennefer, mayor of Thebes under Amenophis II, with his "beloved sister and songstress of Amun," Meret. Their hands are raised in adoration to Osiris and Anubis. Meret is painted yellow, as is customary for women. A sistrum hangs from her arm, which indicates her status as a songstress in the cult of Amun. Sennefer wears a long transparent linen garment over his kilt. In front of him is a small offering stand with lotus flowers.*

143

144

145

146

147

147. *Spell 151 of the Book of the Dead in the tomb of Sennefer. The spell concerns the embalming and protection of the deceased in the hall, where he is cared for by Anubis. In the center Anubis places his hand on the mummy, beneath which stands the bird-formed* ba *of the deceased. Nephthys kneels at the head of the mummy; Isis is at his feet. Surrounding the center panel are other scenes of* ba *birds and* shawabty *figures. The four sons of Horus are placed at the four corners of the center square as the protectors of the mummy's internal organs.*

148. *A vulture flies among grapevines on the ceiling of the tomb of Sennefer.*

149. *Another painting from the tomb of Sennefer. A papyrus boat above carries Sennefer and the "Lady of the House," Meret, seated in a shrine. A priest with offerings on a small table pours purified water before them. A wooden boat below escorts the deceased to the Beyond.*

148

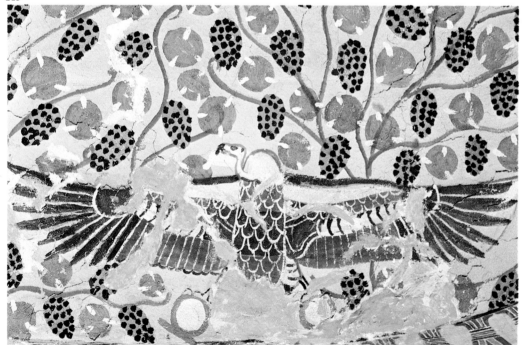

149

150

151

150. *Tomb of Nofretari. The seven celestial cows and their bull with three of the four "control rudders of the sky" below. The representation belongs to spell 148 of the Book of the Dead, which effects nourishment and protection in the Beyond. Nofretari limits herself to naming the cows and rudder, and omits the text of the spell.*

151. *"Osiris Queen Nofretari" is led by a hippopotamus-headed goddess of the Beyond. Both have the yellow skin used for women, although Nofretari has red skin when represented elsewhere in the tomb, as is shown in plate 143.*

The south wall of the Dynasty 18 tomb of the scribe Nakht. Three rows of offering bearers on the sides and two additional bearers accompanied by tree goddesses below hold food and supplies. These are directed toward a false door painted to simulate granite through which the soul of the deceased could receive the offerings. The ceiling above is painted with colorful imitation mats.

APPENDIX

ABBREVIATIONS

The following abbreviations are used throughout the appendix.

AbhHeidelberg	Abhandlungen der Heidelberger Akademie der Wissenschaften, Philosophische-Historische Klasse	JdI	Jahrbuch des Deutschen Archäologischen Instituts
AbhKairo	Abhandlungen des Deutschen Archäologischen Instituts Kairo: Ägyptologische Reihe	JEA	Journal of Egyptian Archaeology
		JEOL	Jaarbericht van het Vooraziatisch-Egyptisch Gezelschap Ex Oriente Lux
AbhLeipzig	Abhandlungen der Sächsischen Akademie der Wissenschaften zu Leipzig, Philologische-Historische Klasse	JNES	Journal of Near Eastern Studies
		KV	Valley of the Kings tomb number
ÄDS	Ägyptische Denkmäler in der Schweiz	LÄ	Lexikon der Ägyptologie
ÄgAbh	Ägyptische Abhandlungen	LÄS	Leipziger Ägyptologische Studien
ÄgFo	Ägyptologische Forschungen	MÄS	Münchner Ägyptologische Studien
AH	Aegyptiaca Helvetica	MDAIK	Mitteilungen des Deutschen Archäologischen Instituts, Abteilung Kairo
APAW	Preussische Akademie der Wissenschaften, Abhandlungen der Philosophischen-Historischen Klasse	MIFAO	Mémoires publiées par les Membres de l'Institut Français d'Archéologie Orientale du Caire
APSM	American Philosophical Society Memoirs	NachAkGött	Nachrichten der Akademie der Wissenschaften in Göttingen, I. Philologische-Historische Klasse
ASAE	Annales du Service des Antiquités de l'Égypte	OBO	Orbis Biblicus et Orientalis
AVDAIK	Archäologische Veröffentlichungen des Deutschen Archäologischen Instituts, Abteilung Kairo	OCG	Ostraca Hiératiques of the Catalogue Générale des Antiquités égyptiennes du Musée du Caire
BdÉ	Bibliothèque d'Étude of the Institut Français d'Archéologie Orientale du Caire	ODM	Ostraca Hiératiques non littéraires de Deir el Médineh
Beiträge Bf	Beiträge zur ägyptologischen Bauforschung und Altertumskunde	OIP	Oriental Institute Publications, Chicago
		OLZ	Orientalistische Literaturzeitung
BIE	Bulletin de l'Institut Égyptien	PÄ	Probleme der Ägyptologie
BIFAO	Bulletin de l'Institut Français d'Archéologie Orientale	P–W	Pauly–Wissowa, Realencyclopädie der Classischen Altertumswissenschaft
BiOr	Bibliotheca Orientalis	QV	Valley of the Queens tomb number
BS	Bollingen Series	RdÉ	Revue d'Égyptologie
BSFE	Bulletin de la Société Française d'Égyptologie	SAK	Studien zur Altägyptischen Kultur
CAH	Cambridge Ancient History	SAOC	Studies in Ancient Oriental Civilization
Catalogue général	Catalogue Général des Antiquités égyptiennes du Musée du Caire	SHR	Studies in the History of Religions
		TSBA	Transactions of the Society of Biblical Archaeology
CdÉ	Chronique d'Égypte	TT	Theban Tomb (numbering system for private tombs in the Theban Necropoleis, cf. KV, QV)
FIFAO	Documents de Fouilles publiées par les membres de l'Institut Français d'Archéologie Orientale du Caire	TTSO	Tut'ankhamun's Tomb Series, Oxford
GM	Göttinger Miszellen	ZÄS	Zeitschrift für ägyptische Sprache und Altertumskunde
HÄB	Hildesheimer Ägyptologische Beiträge		
JAOS	Journal of the American Oriental Society		

REFERENCES AND FURTHER READING

Before the appearance of the German edition of this book, *The Royal Necropoleis of Thebes* by Elizabeth Thomas (Princeton, 1966) was the only scholarly study devoted to the Valley of the Kings and the other royal cemeteries of Thebes. Equally valuable and likewise indispensable is the *Topographical Bibliography of Ancient Egyptian Hieroglyphic Texts, Reliefs and Paintings, Volume I, Part 2: Royal Tombs and Smaller Cemeteries* by Bertha Porter and Rosalind L. B. Moss (2nd revised edition, Oxford, 1964).

Quoted passages in this book have been translated from Egyptian and German sources. Published English translations are cited below for the convenience of the reader.

CHAPTER 1

Elizabeth Thomas's survey of the history of the Valley in chapter 4 of *The Royal Necropoleis* includes numerous quotations from early travelers. See also K. W. Marek, *Gods, Graves and Scholars* (New York, 1951, 2nd ed., 1967), chaps. 14–17; and John Romer, *Valley of the Kings* (New York, 1981).

The Greek and Latin graffiti in the tombs were compiled by Jules Baillet, *Inscriptions grecques et latines des tombeaux des rois ou syringes* (Cairo, MIFAO 42, 1926). The inscriptions on the northern Colossus of Memnon can be found in André and Étienne Bernand, *Les inscriptions grecques et latines du Colosse du Memnon* (Paris, 1960).

Diodorus dealt with the royal tombs in book 1, chapter 46, of his *Bibliotheca historica* (including the remarks of Egyptian priests to the effect that only 17 of the 47 tombs were preserved down to the beginning of the Ptolemaic era); Strabo mentions them in book XVII, chapter 1, 46, of his *Geography*.

For Protais and François, see Serge Sauneron, "Villes et Légendes d'Égypte," BIFAO 67 (1969): 122ff. For the proper translation of the Arabic "Biban el Meluk" (*bab* here being derived from an ancient Egyptian word for "cave," rather than from the Arabic for "door,"and thus today "tomb"), see Ahmed Fakhry, "Miscellanea," ASAE 37 (1937): 31, n. 1.

Concerning Claude Sicard, see his *Oeuvres*, ed. M. Martin (Cairo, BdÉ 83–85, 1982). The other accounts dating to the eighteenth century are in Richard Pococke, *A Description of the East, Part I: Observations on Egypt* (London, 1743), p. 98 for the descriptions of the texts and pictures of the royal tombs; James Bruce, *Travels to Discover the Sources of the Nile* (Edinburgh, 1790); William George Browne, *Travels in Africa, Egypt and Syria* (1798). Vivant Denon's account is in *Voyage dans la Basse et la Haute Égypte, pendant les campagnes du Général Bonaparte* (Paris, 1802). The notes of E. Jomard and L. Costaz are in *Description de l'Égypte: Antiquités*, vol. 3 (Paris, 1821).

Giovanni Battista Belzoni's *Narrative of the Operations and Recent Discoveries Within the Pyramids, Temples, Tombs and Excavations in Egypt and Nubia* (London, 1820) includes the description of the tomb of Sety I (pp. 230–246),. and is supplemented by Stanley Mayes, *The Great Belzoni* (London, 1959). Joseph Bonomi and Samuel Sharpe provided very careful copies of Sety's sarcophagus in *The Alabaster Sarcophagus of Oimenepthah I, King of Egypt* (London, 1864). Robert Hay's story has been told by Selwyn Tillett in *Egypt Itself: The Career of Robert Hay* (London, 1984). Unpublished manuscripts by James Burton and Robert Hay are in the British Library in London, while those of John Gardner Wilkinson are at the Griffith Institute in Oxford, and those of Nestor l'Hôte are in the Louvre and the Bibliothèque Nationale in Paris. Jeanne Vandier d'Abbadie presented a selection in *Nestor l'Hôte* (Leiden, 1963). A detailed list of unpublished material relating to the Valley of the Kings is in Porter-Moss, *Topographical Bibliography*, pp. xxxv–xxxvii, now supplemented by the recently discovered Wilkinson squeezes in the British Museum.

Champollion's letters from the Valley of the Kings were published in *Lettres écrites d'Égypte et de Nubie en 1828 et 1829* (Paris, 1833; 2nd ed., Paris, 1868) and are now available in J. F. Champollion, *Lettres et journaux écrits pendant le voyage d'Égypte*, ed. H. Hartleben (Paris, 1986), pp. 245ff. His copies are in *Monuments de l'Égypte et de la Nubie* (Paris, 1835–1845; reprint, Geneva, n.d.), and *Notices descriptives* (Paris, 1835–1872; reprint, Geneva, 1973–1974). The expedition's materials are also available in Ippolito Rosellini, *I Monumenti dell'Egitto e della Nubia* (Pisa, 1832–1844; reprint, Geneva, 1977).

The drawings of Carl Richard Lepsius's Prussian expedition were published in *Denkmaeler aus Aegypten und Aethiopien* (Berlin, 1849–1850; reprint, Geneva, 1972–1973), with the text volumes edited by Édouard Naville (Leipzig, 1897–1913; reprint, Geneva, 1975).

The cache with the royal mummies was discussed most recently by Michel Dewachter,"Contribution à l'histoire de la cachette royale de Deir el-Bahri," BSFE 74 (1975): 19–32.

Early text editions: Édouard Naville, *La Litanie du soleil* (Leipzig, 1875); "La destruction des hommes par les dieux," TSBA 4 (1875): 1–19 (Book of the Celestial Cow in the tomb of Sety I); and TSBA 8 (1885): 412–420 (the version in the tomb of Ramesses III). The copies by E. Lefébure and his colleagues are in *Les Hypogées royaux de Thèbes* (Paris, 1886–1889), and his translations of the Book of Gates ("Book of Hades") are in *Records of the Past*, vols. 10, pp. 79–134, and 12, pp. 1–35 (London 1874–1881). Gaston Maspero's fundamental *Les Hypogées royaux de Thèbes*, in *Revue de l'histoire des religions* 17 (1888): 251–310 and 18 (1889): 1–67, was reprinted in his *Études de mythologie et d'archéologie égyptienne*, vol. 2, pp.1–181 (Paris, 1893). The first edition of the abridged version of the Amduat is Gustave Jéquier, *Le Livre de ce qu'il y a dans l'Hadès* (Paris, 1894). The quote in Chantepie de la Saussaye's textbook (vol. 1, p. 98) is from H. O. Lange.

Victor Loret recorded his discoveries in BIE 3, 9 (1898): 91–112. Georges Daressy published the finds from these newly discovered tombs in *Fouilles de la Vallée des Rois* (Cairo, Catalogue général, 1902).

Theodore M. Davis published several volumes on his excavations, aided by Gaston Maspero, Howard Carter, and others. (See the literature concerning the individual tombs below.) The original story of the discovery of the tomb of Tutankhamun was recounted by Howard Carter and A. C. Mace, *The Tomb of Tut.Ankh.Amen*, 3 vols. (London, 1923–1933), now supplemented by I. E. S. Edwards, *Tutankhamun: His Tomb and Its Treasures* (New York, 1976). Oxford's Tut'ankhamun's Tomb series has published some of the treasures; and Alexandre Piankoff has published the texts and illustrations of the golden shrines in *Les Chapelles de Tout-Ankh-Amon* (Cairo, MIFAO 72, 1951–52) and *The Shrines of Tut-Ankh-Amon* (New York, BS 40, no. 2, 1955; and Harper Torchbook, 1962).

E. A. Wallis Budge translated extensively from the Royal Tombs in his three-volume opus *The Egyptian Heaven and Hell* (London, 1906). Adolf Erman's condemnation is in *Die ägyptische Religion* (Berlin, 1934/1978, p. 237); Hermann Kees's remark was made in OLZ, 1936, col. 682.

Alexander Piankoff's text editions include *Le Livre des Portes* (Cairo, MIFAO 74, 75, 90, 1939–1962); *Le Livre des Quererts* (Cairo, 1946, a reprint from BIFAO 41–45); *La Création du disque solaire* (Cairo, 1953); and *The Litany of Re* (New York, BS 40, no. 4, 1964). Royal funerary texts were also examined by Hermann Grapow, "Studien zu den thebanischen Königsgräbern," ZÄS 72 (1936): 12–39, and Siegfried Schott, *Die Schrift der verborgenen Kammer in Königsgräbern der 18. Dynastie* (NAG, 1958, no. 4), and *Zum Weltbild der Jenseitsführer des neuen Reiches* (NAG, 1965, no. 11).

Erik Hornung's own text editions include *Das Amduat: Die Schrift des verborgenen Raumes* (Wiesbaden, ÄgAbh 7 and 13, 1963–1967); *Das Buch der Anbetung des Re im Westen* (Geneva, AH 2 and 3, 1975–1976); with Andreas Brodbeck and Elisabeth Staehelin, *Das Buch von den Pforten des Jenseits*, (Geneva, AH 7 and 8, 1979, 1980). Translations of these by Erik Hornung appear in *Ägyptische Unterweltsbücher* (Zurich and Munich, 1972; 2nd ed., 1984).

Part of the corpus of royal texts edited by Erik Hornung has now been presented in English by Marshall Clagett, in *Ancient Egyptian Science* (Philadelphia, APSM 184, 1989), vol. 1. This volume was published during the translation of the English edition of Valley of the Kings and was not consulted during the preparation of the text.

CHAPTER 2

A survey of the development of the royal tombs is provided by Dieter Arnold and Erik Hornung in LÄ 3: 496–514. For tombs of the early periods, see Walter B. Emery, *Archaic Egypt* (Harmondsworth, 1961). The problem of Menes was presented by H. Brunner, LÄ 4: 46–48; the mastaba by J. Brinks, LÄ 3: 1214–1231; and the *sed* festival by Erik Hornung and Elisabeth Staehelin, *Studien zum Sedfest* (Geneva, AH 1, 1974).

The pyramids are masterfully handled by I. E. S. Edwards, *The Pyramids of Egypt* (rev. ed., Harmondsworth, 1985); Rainer Stadelmann, *Die ägyptischen Pyramiden* (Mainz, 1985); J.-P. Lauer, *Le Mystère des pyramides* (Paris, 1974). The Pyramid of Cheops has produced a flood of occult literature, but a scientific study has yet to appear. Raymond O. Faulkner has provided a complete translation of the Pyramid Texts, *The Ancient Egyptian Pyramid Texts* (Oxford, 1969; reprinted, Warminster, n.d.); Kurt Sethe's translation and commentary, *Übersetzung und Kommentar zu den altägyptischen Pyramidentexten* (Glückstadt, 1935–1962) is incomplete.

The royal tombs of Dynasty 11 have been newly examined by Dieter Arnold in *Gräber des alten und mittleren Reiches in El-Tarif* (Mainz, AVDAIK 17, 1976) and *Der Tempel des Königs Mentuhotep von Deir el-Bahari* (Mainz, AVDAIK 8 and 11, 1974). The Coffin Texts of the Middle Kingdom are translated by Raymond O. Faulkner, *The Ancient Egyptian Coffin Texts* (Warminster, 1973–1978).

For the royal cemetery at Dra abu'l Naga see Herbert E. Winlock, ''The Tombs of the Kings of the Seventeenth Dynasty at Thebes,'' JEA 10 (1924): 217–277; Walther Wolf, *Funde in Ägypten* (Göttingen, 1966), pp. 150ff; and Elizabeth Thomas, *The Royal Necropoleis of Thebes* (Princeton, 1966), chap. 3.

For the New Kingdom, see Aidan Dodson, ''The Tombs of the Kings of the Eighteenth Dynasty at Thebes,'' ZÄS 115 (1988): 110–123. For the different canons for royal and non-royal tombs, and the principle of the ''Extension of the Existing,'' see Erik Hornung, ''Struktur und Entwicklung der Gräber im Tal der Könige,'' ZÄS 105 (1978): 59–66. The problem of the tomb of Tuthmosis II is discussed by Erik Hornung in ''Das Grab Thutmosis II,'' RdÉ 27 (1975): 125–131. The shafts were taken up in Friedrich Abitz, *Die religiöse Bedeutung der sogenannten Grabräuberschächte in den ägyptischen Königsgräbern der 18. bis 20. Dynastie* (Wiesbaden, ÄgAbh 26, 1974). The development of the decoration from Tuthmosis I to Haremheb is studied in Erik Hornung, *Das Grab des Haremhab im Tal der Könige* (Bern, 1971). Geoffrey T. Martin, J. van Dijke, and H. D. Schneider are working on *The Memphite Tomb of Horemhab* (forthcoming). The tomb of his successor was published by Alexandre Piankoff, ''La tombe de Ramsès Ier,'' BIFAO 56 (1957): 189–200.

The temenos tombs of the Third Intermediate Period were studied by Rainer Stadelmann, ''Das Grab im Tempelhof,'' MDAIK 27 (1971): 111–123; and Pierre Montet, *La Nécropole royale de Tanis* (Paris, 1947–1960). Those of the divine consorts on the Theban west bank remain to be published. The most thorough study of the tombs of Alexander and his Ptolemaic successors remains H. Thiersch, ''Die alexandrinische Königsnekropole,'' JdI 25 (1910): 55–97.

CHAPTER 3

The reference from the tomb of Ineni is translated from the original text in Kurt Sethe, *Urkunden der 18. Dynastie* (Urkunden des ägyptischen Altertums, Abt. IV, Leipzig, 1906ff, with reprints), p. 57, ll. 3–5, and the titles, pp. 69, 72. See E. Dziobek, *Das Grab des Ineni: Theben Nr. 81* (Mainz, AVDAIK 68, 1989). Maya and his associates are mentioned in Erik Hornung, *Das Grab des Haremhab im Tal der Könige* (Bern, 1971), pp. 21–23.

The crew, their work and their lives are the theme of: Jaroslav Cerny, *A Community of Workmen at Thebes in the Ramesside Period* (Cairo, BdÉ 50, 1973); and *The Valley of the Kings* (Cairo, BdÉ 61, 1973); Dominique Valbelle in ''*Les

Ouvriers de la tombe''*: Deir el-Médineh à l'Époque Ramesside* (Cairo, BdÉ 96, 1985); Morris Bierbrier, *The Tomb-Builders of Pharaoh* (New York, 1984); John Romer, *Ancient Lives: Daily Life in Egypt of the Pharaohs* (New York, 1984); Raphael Ventura, *Living in a City of the Dead* (Fribourg and Göttingen, OBO 69, 1986); and E. S. Bogoslovsky, *Ancient Egyptian Masters* (Moscow, 1983, in Russian). The village is also discussed by T. G. H. James, *Pharaoh's People* (London, 1984), pp. 230ff; and Kenneth A. Kitchen, *Pharaoh Triumphant: the Life and Times of Ramesses II* (Warminster, 1982), chap. 9. The economic aspects of the workmen's lives are discussed by Barry J. Kemp, *Ancient Egypt: Anatomy of a Civilization* (London, 1989), pp. 258ff; and treated in detail by J. J. Janssen, *Commodity Prices from the Ramesside Period* (Leiden, 1975); and by Schafik Allam, *Hieratische Ostraka und Papyri aus der Ramessidenzeit* (Tübingen, 1973).

The work in the tombs is covered by Frank Teichmann in Erik Hornung, *Das Grab des Haremhab* (Bern, 1971), pp. 32–37; Erik Hornung, *Zwei Ramessidische Königsgräber: Ramses IV und Ramses VII* (Mainz, Theben VI, 1990); and Dieter Arnold, ''Grabbau,'' LÄ 2: 847–851. Additional observations have been made by Elisabeth Schmid. The preserved plans and sketches are discussed by Elizabeth Thomas, *The Royal Necropoleis* (Princeton, 1966), pp. 277ff; and Jaroslav Cerny, *Valley of the Kings* (Cairo, 1973), pp. 23ff. The beginning of work on the tomb of Ramesses IV is from ODM 45, ll. 16f (Jaroslav Cerny, *Catalogue des ostraca hiératiques non littéraires de Deir el-Médineh I*, Cairo, FIFAO 3, 1935). For Sety II's tomb, see Jaroslav Cerny and Alan H. Gardiner, *Hieratic Ostraca I* (Oxford, 1957), pl. 64, 1, 4f. The conventions of color are discussed by Caroline Ransom Williams, *The Decoration of the Tomb of Per-Neb* (New York, 1932); and Elisabeth Staehelin, ''Zu den Farben der Hieroglyphen,'' GM 14 (1974): 49–53. Lighting arrangements are described by Jaroslav Cerny, *Valley of the Kings* (Cairo, 1973), pp. 43–54.

The Amenmesse episode is discussed in Rolf Krauss, ''Untersuchungen zu König Amenmesse,'' SAK 4 (1976): 161–199 and SAK 5 (1977): 131–174. Paneb's activities are recounted by Jaroslav Cerny in *A Community of Workmen*, pp. 300–305; and by John Romer, *Ancient Lives*, pp. 60ff. The accusations against Paneb were edited by Jaroslav Cerny, ''Papyrus Salt 124,'' JEA 15 (1929): 243–258. Schafik Allam, *Hieratische Ostraka und Papyri*, provides German translations of Papyrus Salt (pp. 281–287), the court protocols (OCG, 25, 556, pp. 61–63), and Parahotep's letter (ODM 303, p. 114). English translations of some of the strike papyrus and the Berlin ostracon were made by William F. Edgerton, ''The Strikes in Ramses III's Twenty-ninth Year,'' JNES 10 (1951): 137–145. The Chicago ostracon was translated by Edward F. Wente, ''A Letter of Complaint to the Vizier To,'' JNES 20 (1961): 252–257.

T. E. Peet published the court records and notes in *The Great Tomb-Robberies of the Twentieth Egyptian Dynasty* (Oxford, 1930; reprinted Hildesheim, 1977). Jean Capart, Alan H. Gardiner, and B. van de Walle provided clinching evidence of the other half of Papyrus Amherst in ''New Light on the Ramesside Tomb-Robberies,'' JEA 22 (1936): 169–193. Whether and when Tutankhamun's tomb was broken into was investigated by Rolf Krauss, ''Zum archäologischen Befund im thebanischen Königsgrab Nr. 62,'' MDOG, 18 (1986): 165–181; and popularly by Thomas Hoving, *Tutankhamun: The Untold Story* (New York, 1978).

The discovery of the royal mummies was discussed in Chapter 1, and the results of the recent examinations of them are presented by James E. Harris and Edward F. Wente, *An X-Ray Atlas of the Royal Mummies* (Chicago and London, 1980).

An account of the episodes in Dynasty 20 is in John A. Wilson, *The Burden of Egypt* (Chicago, 1951, reprinted as *The Culture of Ancient Egypt*), chap. 10. The end of the Ramesside period is described by Jaroslav Cerny, ''Egypt from the Death of Ramesses III to the End of the Twenty-First Dynasty,'' CAH 2: chap. 35; and by Kenneth A. Kitchen, *The Third Intermediate Period* (Warminster, 1973; rev. ed., 1986). The last burial in the royal cache would appear to have taken place in about 934 B.C, or regnal year 11 of Sheshonk I, founder of Dynasty 22.

CHAPTER 4

The divine scenes in the royal tombs up to Ramesses III are collected and discussed by Friedrich Abitz, *König und Gott* (Wiesbaden, ÄgAbh 40, 1984).

The nature of Egyptian belief is presented by Erik Hornung, *Conceptions of God in Ancient Egypt: The One and the Many*, trans. John Baines (Ithaca, 1982; London, 1983), with recommendations for further reading. For individual divinities, see Hans Bonnet, *Reallexikon der ägyptischen Religionsgeschichte* (Berlin, 1952, 1971) and the LÄ.

Marie-Louise Buhl examined the tree goddess "The Goddesses of the Egyptian Tree Cult," JNES 6 (1947): 80–97, as did Ramses Moftah in *Die heiligen Bäume im alten Ägypten* (unpublished dissertation, Göttingen, 1959).

The dead king devours the gods in spells 273–274 of the Pyramid Texts, translated by Miriam Lichtheim, *Ancient Egyptian Literature* (Berkeley, 1975), vol. 1, 36–38; and Raymond O. Faulkner, *The Ancient Egyptian Pyramid Texts* (Oxford, 1969), pp. 79–84; and Erik Hornung, *Meisterwerke der altägyptischen Dichtung* (Zurich and Munich, 1978), pp. 59–61. The text on member divinification has been translated by Alexandre Piankoff, *The Litany of Re* (New York, BS 40, no. 4, 1964), pp. 38–39; and Erik Hornung, *Das Buch der Anbetung des Re im Westen* (Geneva, AH 2 and 3, 1975–1976), 1: 209–216, 2: 87–88, 142ff. Friedrich Abitz brought the details of the tomb of Tausert to my attention.

For Hathor as a goddess of regeneration, see Elisabeth Staehelin, "Zur Hathorsymbolik in der altägyptischen Kleinkunst," ZÄS 105 (1978): 76–84. Isis's role from the Old Kingdom to the end of the New Kingdom was the object of Maria Münster's study, *Untersuchungen zur Göttin Isis* (Berlin, MÄS 11, 1968). Horus's role as the supporter of Osiris is especially clear in spell 78 of the Book of the Dead (Raymond O. Faulkner, *Book of the Dead*, pp. 74–78; Erik Hornung, *Totenbuch*, pp. 157–164 and 462–464, with its predecessor, spell 312 of the Coffin Texts (Raymond O. Faulkner, *Coffin Texts*, vol. 1, pp. 229–233). A work on the sons of Horus remains to be written, but their parents would appear to be Isis and Horus (Book of the Dead, spell 112, li. 31; the "oldest Horus," according to spell 157 of the Coffin Texts; see, Faulkner, *Coffin Texts*, vol. 1, p. 135).

Lines 74ff of the Hymn to Ptah refer to the Beyond. See Walther Wolf, "Der Berliner Ptah-Hymnus," ZÄS 64 (1929): 17–44. Hermann Schlögl dated the "Philosophy of a Memphite Priest" to the reign of Ramesses II in *Der Gott Tatenen* (Fribourg and Göttingen, OBO 29, 1980), and investigated Ptah's relation to Tatenen.

The Ennead is discussed by Winfried Barta, *Untersuchungen zum Götterkreis der Neunheit* (Berlin, MÄS 28, 1973). For the animals intended to assure regeneration, see chap. 11 below.

CHAPTER 5

A German translation of the Amduat and the other books of the Netherworld is in Erik Hornung, *Ägyptische Unterweltsbücher* (Zurich and Munich, 1972; 2nd ed., 1984). For an English translation see Marshall Clagett, *Ancient Egyptian Science* (Philadelphia, APSM 184, 1989), pp. 471ff. The individual text editions appearing under the names of Erik Hornung and Alexandre Piankoff are listed at the close of the literature references for chapter 1. The Middle Kingdom "Book of Two Ways" is translated by Leonard H. Lesko, *The Ancient Egyptian Book of Two Ways* (Berkeley and Los Angeles, 1972), and Alexandre Piankoff, *The Wandering of the Soul* (Princeton, BS 40, 6, 1974), pp. 2–37; the Egyptian text is mostly in volume 7 of Adriaan de Buck's edition of *The Egyptian Coffin Texts* (Chicago, OIP 1935–1961); and translated by Raymond O. Faulkner, *The Ancient Egyptian Coffin Texts*, vol. 3, pp. 127–189. The various versions of spell 168 of the Book of the Dead were assembled and translated by Alexandre Piankoff in *The Wandering of the Soul*, pp. 39–114; and a single version of spell 168 by Raymond O. Faulkner, *The Ancient Egyptian Book of the Dead* (London, 1985), pp. 162–166. The Book of the Gates is now complete in the definitive edition by Erik Hornung, with Andreas Brodbeck and Elisabeth Staehelin, *Das Buch von den Pforten des Jenseits* (Geneva, AH 7–8, 1979–1980).

For the gate spells of the Book of the Dead see Erik Hornung, *Das Totenbuch der Ägypter* (Zurich and Munich, 1979), pp. 276–298, 502–505; and Faulkner, *Book of the Dead*, pp. 133ff. The name quoted at length is at the eighth gate (Hornung, *Totenbuch*, spell 145, p. 286; Faulkner, *Book of the Dead*, spell 144, p. 136).

For the sarcophagus of Ankhnesneferibre, see C. E. Sander-Hansen, *Die religiösen Texte auf dem Sarg der Anchnesneferibre* (Copenhagen, 1937), p. 111. The quote following, from about the time of Sety I, is on a stele in Abydos, for which see G. A. Gaballa, "Three Funerary Stelae from the New Kingdom," MDAIK 35 (1979): 79, after A. Mariette, *Catalogue général des monuments d'Abydos* (Paris, 1880), p. 455. On ancient Egyptian mourning see, Erich Lüddeckens, "Untersuchungen über religiösen Gehalt, Sprache und Form der ägyptischen Totenklagen," MDAIK 11 (1943); selections have been translated into German by Siegfried Schott, *Altägyptische Liebeslieder* (Zurich, 1950), pp. 140–143.

The luxurious grain and the reapers of the Beyond are described in spells 109 and 149 of the Book of the Dead (Hornung, *Totenbuch*, pp. 209f, 302f.; Faulkner, *Book of the Dead*, pp. 102, 137ff). On the "offering fields" of the Coffin Texts, see A. de Buck, *Coffin Texts*, vol. 5, spell 466; R. O. Faulkner, *Coffin Texts*, vol. 2, spells 466–467, pp. 93ff. An Egyptian mile (*iteru*) is approximately 6.5 English miles. For the Book of Nut, see O. Neugebauer and R. Parker, *Egyptian Astronomical Texts* (Providence and London, 1960), vol. 1, pp. 36–94. The parallels in scene 8 of the Book of Gates are in Hornung, *Unterweltsbücher*, p. 205.

The exulting baboons in Amduat are discussed by Hornung, *Unterweltsbücher*, pp. 67f; the "Divine Ennead with echoing silence" (Book of Caverns 5, 3), ibid., p. 316; the Beyond as Igeret, "the silent one," Hornung, *Das Amduat*, vol. 2, p. 162 (8).

For the tomb of User (TT 61), see Erik Hornung, "Die Grabkammer des Vezirs User," NachAkGött 1961, no. 5; and "Zur Familie des Vezirs User," ZÄS 92 (1965): 75–76. On the Books of the Heavens see Alexandre Piankoff, *Le livre du jour et de la nuit* (Cairo, BdÉ 13, 1942); the Book of Nut is in O. Neugebauer and R. A. Parker, *Egyptian Astronomical Texts* (Providence and London, 1960), vol. 1, pp. 36–94.

For statements concerning the purpose of the voyage through the Netherworld, see Hornung, *Unterweltsbücher*, pp. 91, 204, 255, 320. Light as the overflowing seed of the sun god is discussed by Erik Hornung, *Das Buch der Anbetung des Re im Westen*, vol. 2, p. 109 (96).

CHAPTER 6

Erik Hornung's annotated text and German translation of the Litany of Re are in *Das Buch der Anbetung des Re im Westen I-II* (Geneva, AH 2 and 3, 1975–1976). The quoted passages are from pp. 101–105, 155–156, 176 of the text volume; the quotation about the freedom of the *ba* soul is on p. 143. For the English translations see Alexandre Piankoff, *The Litany of Re* (New York, BS 40, no. 4, 1964); and Marshall Clagett, *Ancient Egyptian Science* (Philadelphia, APSM 184, 1989), pp. 511ff.

Book of the Dead spells for boarding and voyaging on the solar bark are nos. 100–102, 134, 136, 140. The solar cycle has been most recently studied by Erik Hornung, "Die Tragweite der Bilder: Altägyptische Bildaussagen," *Eranos-Yearbook* 48 (1979): 183–237; and "Zu den Schlussszenen der Unterweltsbücher," MDAIK 37 (1981): 217–226.

For the Books of the Heavens, see Alexandre Piankoff, *Le Livre du jour et de la nuit* (Cairo, BdÉ 13, 1942); for the Book of Nut see O. Neugebauer and R. A. Parker, *Egyptian Astronomical Texts* (Providence and London, 1960), vol. 1, pp. 36–94.

Scenes of renewal in the Amduat and the Book of Gates are discussed in Erik Hornung, *Ägyptische Unterweltsbücher* (Zurich and Munich, 1972; 2nd ed., 1984), pp. 185ff (the Amduat serpent); pp. 212ff (the Earth Bark); pp. 295ff (closing scene of the Book of Gates). In English see Marshall Clagett, *Ancient Egyptian Science*, pp. 506, 851. The final scenes of the other Books of the Netherworld are discussed in "Zu den Schlussszenen der Unterweltsbücher," MDAIK 37 (1981): 217–226. The mummy depicted as a fish is in the tomb of Khabekhnet (TT 2), published in Georg Steindorff und Walther Wolf, *Die thebanische Gräberwelt* (LÄS 4, 1936), pl. 14 (b).

The nightly voyage through a crocodile was examined by Alexandre Piankoff, *Création du disque solaire* (Cairo, BdÉ 19, 1953) and Emma Brunner-

Traut, ''Ägyptische Mythen im Physiologus (zu Kapitel 26, 25 und 11),'' in Wolfgang Helck (ed.), *Festschrift für Siegfried Schott zu seinem 70. Geburtstag* (Wiesbaden, 1968), pp. 32–36. Taking the solar circuit into the tomb itself is Hellmut Brunner, ''Illustrierte Bücher im alten Ägypten,'' Hellmut Brunner, Richard Kannicht and Klaus Schwager (eds.), *Wort und Bild* (Munich, 1979), pp. 201–218, esp. 212f; and Jaroslav Cerny, *Valley of the Kings* (Cairo, BdÉ 61, 1973), p. 27, where the ancient Egyptian names of the rooms in the tombs are discussed. For the sun in a god's mouth see Adriaan de Buck, ''Een merkwaardige Egyptische voorstelling van zonsop- en ondergang,'' JEOL 5 (1937/1938): 306, fig. 3.

The copy from Ramesses III's burial chamber is in Jean-François Champollion, *Notices Descriptives* (Paris, 1835–1872; Geneva, 1973–1974), vol. 1, pp. 422f. A slightly altered version of the scene without the royal name was incorporated in the Book of the Earth in the tomb of Ramesses VI; see Erik Hornung, *Ägyptische Unterweltsbücher*, p. 461, fig. 98.

CHAPTER 7

A comprehensive investigation of Re's encounter with Apophis remains to be written, but glimpses of it are in Hornung, *Unterweltsbücher*, pp. 45–47; under ''Apophis'' in the LÄ 1: 350–352; and in Clagett, *Egyptian Science*, p. 688, (''Apep'').

The literary reaction to the collapse at the end of the Old Kingdom and the Egyptians' struggle with its causes is a favorite theme, see Eberhard Otto, *Der Vorwurf an Gott* (Hildesheim, 1951); Gerhard Fecht, *Der Vorwurf an Gott in den ''Mahnworten des Ipu-wer''* (AbhHeidelberg 1972, no. 1); Winfried Barta, ''Die Erste Zwischenzeit im Spiegel der pessimistischen Literatur,'' JEOL 24 (1976): 50–61; Friedrich Junge, ''Die Welt der Klagen,'' in Jan Assmann (ed.), *Fragen an die altägyptische Literatur* (Wiesbaden, 1977), pp. 275–284; Erik Hornung, ''Verfall und Regeneration der Schöpfung,'' *Eranos-Yearbook* 46 (1977): 411–449. English translations of the Egyptian literature in question will be found in William K. Simpson (ed.), *The Literature of Ancient Egypt* (New Haven, 1973), pp. 180–233, as well as in Miriam Lichtheim, *Ancient Egyptian Literature* (Berkeley, 1973), vol. 1, pp. 58ff, 134ff. Some notes on the subject with additional literature are in Ronald J. Williams, ''The Sages of Ancient Egypt in the Light of Recent Scholarship,'' JAOS 101 (1981): 1–19.

Coffin Text spell 414 is translated by Raymond O. Faulkner, *The Ancient Egyptian Coffin Texts* (Warminster, 1977), vol. 2, p. 65; spell 108 of the Book of the Dead, by Hornung, *Totenbuch*, pp. 206–208, 481f, with the more detailed descriptions from spell 39 in Hornung, *Totenbuch*, pp. 107–110, 439–441; and Faulkner, *Book of the Dead*, pp. 101–102 (spell 108); 60–61 (spell 39). For the Apophis scenes in the Books of the Netherworld, see the literature cited at the beginning of the list for this chapter. The ''Apophis Book'' was translated by Raymond O. Faulkner, ''''The Bremner-Rhind Papyrus: The Book of Overthrowing Apep,'' JEA 23 (1937): 166–185, and 24 (1938): 41–53; and by Clagett, *Egyptian Science*, pp. 591ff.

Seth's complex nature is treated in Herman te Velde, *Seth, God of Confusion* (Leiden: PÄ 6, 1967; 2nd ed., 1977), and Erik Hornung, ''Seth: Geschichte und Bedeutung eines ägyptischen Gottes,'' *Symbolon* n.s., no. 2 (1974): 49–63. The Ouroborus is encountered for the first time on one of Tutankhamun's gilded shrines: Alexandre Piankoff, *The Shrines of Tut-Ankh-Amon* (New York, BS 40, 2, 1955), pl. 48; and more generally, B. H. Stricker, *De grote Zeeslang* (Leiden, 1953), with English summary, p. 28.

The Book of the Celestial Cow appears likewise for the first time—but incompletely—on one of Tutankhamun's golden shrines (Alexandre Piankoff, *The Shrines of Tut-Ankh-Amon*, pp. 26–37 and pl. 56). The most recent publications are the annotated translation by Erik Hornung et al., *Der ägyptische Mythos von der Himmelskuh: Eine Ätiologie des Unvollkommenen* (Freiburg and Göttingen, OBO 46, 1982); and in Clagett, *Egyptian Science*, pp. 531ff.

CHAPTER 8

A single book dealing with Osiris and his myth remains to be written, but the articles under ''Osiris'' in LÄ 4: 623–633 (by John Gwyn Griffiths in English) and P–W suppl. vol. 9: 469–513 (by Wolfgang Helck in German) can be read with profit; see also John Gwyn Griffiths, *The Origins of Osiris and his Cult* (Leiden, SHR 40, 1980); Griffiths also translated Plutarch's *De Iside et Osiride* (Cardiff, 1970) into English. The Ramesside tale of the ''contendings of Horus and Seth'' is translated by Edward F. Wente, in William K. Simpson (ed.), *The Literature of Ancient Egypt* (New Haven, 1973), pp. 108–126; and by Miriam Lichtheim, *Ancient Egyptian Literature* (Berkeley, 1976), vol. 2, pp. 214ff.

Spell 154 of the Book of the Dead is rendered into German by Hornung, *Totenbuch*, pp. 331–334; and into English by Faulkner, *Book of the Dead*, p. 152. The positive aspects of decomposition are discussed in chapter 9. The quote from the Book of Caverns is taken from Alexandre Piankoff, *Livre des Quererets*, pl. 35, 3 (Hornung, *Unterweltsbücher*, p. 353). The emanations of Osiris are particularly important in spell 63B (Hornung, *Totenbuch*, p. 134; Faulkner, *Book of the Dead*, p. 69), but their significance is far from clear (and the translations correspondingly divergent).

For the scene with Osiris's casket in the Book of the Earth, see Hornung, *Unterweltsbücher*, pp. 458–461; the scene with Horus, ibid., pp. 468f; Osiris's corpse in the Book of Caverns, ibid., pp. 352f, 418f. Osiris is praised in a Ramesside song as the ''mummy with long phallus'' (Adolf Erman, ''Gebete eines ungerecht Verfolgten und andere Ostraka aus den Königsgräbern,'' ZÄS 38 [1900]: 30–31). For spell 78 of the Book of the Dead see Hornung, *Totenbuch*, pp. 157–164, 462–464. For Osiris with bull's head, see Hornung, *Unterweltsbücher*, p. 313f. The meaning of the name Wennefer (''existing on perfection'') is discussed by Gerhard Fecht, *Wortakzent und Silbenstruktur* (Glückstadt: ÄgFo 21, 1960), pp. 58f, section 107. For the illustration on the coffin in the Fitzwilliam Museum (Cambridge, England), see R. T. Rundle Clark, *Myth and Symbol in Ancient Egypt* (London, 1959), pp. 254f, pl. 18. ''Osiris beds'' (see ''Kornosiris'' in LÄ 3: 744–746, by Christine Seeber-Beinlich) were found in the tombs of Amenophis II, Tutankhamun, Maiherperi, and Yuya/Tuya in the Valley of the Kings.

For the specific connection between Re and Osiris, see Hornung, *Amduat*, vol. 2, p. 124; and Erik Hornung, *Conceptions of God* (Ithaca, 1982), pp. 93–96. For the resurrection scenes in the royal burial chamber, see Hornung, ''Zu den Schlussszenen der Unterweltsbücher,'' MDAIK 37 (1981): 217–226; and Hornung, *Unterweltsbücher*, pp. 429–431 (Book of the Earth). For the ''breathing through the solar disk,'' ibid., p. 395.

The Papyrus of Padiamun was published by Alexandre Piankoff and N. Rambova, *Mythological Papyri* (New York, BS 40, 3, 1957), no. 10. The quotation from the shrine of Tutankhamun is from Alexandre Piankoff, *Shrines of Tut-Ankh-Amon*, pl. 21. The reference from the Litany of Re is from Erik Hornung, *Buch der Anbetung des Re*, vol. 2, p. 87. For worshipping Osiris in Rosetau, see Hornung, *Totenbuch*, p. 228; and Faulkner, *Book of the Dead*, p. 113 (spell 119). Alexandre Piankoff published *The Funerary Papyrus of Tent-Amon in Egyptian Religion* 4 (1936): 49–70.

CHAPTER 9

On the general theme of Egyptian thoughts about the nature of man and his fate, see Erik Hornung, ''Fisch und Vogel: zur altägyptischen Sicht des Menschen,'' *Eranos-Yearbook* 52 (1983): 455–496.

There are a number of works dealing with mummification, but A. T. Sandison's article (in English) ''Balsamierung,'' LÄ 1: 610–614 mentions the most important ones. Ange-Pierre Leca's *Les Momies* (Paris, 1976) has appeared since then. On religious anthropology, see Erik Hornung, *Einführung in die Ägyptologie* (Darmstadt, 1967), section 33, with earlier literature. For the *ba* soul in particular, see Elske Marie Wolf-Brinkmann, *Versuch einer Deutung des Begriffs ''b3'' anhand der Überlieferung der Frühzeit und des Alten Reiches* (Freiburg, 1968); and Louis V. Zabkar, *A Study of the Ba Concept in Ancient Egyptian Texts* (Chicago, 1968); the shade, Beate George, *Zu den altägyptischen Vorstellungen* vom Schatten als Seele (Bonn, 1970); and the akh (referring to the blessed Dead as "enlightened ones"), Gertie Englund, Akh—une notion religieuse dans l'Égypte pharaonique (Uppsala, 1978). The quote about the importance of the name is from spell 316 of the Coffin Texts (Adriaan de Buck, Coffin Texts, vol. 4, p. 109 f–g; Raymond O. Faulkner, Ancient Egyptian Coffin Texts, vol. 1, p. 239). Similar phrases were collected by Siegfried Schott, "Zur Unvergänglichkeit des Namens," MDAIK 25 (1969): 135. On the otherworldly significance of the name, spell 25 of the Book of the Dead (Hornung, Totenbuch, pp. 88f; Faulkner, Book of the Dead, p. 52).

The material relating to the Egyptian decans was collected by Otto Neugebauer and Richard A. Parker, Egyptian Astronomical Texts (Providence and London, 1960–1969). See also Erik Hornung, "Zur Bedeutung der ägyptischen Dekangestirne," GM 17 (1975): 35–37 (where it is also made clear that the "star clocks" in the tombs are there to assure that the departed join in the celestial revolutions; they are not intended as precise instruments for the measurement of time).

Concerning the representation of mummies in the Amarna Period, see Marianne Guentch-Ogloueff, "Fragments de sarcophage du temps d'Akhenaton," RdÉ 4 (1940): 75–80. The quote from the Book of Gates (scene 40) is in Erik Hornung, Unterweltsbücher, p. 248; similar addresses to the mummies, ibid., pp. 209f, 222. For the various phases of the straightening out of the sleep of death, ibid., pp. 118, 264, 361, 449, 468; the substitution of the head, Book of Caverns, ibid., pp. 414f.

The deliberate mutilation of mummies was discussed by Alfred Hermann, "Zergliedern und Zusammenfügen: Religionsgeschichtliches zur Mumifizierung," Numen 3 (1956): 81–96; see also G. R. H. Wright, "The Egyptian Sparagmos," MDAIK 35 (1979): 345–358. On the positive aspects of decomposition see Ingeborg Clarus, Du stirbst, damit du lebst: Ägyptische Mythologie in tiefenpsychologischer Sicht (Fellbach, 1980): pp. 62–64 (this book gives particular attention to a Jungian psychological analysis of the Amduat).

For the gods with the measuring cord, see Erik Hornung, Unterweltsbücher, pp. 229f; and pp. 69, 72, and 81 for the assignment of fields to the blessed dead in the Amduat. The "shining" grain is in the Book of Gates, scene 46 (ibid., p. 256). The scene with the foreign peoples (ibid., pp. 233–235) was almost complete when Belzoni copied it, and today it is almost entirely lost. References to humankind as the "Cattle of Re" and the like are entirely favorable in Egyptian.

The joyous cry "the doors are open. . ." is in the Litany of Re. See Hornung, Buch der Anbetung des Re , vol. 1, p. 194, and Alexandre Piankoff, The Litany of Re (New York, 1964), p. 37. The complaint following is from scene 14 of the Book of Gates (Hornung, Unterweltsbücher, p. 217).

The problems of the existence and limits of time were tackled by Jan Assmann, Zeit und Ewigkeit im alten Ägypten: Ein Beitrag zur Geschichte der Ewigkeit (AbhHeidelberg 1975, no. 1); and Erik Hornung, "Zeitliches Jenseits im alten Ägypten," Eranos-Yearbook 47 (1978): 269–307.

CHAPTER 10

The content and sources for this chapter were assembled mainly from Jan Zandee, Death as an Enemy (Leiden, 1960) and Erik Hornung, Altägyptische Höllenvorstellungen (AbhLeipzig 59, 1968, fascicle 3). For the Judgment of the Dead in the Book of the Dead, see Christine Seeber, Untersuchungen zur Darstellung des Totengerichts im Alten Ägypten (Berlin, MÄS 35, 1976). Earlier conceptions are treated by Reinhard Grieshammer, Das Jenseitsgericht in den Sargtexten (Wiesbaden, ÄgAbh 20, 1970).

The quote from the Teaching of Merikare was adapted from Wolfgang Helck, Die Lehre für König Merikare (Wiesbaden, 1977), p. 31, and Raymond O. Faulkner, "The Teaching for Merikare," in William K. Simpson (ed.), The Literature of Ancient Egypt (New Haven, 1973), pp. 183–184. German translations of spell 125 of the Book of the Dead are in Erik Hornung, Totenbuch, pp. 233–245, and Meisterwerke altägyptischer Dichtung (Zurich and Munich, 1978), pp. 63–69. English translations are by Raymond O. Faulkner, Book of the Dead, pp. 29–34, and E. A. Wallis Budge, Book of the Dead, pp. 355–378. For the

judgment scene in the Amduat: Erik Hornung, Unterweltsbücher, pp. 129–133; in the Book of Gates: Hornung, Unterweltsbücher, pp. 237–240; in the Book of the Night: Alexandre Piankoff, Le Livre du jour et de la nuit (Cairo, 1942), pp. 66f. The demotic Setne-Khamwas stories dominated by the ancient Egyptian theme of the sorcerers' competition are translated by Miriam Lichtheim, Ancient Egyptian Literature (Berkeley, 1980), vol. 3, pp. 125–151. Osiris's letter is in Papyrus Chester Beatty 1 (Alan H. Gardiner, The Library of A. Chester Beatty: Description of a Hieratic Papyrus [London, 1931], p. 25, pl. 15) and is also translated by Miriam Lichtheim, Ancient Egyptian Literature (Berkeley, 1976) vol. 2, p. 222; and by Edward F. Wente in William K. Simpson (ed.), The Literature of Ancient Egypt (New Haven, 1973), pp. 124–125.

For bound victims in the Book of Gates see Hornung, Unterweltsbücher, pp. 205–207, 270f.; the "posts of Geb" (scene 45), ibid., pp. 254f. The sun god as the "fetterer" (address 64 of the Litany of Re), Hornung, Buch der Anbetung des Re, vol. 2, p. 18 (176 and 178); and Clagett, Egyptian Science, p. 524; as well as Hornung, Amduat, vol. 3, p. 63. "He who is bound there is not released," is a phrase from a later papyrus cited by Siegfried Schott, "Totenbuchspruch 175 in einem Ritual zur Vernichtung von Feinden," MDAIK 14 (1956): 187.

For references to the tearing out of hearts, see Hornung, Buch der Anbetung des Re II, p. 132 (341). The reference to the Book of Caverns is from Alexandre Piankoff, Le Livre des Quererets (Cairo, 1946), pl. 49, 3. For the squeezing of blood, see Siegfried Schott, "Das blutrünstige Keltergerät," ZÄS 74 (1938): 88–93.

For the "Great Fiery One" in the Book of Gates (scenes 59/60), see Hornung, Unterweltsbücher, pp. 270–272; the three serpents of the Book of Caverns, ibid., pp. 320f; the fire pits of the Amduat, ibid., pp. 179–181 (also Clagett, Egyptian Science, pp. 504 and 850); the traps in the Book of Gates, ibid., p. 227; the fire hole (scene 41), ibid., pp. 249f; and the text for the kettles, ibid., p. 392. The second century A.D. tomb fresco from Akhmim was published by F. W. von Bissing, "Tombeaux d'époque romaine à Akhmîm," ASAE 50 (1950): 557, pl. I.

On the nonexistence of the damned, see Erik Hornung, Altägyptische Höllenvorstellungen (AbhLeipzig 59, 1968, fascicle 3), p. 32. The reference to the Eye of Horus is from Alexandre Piankoff, Le Livre de Quererts (Cairo, 1946), pl. 48, 6.

CHAPTER 11

A comprehensive work devoted to the objects accompanying the dead into the tomb remains to be written, but Howard Carter's The Tomb of Tut.Ankh.Amen and Oxford's Tut'ankhamon's Tomb series give an idea of what was found in the representative tomb of Tutankhamun.

The objects found in predynastic and archaic Egyptian tombs are presented by William C. Hayes, The Scepter of Egypt (New York, 1953) vol. 1, pp. 3–31, including the cosmetic palettes (for which see also "Palette," in LÄ 4: 654–658, by Wolfhart Westendorf). Hayes details many objects customarily placed in tombs over the millennia, and the special significance of some of the animal shaped objects is discussed exhaustively by Erik Hornung and Elisabeth Staehelin et al., Skarabäen und andere Siegelamulette aus Basler Sammlungen (Mainz, ÄDS 1, 1976), pp. 106–163. For the interpretation of the decoration of the Negada painted vessels, see Emma Brunner-Traut, "Drei altägyptische Totenboote und vorgeschichtliche Bestattungsgefässe (Negade II)," RdÉ 27 (1975): 41–55. Some of the animals mentioned also enjoyed popularity during the immediately preceding phase. Peter J. Ucko, Anthropomorphic Figurines of Predynastic Egypt and Neolithic Crete (London, 1968), pp. 409ff; and Erik Hornung, Conceptions of God (Ithaca, 1982), pp. 102ff, tackle the interpretation of early anthropomorphic figurines.

The most thorough study of Egyptian art is that by Walther Wolf, Die Kunst Ägyptens (Stuttgart, 1957). John Baines's translation of the redoubtable Heinrich Schäfer's Principles of Egyptian Art (Oxford, 1986) presents continental conceptions of art to the English-speaking world. W. Stevenson Smith's standard text, The Art and Architecture of Ancient Egypt has been revised by William K. Simpson (Harmondsworth, 1981). C. W. Ceram provides a popular account of the discovery of several tombs in Gods, Graves and Scholars. For lists of offerings see Winfried Barta, Die altägyptische Opferliste (Berlin, MÄS 3, 1963);

for representations of objects, see Gustav Jéquier, *Les Frises d'objects des sarcophages du Moyen Empire* (Cairo, MIFAO 47,1921). Funerary processions and rites are discussed in Jürgen Settgast, *Untersuchungen zu Altägyptischen Bestattungsdarstellungen* (Glückstadt, AbhKairo 3, 1963). Statuettes from the tombs of Sety II, Tutankhamun, and others were collected by Friedrich Abitz, *Statuetten in Schreinen als Grabbeigaben in den ägyptischen Königsgräbern der 18. und 19. Dynastie* (Wiesbaden, ÄgAbh 35, 1979).

The expression "Beware, Earth!" (tomb of Tutankhamun) is frequent in ritual texts and should open the way for the approaching king or god. For the ritual of the Opening of the Mouth, see Eberhard Otto, *Das ägyptische Mundöffnungsritual* (Wiesbaden, ÄgAbh 3, 1960). Jar labels are translated by Jaroslav Cerny, *Hieratic Inscriptions from the Tomb of Tut'ankhamun*, (Oxford, TTSO 2, 1965); cosmetics are interpreted by Erik Hornung and Elisabeth Staehelin, *Skarabäen* (see above), pp. 140–141; mirrors, by Christine Lilyquist, *Ancient Egyptian Mirrors from the Earliest Times Through the Middle Kingdom* (Berlin, MÄS 27, 1979); and Tutankhamun's staffs decorated with Egyptian foes, by Raphael Giveon (Review of Hassan, *Stöcke und Stäbe*), CdÉ 54 (1979): 90ff. It is only with Merneptah and his successors that the pharaoh wears a crown in the entrance scenes of the first corridor: Sety I and Ramesses II wear only head cloths.

Hans D. Schneider presents many aspects of the shawabtys in *Shabtis* (3 parts, Leiden, 1977). William C. Hayes published *The Royal Sarcophagi of the XVIII Dynasty* (Princeton, 1935), while a supplement dealing with Dynasties 19 and 20 remains to be done. Scarabs and other amulets have been examined by Erik Hornung and Elisabeth Staehelin et al., in *Skarabäen und andere Siegelamulette aus Basler Sammlungen* (Mainz, ÄDS 1, 1976). It is impossible here to discuss all of the objects which were put into the tombs: musical instruments, board games, writing utensils, flowers, and so on. The final quotation is adapted from Raymond O. Faulkner, "The Teaching for Merikare," in William K. Simpson (ed.) *The Literature of Ancient Egypt* (New Haven, 1973), p. 184; also translated by Miriam Lichtheim, *Ancient Egyptian Literature* (Berkeley, 1973), vol. 1, p. 101.

CHAPTER 12

The literature for the cemeteries of Abydos and Saqqara is cited above under chapter 2. The Dynasty 11 stele with Antef II's hounds is Cairo CG no. 20512. The legend characterizes the god also as Shu, who separates sky from earth in the Creation, and promises the king, "I set your soul [ba, written with a ram hieroglyph] in the sky and your body in the underworld, for all eternity." published by H. O. Lange and Heinrich Schäfer, *Grab- und Denksteine des Mittleren Reiches im Museum von Kairo* (Berlin, Catalogue général, 1902ff). George A. Reisner and William St. Smith's *The Tomb of Queen Hetep-heres, the Mother of Cheops* (Cambridge, Mass., A History of the Giza Necropolis II, 1955) deals with her treasures. Hermann Junker's twelve-volume work *Gîza* (Vienna, 1929–1955), covers the details of the tombs. The arrangement of the cemetery is discussed by W. Helck, "Zur Entstehung des Westfriedhofs an der Cheops-Pyramide," ZÄS 81 (1956): 62–65. Prentice Duell published *The Mastaba of Mereruka* (OIP 31 and 39, 1938). The more modest burials are widely distributed in the literature and have not been systematically assembled.

For the pyramids of the queens of the late Old Kingdom, see Gustave Jéquier, *La Pyramide d'Oudjebten* (Cairo, 1928) and *Les Pyramides des reines Neit et Apouit* (Cairo, 1933). For the excavations of the oasis tomb of Governor Medunefer, see Michel Vallogia, "La Fouille de mastaba V de Balat (Oasis de Dakhleh)," BSFE 84 (1979): 6–20, and "Rapport préliminaire sur la deuxième campagne de fouilles du mastaba V à Balat (Oasis de Dakhleh)," BIFAO 79 (1979): 51–61. Rock tombs are the theme of Helmut Brunner's *Die Anlagen der*

ägyptischen Felsgräber bis zum Mittleren Reich (Glückstadt, AgFo 3, 1936), while some Dynasty 11 tombs were published by Dieter Arnold in *Gräber des Alten und Mittleren Reiches in El-Tarif* (Mainz, AVDAIK 17, 1976). N. Farag and Zaky Iskander published *The Discovery of Neferwptah* (Cairo, 1971). Recent discoveries at the pyramid of Amenemhat III in Dahshur are covered by Dieter Arnold, *Der Pyramidenbezirk des Königs Amenemhat III. in Dahschur, Vol. I: Die Pyramide* (Mainz, AVDAIK 53, 1987).

The Theban necropolis is the subject of Georg Steindorff and Walther Wolf, *Die thebanische Gräberwelt* (LÄS 4, 1936), while the private tombs in the Valley of the Kings are treated in Elizabeth Thomas, *The Royal Necropoleis of Thebes* (Princeton, 1966), chap. 9. Hatshepsut's first tomb was investigated and described by Howard Carter, "A Tomb prepared for Queen Hatshepsuit," JEA 4 (1917): 114–118. For Yuya and Tuya, see below under KV 46. For the provincial tombs of royal offspring, see Barry J. Kemp, "The Harim Palace at Medinet el-Ghurab," ZÄS 105 (1978): 122–133; and Geoffrey T. Martin, "Excavations at the Memphite Tomb of Horemhab," JEA 65 (1979): 15–16 (the latter includes a reference to the burial of Haremheb's wife).

The tomb of Queen Nofretari is available in a comprehensive publication by Gertrud Thausing and Hans Goedicke, *Nofretari: Eine Dokumentation der Wandgemälde ihres Grabes* (Graz, 1971). Most of its motifs are also in Edmund Dondelinger, *Der Jenseitsweg der Nofretari* (Graz, 1973), and remarks on the arrangement and decoration by Erik Hornung, "Das Grab einer ägyptischen Königin," BiOr 32 (1975): 143–145. Hartwig Altenmüller's work on the tomb of Queen Tausert is in preparation, and only preliminary reports have appeared: "Das Grab der Königin Tausert im Tal der Könige von Theben" SAK 10 (1983): 1–24; and "Das Grab der Königin Tausret (KV 14)," GM 84 (1985): 7–17. For the historical background of this period, see Rosemarie Drenkhahn, *Die Elephantine-Stele des Sethnacht und ihr historischer Hintergrund* (Wiesbaden, ÄgAbh 36, 1980). For other tombs in the Valley of the Queens, see Friedrich Abitz, *Ramses III in den Gräbern seiner Söhne* (Fribourg and Göttingen: OBO 72, 1986).

For the tomb of User (TT 61), see Erik Hornung, "Die Grabkammer des Vezirs User," NachAkGott, 1961, no. 5; and "Zur Familie des Vezirs User," ZÄS 92 (1965): 75–76.

The treasure of the tomb of Maiherperi was presented by Georges Daressy, *Fouilles de la Vallée des Rois*, (Cairo: Catalogue général, 1902), pp. 1–61. For the Book of the Dead generally and for translation, see Erik Hornung, *Das Totenbuch der Ägypter*, (Zurich and Munich, 1979); Raymond O. Faulkner, *The Ancient Egyptian Book of the Dead* (revised edition, London, 1985); Thomas G. Allen, *The Book of the Dead or Going Forth by Day* (Chicago, SAOC 37, 1974); E. A. Wallis Budge, *The Book of the Dead* (numerous eds. since 1899).

The burial chamber of Sennefer's tomb (TT 96) has been published in a small volume, *Reconstitution du caveau de Sennefer dit "Tombe aux vignes"* (Paris, 1985), and in Christiane Desroches Noblecourt et al., *Sen-nefer: Die Grabkammer des Bürgermeisters von Theben* (Mainz, 1986). Amenophis the son of Hapu is the topic of Alexandre Varille, *Inscriptions concernant l'architecte Amenhotep, fils de Hapou* (Cairo, 1968), and is discussed by Dietrich Wildung, *Egyptian Saints* (New York, 1977), pp. 83–110. Keith Seele published *The Tomb of Tjanefer at Thebes* (OIP 86, 1959).

Various aspects of the second cachette of Deir el-Bahri have been examined by Andrzej Niwinski in *21st Dynasty Coffins from Thebes: Chronological and Typological Studies* (Mainz, Theben V, 1988); "Untersuchungen zur ägyptischen religiösen Ikonographie der 21. Dynastie," GM 49 (1981): 47–59, and GM 65 (1983): 75–89; "The Bab al-Gusus Tomb and the Royal Cache in Deir el-Bahri," JEA 70 (1984): 73–81; and "Miscellanea de Deir el-Bahri," MDAIK 41 (1985): 197–227. An example of a Theban tomb from the period of Dynasties 25–26 is published in Manfred Bietak and Elfriede Reiser-Haslauer, *Das Grab des Anchhor* (Vienna, 1978).

The Most Important Literature on the Individual Tombs in the Valley of the Kings, by KV number

KV 1. Ramesses VII: Alexandre Piankoff, "La Tombe No. 1 (Ramsès VII)," ASAE 55 (1958): 145–156; Erik Hornung, "Zum Grab Ramses VII," SAK 11 (1984): 419–424; Erik Hornung, *Zwei Ramessidische Königsgräber: Ramses IV. und Ramses VII.* (Mainz, Theben VI, 1990).

KV 2. Ramesses IV: Eugène Lefébure, *Les Hypogées royaux de Thèbes, Part II: Notices des hypogées* (Paris 1889); Erik Hornung, *Zwei Ramessidische Königsgräber: Ramses IV. und Ramses VII.* (Mainz, Theben VI, 1990).

KV 4. Ramesses XI: A publication is being prepared by John Romer.

KV 6. Ramesses IX: Félix Guilmant, *Le Tombeau de Ramsès IX* (Cairo, MIFAO 15, 1907). Aside from a few decorated ceilings, the decoration is almost completely reproduced in drawings.

KV 7. Ramesses II: Charles Maystre, "Le Tombeau de Ramsès II," BIFAO 38 (1939): 183–190. A survey.

KV 9. Ramesses VI: Alexandre Piankoff and N. Rambova, *The Tomb of Ramesses VI* (New York, BS 40, 1, 1954). Complete photographic documentation, with translations. Friedrich Abitz, *Baugeschichte und Dekoration des Grabes Ramses' VI.* (Fribourg and Göttingen, OBO 89, 1989).

KV 11. Ramesses III: A publication is being prepared by Marek Marciniak.

KV 14. Hartwig Altenmüller's preliminary reports: "Das Grab der Königin Tausret im Tal der Könige von Theben" SAK 10 (1983): 1–24; and "Das Grab der Königin Tausret (KV 14)," GM 84 (1985): 7–17.

KV 16. Ramesses I: Alexandre Piankoff, "La Tombe de Ramsès Ier," BIFAO 56 (1957): 189–200. Complete photographic documentation.

KV 17. Sety I: Eugène Lefébure, *Les Hypogées royaux de Thèbes, Part I* (Paris, 1886). Complete but not faultless copies.

KV 20. Hatshepsut: Theodore M. Davis et al., *The Tomb of Hâtshopsîtû* (London, 1906).

KV 22. Amenophis III: Alexandre Piankoff and Erik Hornung, "Das Grab Amenophis' III. im Westtal der Könige," MDAIK 17 (1961): 111–127.

KV 23. Aye: Alexandre Piankoff, "Les peintures dans la tombe du roi Aï," MDAIK 16 (1958): 247–251. Complete photographic documentation.

KV 34. Tuthmosis III: Paul Bucher, *Les Textes des tombes de Thutmosis III et d'Aménophis II* (Cairo, MIFAO 60, 1932). Complete photographic documentation, texts typeset. John Romer, "The Tomb of Tuthmosis III," MDAIK 31 (1975): 315–351. A. Fornari and M. Tosi, *Nella sede della verità* (Milan, 1987).

KV 35. Amenophis II: Paul Bucher, *Les Textes des tombes de Thutmosis III et d'Aménophis II* (Cairo, MIFAO 60, 1932). Near-complete photographic documentation (aside from some pillar faces); texts typeset.

KV 43. Tuthmosis IV: Howard Carter, Percy E. Newberry, and Gaston Maspero, *The Tomb of Thoutmôsis IV* (Westminster, 1904). Finds only; appeared in identical form, without the introduction by Maspero, under same title as vol. 15 of the Catalogue général.

KV 46. Yuya/Tuya: Theodore M. Davis et al., *The Tomb of Iouiya and Touiyou* (London, 1907). The treasures were published by James E. Quibell, *The Tomb of Yuaa and Thiuiu* (Cairo, Catalogue général 43, 1908).

KV 47. Siptah: Theodore M. Davis et al., *The Tomb of Siphtah* (London, 1908). Only a few scenes in the tomb.

KV 55. Teye/Semenkhkare: Theodore M. Davis et al., *The Tomb of Queen Tiyi* (London, 1910). Alan H. Gardiner, "The So-called Tomb of Queen Tiye," JEA 43 (1957): 10–25 (attributing the tomb to Akhenaton). G. Perepelkin, *The Secret of the Gold Coffin* (Moscow, 1978). C. N. Reeves, "A Reappraisal of Tomb 55 in the Valley of the Kings," JEA 67 (1981): 48–55.

KV 57. Haremheb: Theodore M. Davis et al., *The Tombs of Harmhabi and Touatânkhamanou* (London, 1912): complete black-and-white photographic documentation. Erik Hornung, *Das Grab des Haremhab im Tal der Könige* (Bern, 1971): complete color photographic documentation.

KV 62. Tutankhamun: Georg Steindorff, "Die Grabkammer des Tutanchamun," ASAE 38 (1938): 641–667. Complete photographic documentation.

Chronological Overview

Archaic Period, c. 3000–2640 B.C.
    Dynasties 1–2
Old Kingdom, 2640–2134 B.C.
    Dynasties 3–8
First Intermediate Period, 2134–2040 B.C.
    Dynasties 9–10
Middle Kingdom, 2040–1650 B.C.
    Dynasties 11–14
Second Intermediate Period, 1650–1540 B.C.
    Dynasties 15–17
    (Hyksos Period)
New Kingdom, 1540–1070 B.C.
    Dynasty 18, 1540–1295 B.C.
      Amarna Period 1352–1325 B.C.
    Dynasties 19–20, 1295–1070 B.C.
    (Ramesside Period)
Third Intermediate Period, 1070–664 B.C.
    Dynasties 21–25
Late Period, 664–305 B.C.
    Dynasties 26–30
Ptolemaic Period, 305–30 B.C.
Roman Period, 30 B.C.

The Tombs in the Valley of the Kings

The sequence is chronologically arranged with the tomb number (KV = Kings' Valley) followed by the pharaoh's name and the dates of his reign. The names in parentheses are those of commoners with tombs in the Valley.

KV	Dynasty 18	
38	Tuthmosis I	1494–1482
42	Tuthmosis II	1482–1479
20	Hatshepsut	1479–1457
34	Tuthmosis III	1479–1425
35	Amenophis II	1427–1401
36	(Maiherperi)	
48	(Amenemope)	
43	Tuthmosis IV	1401–1391
22	Amenophis III	1391–1353
45	(Userhet)	
46	(Yuya and Tuya)	
55	(Teye/Semenkhkare)	
62	Tutankhamun	1335–1326
23	Aye	1326–1322
57	Haremheb	1322–1295

KV	Dynasty 19	
16	Ramesses I	1295–1293
17	Sety I	1293–1279
7	Ramesses II	1279–1213
8	Merneptah	1213–1203
15	Sety II	1203–1196
10	Amenmesse	ca.1200
47	Siptah	1196–1190
14	Tausert/Sethnakht	1190–1184
13	(Biya)	

KV	Dynasty 20	
11	Ramesses III	1184–1153
2	Ramesses IV	1153–1146
9	Ramesses V/VI	1146–1135
1	Ramesses VII	1135–1129
6	Ramesses IX	1127–1109
19	(Montuherkhepeshef)	
18	Ramesses X	1109–1099
4	Ramesses XI	1099–1070

GLOSSARY

GODS AND GODDESSES

Aker. Ancient personification of the earth as well as the Netherworld, known since the Pyramid Texts of the Old Kingdom. Depicted as a strip of land with human head or as a double lion or double sphinx with two heads, he is the ambivalent guardian of the entrance to and exit from the Netherworld. He may be either threatening or helpful to the deceased. His role in the Books of the Netherworld, except in the Book of the Earth, is limited, and he did not enjoy an independent cult.

Akhty. ''He of the horizon''; appellation of the sun god when manifest on the horizon. *See also* Harakhty.

Amun. ''The hidden one''; deity usually shown in anthropomorphic form wearing a tall feather crown, but sometimes as ram or as a goose. His cult is attested to first in the Theban district, but he is mentioned earlier as a primeval deity. Preeminent among deities from 2000 to 1360 B.C., he unites all the characteristics of the creator and sustainer of the world. Amun plays virtually no role in the royal texts of the Valley of the Kings.

Anubis. Funerary god usually depicted as a black canine (jackal) or as a human body with a dog's head. The dead pharaoh's mummy was entrusted to Anubis; he thus plays a prominent role as a protective deity in the royal tombs. However, he plays no role in the actual texts of the Beyond.

Apophis. Serpentine foe of the sun god, embodying the perpetual menace of disorder to the ordered world. He is a constant threat to the solar bark and, in a never ending struggle, must be continually warded off by magic.

Aton. The disk of the sun; not worshiped as a deity until the New Kingdom, and raised by Akhenaton to the status of the unique, exclusive god, Aton was depicted initially with a falcon's head and later as a sun disk, with rays terminating in human hands. ''The great disk'' is mentioned occasionally in the Books of the Netherworld, but not as the separate deity Aton; the disk is merely one manifestation of the sun god himself.

Atum. ''The undifferentiated one''; both the primeval being and the creator of the world. His mythological origin placed him at the head of the Ennead of Heliopolis, but in later periods he was worshiped as the evening manifestation of the sun god opposite Khepri, the morning manifestation. Usually represented in purely human form, he is a major figure in the Egyptian pantheon.

Bes. General term for various dwarf gods with monstrous faces, often wearing feather crowns and a lion's mane. They are friendly deities who repel evil, especially at the birth of a child.

Geb. Earth god of a more universal character than Aker, and depicted in purely human form. As god of the earth Geb is ''hereditary prince'' as well as ''ancestor'' of the gods. Husband of the sky goddess, Nut, he is the father of Osiris. Offerings were made to the dead through him, but he was not worshiped extensively.

Harakhty. ''Horus of the horizon''; daytime form of the sun god. He is depicted as a falcon, or in human form with a falcon's head surmounted by a sun disk.

Hathor. ''House of Horus''; probably the most universal Egyptian goddess. She has the marked characteristics of a mother, and as the ''eye of Re,'' she brings ruin to all enemies. She is shown usually as a woman with cow's horns and sun disk, or as a cow. In Thebes, and especially in the Valley of the Kings, she merges into the goddess of the pharaoh and Isis, losing her specific identity to Isis, but acquiring another role as mistress of the West, and thus of the Realm of the Dead.

Hika. Anthropomorphic personification of magic. Hika is one of the two constant companions (with Sia) of the sun god in the Book of Gates, and is indispensable in the defeat of Apophis.

Horus. Possibly identified with ''the distant one,'' Horus is an ancient god of the sky and kingship. His close links with the sun god and later with Osiris and Isis lead to many new associations, and his martial and youthful aspects become especially prominent. The living pharaoh is Horus, the son and avenger of Osiris; the deceased pharaoh becomes Osiris.

Hu. Personification of the ''utterance'' with which the creator god calls things into being. With Hika and Sia he is one of the creative forces that constantly accompany the sun god in the Netherworld. Hu is not worshiped.

Isis. Sister-spouse of Osiris and mother of Horus. Her name is written with the sign for ''throne.'' She protects the youthful Horus, but also helps the sun god. She is shown usually as a woman with the ''throne'' sign on her head, but because of her multiple connections with other goddesses, she is depicted in countless other forms; Isis is thus the ''multiform one'' par excellence. Her role in the royal tombs is manifold; as the wife of Osiris-the-dead-pharaoh, she protects the pharaoh (in the divine scenes and on the royal sarcophagus); as an independent deity, she accompanies the sun god and has her own place in the landscape of the Netherworld.

Iunmutef. ''Pillar of his mother''; he symbolizes the eldest son and is depicted anthropomorphically with a youthful side-lock and wearing the sacerdotal panther skin. The name is used also as a priestly title, intended to signify the god himself as the model for the priest carrying out functions of a filial nature, such as the care of the mummy of a father.

Khepri. ''He who is coming into being''; morning manifestation of the sun god, usually shown as a scarab beetle, and more rarely in human form with a scarab beetle for a head. Like other prominent deities in the Books of the Netherworld, Khepri appears exclusively in the tombs and funerary literature, without an independent cult.

Maat. Personification of the ''order'' of the world established at the Creation, shown as a woman with a feather in her hair. She was considered the daughter of the creator god (Re) and had a widespread cult from early times.

Nefertum. God of the lotus, shown as a human figure with a lotus on his head, and called ''lotus to the the nose of Re.''

Neith. ''The terrifying one''; goddess of war and the chase, her warlike attributes (arrows and shield) never far away. Often depicted as androgynous, Neith's main role was that of a primeval goddess, and she was worshiped from the Archaic Period, mainly in Sais and Esna. While her significance outside Sais diminished, her role as divine protector in the Valley of the Kings grew as she joined Selket, Nephthys, and Isis in the defense of Osiris.

Nephthys. ''Mistress of the House''; anthropomorphic goddess who accompanies Isis in bewailing and protecting Osiris, as well as in worshiping the sun god. Mythologically, she is the sister-spouse of Osiris's murderer, Seth; the pair have no children, Nephthys supposedly being infertile, (although by another tradition Nephthys reputedly bore Anubis to Osiris). As early as the Pyramid Texts, Nephthys joined Isis in serving the sun god. She plays almost no independent role in myth or cult.

Nun. Personification of the primeval waters from which everything arose, and from which the sun daily emerges, renewed and rejuvenated; hence Nun is ''father of the gods.'' With his female counterpart, Naunet, he forms the first generation of the family group of eight gods (the Ogdoad of Hermopolis). Occasionally depicted in human form, he also assumes a frog's head, drawing on his role as a fertility god. The annual inundation of the Nile was associated with a repetition of the Creation and thus with Nun.

Nut. Ancient goddess of the heavens, depicted as a woman arching over her husband, the earth god Geb. She daily gives birth to and then swallows the sun, and all the other celestial bodies; she also takes the deceased into her protection.

Osiris. This god, who suffered a violent death at the hands of his brother Seth, is depicted anthropomorphically in mummy form without indication of limbs. His attributes of crook and flail allude to his ancient links with the kingship and with pastoralism; other features provide analogies with the death and revival of nature. The most important role of this most complex of

205

gods is as ruler of the dead. The dead pharaoh was himself Osiris. With Isis Osiris posthumously begat Horus. In the Middle Kingdom Abydos was the center of Osiris's cult.

Ptah. Ancient god worshipped in Memphis, where he was regarded as creator of the world and god of technology. Ptah was depicted anthropomorphically, without articulated limbs, but with his hands free before him, bearing symbols of power. His role in the Valley of the Kings was negligible.

Ptah-Tatenen. Divinity in which the ancient creator god Ptah was joined to the chthonic deity Tatenen.

Re. Most important and common name of the sun god, who is combined with many other gods. He is depicted usually in human form and was worshipped primarily as the creator and sustainer of the world. His bark traverses the heavens by day, and the Netherworld by night. Heliopolis was his chief cult center from earliest times.

Selket. "She who causes (the throat) to breathe"; female deity who protects the deceased. She is depicted as a woman with a scorpion on her head. Isis too can assume the form of Selket.

Seth. Violent and ambivalent god frequently represented as a fabulous animal (the "Seth animal"), but also as a human with that animal's characteristic head. Associated with the marginal world of the deserts and foreign countries, Seth is engaged in a constant struggle with Osiris and Horus, both of whom symbolize the reestablishment of divine order, and both of whom are his brothers, according to varying traditions. Seth, with Isis, magically wards off Apophis, the serpentine foe of the sun god and symbol of chaos par excellence.

Shu. God of the space separating the earth from the heavens, and of the light in that airy space. Through his separation of earth and sky Shu plays an important role in the creation of the world. He is depicted as a human, sometimes with a feather in his hair; he is represented also with a lion's head.

Sia. Personification of perception who, together with Hu and Hika, makes the world of the Creation possible. With Hika he forms the crew of the solar bark in the Book of Gates.

Sokar. God of craftsmanship and of the dead. Worshipped in Memphis from the Old Kingdom on, he was closely connected with Ptah and later with Osiris as well. Sokar is shown as a falcon or falcon-headed human whose limbs are not delineated.

Tatenen. "Risen land"; embodiment of the depths of the earth. He was combined with Ptah in Memphis from the time of the New Kingdom. Tatenen is depicted in human form, wearing ram's horns and a crown of feathers.

West, goddess of the. Divine personification of the western Realm of the Dead and the desert mountains, depicted with the hieroglyph for "West" on her head, and usually to be understood as a manifestation of Isis or Hathor.

TERMS

Ankh. Egyptian word meaning "life" or "alive" and represented by an amuletic symbol, frequently offered by a divinity to the pharaoh.

Ba. One of several Egyptian words associated with our concept of "soul," but the most important one in the Netherworld. *Ba* is usually depicted as a human-headed bird. The active aspect of a person, it accompanies the sun god during his daily journey and need not be confined to the Netherworld like the mummy. It maintains a physical existence, and thus it is not a real "soul."

Canopic jars. Four jars in which the deceased's viscera (usually liver, stomach or spleen, lungs, and intestines) were placed after having been removed from the mummy. The vessels accompanied the deceased into the tomb, and each was identified with one of the sons of Horus: Imsety, Hapy, Duamutef, and Qebehsenuef.

Cartouche. Decorative frame or an ornamental tablet destined for inscription. The word is used today to designate the elongated rope rings within which the names of Egyptian kings are customarily enclosed. The cartouche is also an amulet.

Cenotaph. A sepulchral monument erected without the intent of burying a person in it. Egyptian kings had cenotaphs at various sacred places in the country; during the New Kingdom these were, apparently, in Memphis or near the delta capital.

Dat, Duat. Egyptian word for the Beyond, where the solar bark went in the evening and whence it emerged in the morning. During the Old Kingdom, the Beyond lay in the heavens; during the New Kingdom *dat/duat* came to signify the Netherworld.

Djed pillar. Egyptian symbol showing a bundle of stalks bound together and the homonym for the words meaning "to be stable," "enduring." Stability was in fact the significance of the amulets shaped in this fashion.

Ennead. Group of nine gods, usually consisting of a creator and three later generations. The great Ennead of Heliopolis originated with Atum who begat Shu und Tefnut, who begat Geb and Nut, whose descendants were Osiris, Isis, Seth, and Nephthys. Lesser Enneads also existed in Heliopolis and included other divinities.

Ka. Egyptian concept referring to one form of the deceased's "soul." This form usually is understood as a kind of double that dwelled within the tomb, providing sustenance and strength.

Ogdoad. Group of eight gods representing four generations, beginning with Nun and Naunet. The Ogdoad of Hermopolis is the most popular of these.

Ostracon. Greek for "sherd," usually understood to refer to an inscribed potsherd. In Egyptology the term is used for inscribed flakes of limestone as well.

Ouroboros. Word of Greek derivation meaning "tail biter" (corresponding almost precisely to the Egyptian term, literally "tail-in-mouth"). It refers to a serpent, which by devouring its own tail, symbolizes at once the outermost borders of the world and the emptiness within which the earth is enclosed. It is also the image of the beginning swallowing the end, and the end emerging from the beginning, and thus the cyclical infinity of time. In Egyptian mythology, however, this same serpent merges into other primeval serpents symbolizing Apophis, the threat to the universe, as well as the "great wriggler" who protects the sun god on his bark.

Sed festival. Jubilee held from earliest times by Egyptian kings after the first thirty years of their reign, and at shorter intervals thereafter. The festival was a celebration of renewal and rejuvenation. Every pharaoh aspired to spend eternity enthroned in the Beyond, celebrating a never-ending series of *sed* festivals.

Shawabty. Genre of funerary statuettes intended to serve in place of the deceased in performing unpleasant tasks in the Beyond.

Uraeus. Latinized Greek rendering of the Egyptian word for the erect and coiled cobra, the fire-breathing serpent accompanying the king and the gods. The uraeus is the sacred animal of the goddess of Lower Egypt and the most powerful defender of the king and kingship.

Wernes, fields of. Luxuriant fields of the first region of the Beyond traversed by the sun god. Here the blessed dead work and live.

TEXTS

Amduat. Egyptian term meaning "that which is in the Netherworld" (*imy-duat*), used as the modern title for a royal composition known to the Egyptians as the Book of the Secret Chamber, intended to initiate the select into the wonders of the Beyond. Its twelve parts are each divided into three registers, each register dominated by a central theme. Each of the twelve parts corresponds to an hour of the night. Dating to the beginning the New Kingdom, the Amduat is the oldest of the texts on the walls of the royal tombs in the Valley of the Kings. It is both a scientific investigation of the Beyond and an hour-by-hour account of the nightly voyage of the sun god through the Netherworld. The Amduat is characterized by illustrated lists of divinities, accompanied by textual commentaries on the events and the participants.

BIBLIOGRAPHY: Erik Hornung, *Das Amduat: Die Schrift des Verborgenen Raumes* (Wiesbaden, ÄgAbh. 7 and 13, 1963–1967); Erik Hornung, ed., *Texte zum Amduat* (Geneva, AH 3, 1987); Erik Hornung, *Ägyptische Unterweltsbücher* (Zurich and Munich, 1984), pp. 57–194; Marshall Clagett, *Ancient Egyptian Science* (Philadelphia, APSM 184, 1989), vol. 1, pp. 471ff.

Book of Caverns. Modern name for a composition dealing with the Netherworld, created during Dynasty 19. The Netherworld is divided into six parts, each with a number of scenes dealing with specific aspects of the Beyond set in caves or pits over which the sun god passes on his journey. This cave setting draws on a motif used in the eighth hour of the Amduat. The entire composition is dominated by pictorial elements, with captions that pertain to the contents of the scenes. The long texts are for the most part acclamations of Osiris. Cryptographic notes accompany some of the scenes.

BIBLIOGRAPHY: Alexandre Piankoff, *Le Livre des Quererets* (Cairo, 1946); Erik Hornung, *Ägyptische Unterweltsbücher* (Zurich and Munich, 1984), pp. 309–424.

Book of the Celestial Cow. Modern name for a work dating originally from the Amarna Period and found in the Valley of the Kings at the end of Dynasty 18. It records the attempt of the sun god to exterminate the rebellious human race, his regrets, and his subsequent withdrawal into the heavens, where he devises an organization corresponding to his own wishes.

BIBLIOGRAPHY: Erik Hornung, *Der Ägyptische Mythos von der Himmelskuh: Eine Ätiologie des Unvollkommenen* (Fribourg and Göttingen, OBO 46, 1982); Marshall Clagett, *Ancient Egyptian Science* (Philadelphia, APSM 184, 1989), vol. 1, pp. 531ff.

Book of the Day. Modern name for a composition of Ramesside date, consisting of a pictorial version of the solar cycle accompanied by lists of divinities and expository captions rather than lengthy texts.

BIBLIOGRAPHY: Alexandre Piankoff, *Le Livre du jour et de la nuit* (Cairo, BdÉ 13, 1942); Erik Hornung, *Ägyptische Unterweltsbücher* (Zurich and Munich, 1984), pp. 486–488.

Book of the Dead. Modern title of an illustrated collection of spells that the Egyptians called the Book of Coming Forth by Day. Essentially a personally inscribed papyrus scroll intended to be placed in the tombs of commoners during the New Kingdom, the Book of the Dead was not an actual text, but a concept. Certain spells were considered essential (such as spell 125, the Declaration of Innocence and the Judgment of the Dead), while others were expendable; some were available in countless variations, their length and quality varying according to the purchaser's prosperity and priorities. Some spells are completely new in the Book of the Dead, while others have antecedents in the Coffin Texts and even in the ancient Pyramid Texts. The guiding principle and sole purpose of these spells was the necessity of magic in assuring the preservation of life and limb of the deceased on the way to the Beyond, as well as within its boundaries. From these texts, scholars today have acquired an understanding of the ordinary Egyptian's hopes and fears concerning the Beyond. The text appears in the Valley of the Kings at the end of Dynasty 19.

TRANSLATIONS: Erik Hornung, *Das Totenbuch der Ägypter* (Zurich and Munich, 1979); Raymond O. Faulkner, *The Ancient Egyptian Book of the Dead* (New York, 1972; London, 1985); Thomas G. Allen, *The Book of the Dead or Going Forth by Day* (Chicago, 1974); E. A. Wallis Budge, *The Book of the Dead* (numerous eds. since 1899).

Book of the Earth. Modern name for a Dynasty 20 royal composition dealing with the sun god's nightly voyage through the Netherworld. The four parts are profusely illustrated with mummiform figures and solar disks, the Netherworld landscape being the earth (in the form of Aker) dominated by tumuli, caves, and sarcophagi containing numerous divine corpses.

BIBLIOGRAPHY: Alexandre Piankoff, *La Création du disque solaire* (Cairo, BdÉ 19, 1953); Erik Hornung, *Ägyptische Unterweltsbücher* (Zurich and Munich, 1984), pp. 425–480.

Book of Gates. Modern name for a royal composition dating to late Dynasty 18, the title referring to the role of the ''gates'' that separate the twelve hours of the night. It is similar to but more sophisticated than the Amduat, upon which it draws. Each of the three registers consists of a number of individual scenes set side by side. The lengthy lists of the Amduat are dispensed with and the plot contains a more intensive examinations of specific problems of the Beyond, such as the threat of Apophis; the nature of time; justice; material blessings; and the demographic composition of the Beyond.

BIBLIOGRAPHY: Erik Hornung, *Das Buch von den Pforten des Jenseits* (Geneva, AH 7 and 8, 1979–1980); Erik Hornung, *Ägyptische Unterweltsbücher* (Zurich and Munich, 1984), pp. 195–308; Jan Zandee, ''The Book of Gates,'' in *Liber Amicorum: Studies in Honour of Prof. Dr. C. J. Bleeker* (Leiden, SHR 17, 1969), pp. 282–324.

Book of the Hidden (or Secret) Chamber: *See* Amduat.

Book of the Night. Modern name for a Ramesside royal composition. The most detailed of the Books of the Heavens where the familiar features of the nightly journey through the Beyond are set within the body of Nut, goddess of the heavens, who swallows the sun at the close of the day and gives birth to it each morning. Formally it resembles its twin, the Book of the Day.

BIBLIOGRAPHY: Alexandre Piankoff, *Le Livre du jour et de la nuit* (Cairo, BdÉ 13, 1942); Erik Hornung, *Ägyptische Unterweltsbücher* (Zurich and Munich, 1984), pp. 489–493.

Books of the Heavens. Ramesside texts that parallel the Books of the Netherworld and deal with the charting of the heavens.

BIBLIOGRAPHY: Erik Hornung, *Ägyptische Unterweltsbücher* (Zurich and Munich, 1984).

Books of the Netherworld. Modern designation for the whole genre of royal texts adorning the walls of the tombs of the Valley of the Kings. In contrast to the commoners' Book of the Dead, which is a miscellaneous collection of assorted magical spells, these are illustrated scientific and theological treatises describing the world of the Beyond, usually from the standpoint of the sun god and his companions. The term encompasses the Amduat, the Book of Gates, the Book of Caverns, and the Book of the Earth.

BIBLIOGRAPHY: Erik Hornung, *Ägyptische Unterweltsbücher* (Zurich and Munich, 1984); Alexandre Piankoff and N. Rambova, *The Tomb of Ramesses VI*, 2 vols. (New York, BS 40, no. 1, 1954); Marshall Clagett, *Ancient Egyptian Science* (Philadelphia, APSM 184, 1989), vol. 1.

Coffin Texts. Anthology of magical spells, a selection of which were inscribed on coffins of commoners during the Middle Kingdom. The spells were intended to assure the survival of the dead into the Beyond, and thus they provide information about Egyptian beliefs about the Beyond for a period from which there are no royal funerary texts.

TRANSLATION: R. O. Faulkner, *The Ancient Egyptian Coffin Texts*, 3 vols. (Warminster, 1973–1978).

Litany of Re. Modern name of a two-part work used in royal tombs since the middle of Dynasty 18 and probably composed at about the same time as the Amduat. The first part is an acclamation of the sun god under 75 different names, each with a different function. The second is a series of litanies in which the pharaoh assumes the nature, role, and person of various deities, but above all that of the sun god.

BIBLIOGRAPHY: Erik Hornung, *Das Buch der Anbetung des Re im Westen*, 2 parts (Geneva, AH 2 and 3, 1975–1976); Erik Hornung, *Ägyptische Unterweltsbücher* (Zurich and Munich, 1984), pp. 483–484; Marshall Clagett, *Ancient Egyptian Science* (Philadelphia, APSM 184, 1989), vol. 1, pp. 511ff.

Pyramid Texts. Oldest known corpus of religious texts. Inscribed on the walls of the innermost chambers of the royal pyramids of Dynasties 5 and 6 kings, they include texts that were already ancient then alongside others that were more recent. Like the royal Books of the Netherworld (and unlike the commoners' spells in the Coffin Texts and the Book of the Dead), most of the utterances of the Pyramid Texts are conveyed as fact, assuring the dead king of a place among the celestial gods. In contrast to the Books of the Netherworld, however, they are (like the Coffin Texts and the Book of the Dead) anthologies of texts and not original compositions with a deliberate framework and design. The texts apparently include parts of rituals and fragments of mythological works considered useful to the dead king, as well as spell-like commands intended to repel evil and safeguard him.

TRANSLATION: R. O. Faulkner, *The Ancient Egyptian Pyramid Texts* (Oxford, 1969; 2nd ed., Warminster, n.d.).

SUMMARY OF THE DECORATIVE PROGRAM IN THE ROYAL TOMBS

In the rock tombs of Dynasty 18 many of the walls were left unfinished and the decorative program was limited to certain focal points—the shaft, antechamber, and burial chamber. Prior to Haremheb the walls of the burial chamber were decorated exclusively with the text of the Amduat written in cursive. Figures of gods were painted on the walls of the shaft, antechamber, and pillars of the burial chamber. At the end of Dynasty 18, Haremheb replaced the Amduat in the burial chamber with the Book of Gates. His tomb was the first to use painted reliefs. The ceilings of the Dynasty 18 tombs were covered with stars, either yellow or white, on a plain background of blue or black signifying heaven.

The tomb of Sety I, early in Dynasty 19, marks a total transformation of the decoration, and introduces a pattern that would be followed with minor variations until the last tombs in the Valley at the end of the Ramesside period. The following description applies to Sety I's tomb and notes some of the important variations. The letters refer to the plan that accompanies this summary. Sety's was the first tomb to be completely decorated in painted relief from the entrance down to the wall behind the sarcophagus. Certain sections received only preliminary stages of work (corridor B and the walls and pillars in room F), which contain outline drawings and the beginning of relief cutting. Here we can see that the preliminary sketches were done in red and corrected in black before the sculptor carved the relief; the painter did the final work. Unlike the walls, the ceilings were painted but never carved.

The exterior of Sety's tomb, as was typical of the earlier tombs, was not decorated; only with Sety's successor, Ramesses II, was the façade embellished with the scene of the solar disk containing the ram-headed nightly manifestation of the sun god and the scarab beetle, his morning manifestation. In Sety's tomb this scene is placed between corridors A and B.

The first corridor (A) is dominated by the sun. The decoration begins on the left with the pharaoh before the falcon-headed sun god, Re-Harakhty. This is followed by the Litany of Re, which begins with a detailed title and frontispiece. The walls are covered with the texts of invocations to Re's various forms and other prayers and litanies. In Sety's tomb, as in most others, the text of the Litany of Re continues into the second corridor (B) and returns to the entrance on the opposite, right wall. The ceiling of corridor A is painted with vultures, some with serpent's heads, all flying into the tomb to protect the dead king on his journey. In later tombs the vultures alternate with other creatures, winged serpents, scarabs, and falcons. Ramesses VI modifies this program and, instead of the Litany of Re, he places the Book of Gates to the left, the Book of Caverns to the right, in the corridors, and astronomical representations on the ceiling.

The Litany of Re in the second corridor (B) consists of two long rows of figures belonging to the seventy-five invocations in painted niches along the upper walls. Below this is the text of the first three hours of the Amduat, containing both the invocations to the sun god made by the mysterious gods of the Netherworld and the the sun god's responses. At the end of the corridor the deceased pharaoh is greeted by Nephthys and Isis, each kneeling and holding the *shen* ring which guarantees eternal existence to the pharaoh. Above, Anubis, the god responsible for the embalming and welfare of the dead, is shown as a reclining jackal. This scene, along with the representation of the four sons of Horus at the entrance to the next corridor, belongs to spell 151 from the Book of the Dead.

The third corridor (C) is reserved exclusively for the fourth and fifth hours of the Amduat. This is the mysterious cavern of the god Sokar, a sandy waterless region populated by numerous snakes and other strange creatures. The bark of the sun god is transformed into a snake in order to facilitate its movement through the sand before it returns to its normal course through the water.

This corridor leads directly to the shaft (D), which is decorated with scenes of the king praying before the divinities from whom he hoped to secure support in the hereafter. The pharaoh is generally shown facing into the tomb, while the gods face outward. The ceiling of the shaft is painted with yellow stars on a blue sky. After the king was buried, the far side of this shaft was closed up and the wall painted with decoration that differed from the relief decoration of the rest of the room and surely did not deceive intruders. All offerings and royal treasures lay beyond this wall.

The shaft adjoins the upper pillared hall (E). Four pillars are adorned with scenes of the pharaoh before a divinity, similar to the images on the walls of the shaft. The walls of the upper pillared hall are decorated with passages from the Book of Gates, the fifth hour to the left (the measuring out of lifetime and the apportioning of the field to the blessed dead) and the sixth hour to the right (the awakening of the mummies). On the rear wall the pharaoh is shown with Horus before an enthroned Osiris. Attached to the upper pillared hall is a second chamber (F), which appears to have had no established decorative requirements. In Sety I's tomb it contains the ninth, tenth, and eleventh hours of the Amduat.

Continuing down from the upper pillared hall are two more corridors (G and H) leading to the antechamber (I). The walls of G and H are decorated with scenes of the archaic ritual of the Opening of the Mouth. The antechamber picks up the program used in the shaft, scenes of the pharaoh before various divinities. Merneptah later dispensed with the antechamber and instead placed a room between corridors G and H, decorating it with spell 125 from the commoners' Book of the Dead. This scheme was then taken over by later Ramesside kings, who put it in the antechamber.

The burial chamber was always the focus of particular attention. After Tuthmosis III, the main hall was divided into an upper part with pillars (J) and a lower part (K) to house the sarcophagus. As mentioned earlier, the Amduat was the only book used in the burial chamber until it was replaced by the Book of Gates in the tomb of Haremheb. Sety I's tomb uses both, three hours from the Amduat in the lower part and three hours from the Book of Gates in the upper. Merneptah, Tausert, and Ramesses III replaced the scenes from the Amduat in the burial chamber with programmatic scenes of the solar path (from the Book of Caverns), the awakening of Osiris by the rays of the sun, the solar voyage through the chthonic deity Aker, and the birth of the hours.

The pillars in Sety's burial chamber, and the adjoining rooms in the cases where they were finished, contained more scenes of the pharaoh before divinities. The walls of these side rooms are related to the main burial chamber. The walls of N were decorated with scenes from the Amduat, while the entrance to O was decorated with a *djed* pillar. The two small side chambers connected to the upper hall (M and L) were decorated with the Book of the Celestial Cow and the Book of Gates, respectively.

The ceiling of the burial chamber contains astronomical scenes. Prior to the tomb of Ramesses III, these consist of the names and images of constellations; subsequently they included scenes from the Books of the Heavens (the Book of Nut, the Book of the Day, and the Book of the Night).

Rooms beyond the burial chamber (such as P) normally were not decorated. Of particular interest is the representation of the tomb inventory on the lower part of the walls of room N in Sety I's tomb. Later tombs placed the inventory depictions along the base of the wall in the burial chamber.

None of the wooden doors closing off various parts of the tomb is preserved, so we cannot know if or how they were decorated. In the Rammeside period, royal sarcophagi were always decorated with scenes and texts from the Books of the Netherworld as were the gold shrines found in the tomb of Tutankhamen.

It should be noted that no effort was made to present the entire text of any book in the tombs.

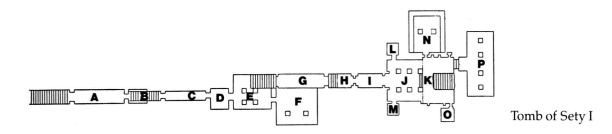

Tomb of Sety I

This chart is based on what still exists supplemented by old records. However, parts of these tombs are still undocumented and inaccessible, while other parts were never finished. The term "divine scenes" is used when the king is shown with various divinities to distinguish these scenes from those containing divinities without the king.

	Tomb	1st Corridor	2nd Corridor	3rd Corridor	Shaft	Upper Pillared Hall	4th and 5th Corridors	Antechamber	Burial Chamber
38	Tuthmosis I								fragments of the Amduat, not found *in situ*
20	Hatshepsut								fragments of the Amduat, not found *in situ*
34	Tuthmosis III				stars on ceiling, decorative frieze on walls			list of divinities	divine scene and Litany of Re on pillars, Amduat on walls
35	Amenophis II								divine scenes, Amduat
43	Tuthmosis IV				divine scenes			divine scenes	
22	Amenophis III				divine scenes			divine scenes	divine scenes, Amduat
62	Tutankhamun								funeral procession, Opening of Mouth, divine scenes, Amduat
23	Aye								fowling, divinities, Amduat, divine scenes
57	Haremheb				divine scenes			divine scenes	Book of Gates
16	Ramesses I								divine scenes, Book of Gates
17	Sety I	Litany of Re	Litany of Re figures, Amduat, Anubis etc.	Amduat	divine scenes	Book of Gates, Osiris shrine	Opening of the Mouth	divine scenes	Book of Gates, Amduat, astronomical ceiling
7	Ramesses II	Litany of Re	Litany of Re figures, Amduat, Anubis etc.	Amduat	divine scenes	Book of Gates, Osiris shrine	Opening of the Mouth	?	Book of Gates, Amduat, astronomical ceiling?
8	Merneptah	Litany of Re	Litany of Re figures, Amduat, Anubis etc.	Amduat	divine scenes	Book of Gates, Osiris shrine	Opening of the Mouth	Book of the Dead, divine scenes	Book of Gates, astronomical ceiling

Tomb	1st Corridor	2nd Corridor	3rd Corridor	Shaft	Upper Pillared Hall	4th and 5th Corridors	Antechamber	Burial Chamber
15 Sety II	Litany of Re	Litany of Re figures, Amduat	Amduat	divinities	Book of Gates, Osiris shrine			Book of Gates
10 Amenmesse	Litany of Re	Litany of Re	?	divine scenes	divine scenes			
47 Siptah	Litany of Re	Litany of Re figures, Amduat, Anubis etc.	Amduat					
14 Tausert/ Sethnakht	divine scenes	Book of the Dead	Book of the Dead	divine scenes	Book of the Dead	Opening of the Mouth	divine scenes	Book of Gates, divinities, astronomical ceiling
11 Ramesses III	Litany of Re	Litany of Re figures, Amduat	Amduat	divine scenes	Book of Gates, Osiris shrine	Opening of the Mouth	Book of the Dead, divine scenes	Book of Gates, divinities, divine scenes, Book of Aker
2 Ramesses IV	Litany of Re	Litany of Re	Book of Caverns				Book of the Dead	Book of Gates, on the ceiling Books of the Heavens
9 Ramesses VI	Book of Gates, Book of Caverns, astronomical ceiling	Book of Gates, Book of Caverns, astronomical ceiling	Book of Gates, Book of Caverns, astronomical ceiling plus Books of the Heavens	Book of Gates, Book of Caverns, astronomical ceiling plus Books of the Heavens	Book of Gates, Book of Caverns, Osiris shrine, astronomical ceiling	Amduat, on the ceiling Books of the Heavens and the cryptographic texts	Book of the Dead, divine scenes, on the ceiling cryptographic texts	Book of the Earth, on the ceiling Books of the Heavens
1 Ramesses VII	Book of Gates, Book of Caverns							Book of the Earth, divine scenes
6 Ramesses IX	Litany of Re, Book of Caverns	Litany of Re, Book of the Dead, Book of Caverns	Amduat, divine scenes, divinities	divine scenes				Book of Caverns, Book of the Earth, Amduat, on ceiling Books of the Heavens
18 Ramesses X	too incomplete							
4 Ramesses XI	too incomplete							

PLANS OF THE ROYAL TOMBS

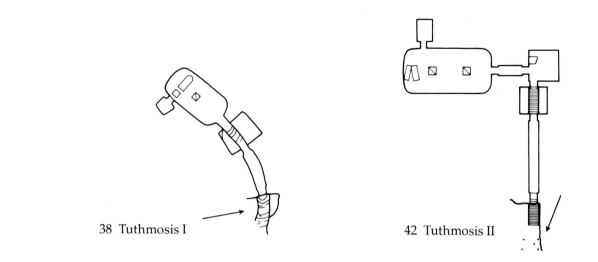

38 Tuthmosis I

42 Tuthmosis II

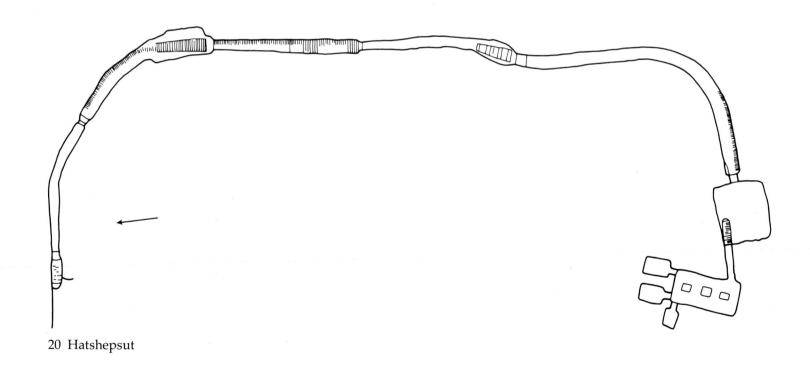

20 Hatshepsut

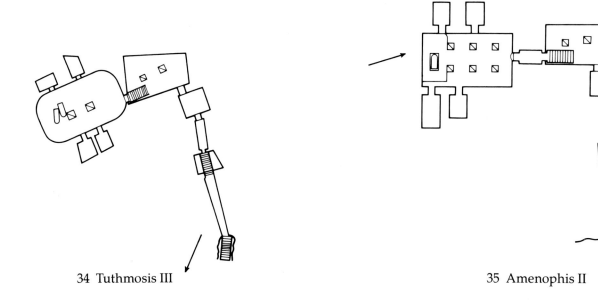

34 Tuthmosis III

35 Amenophis II

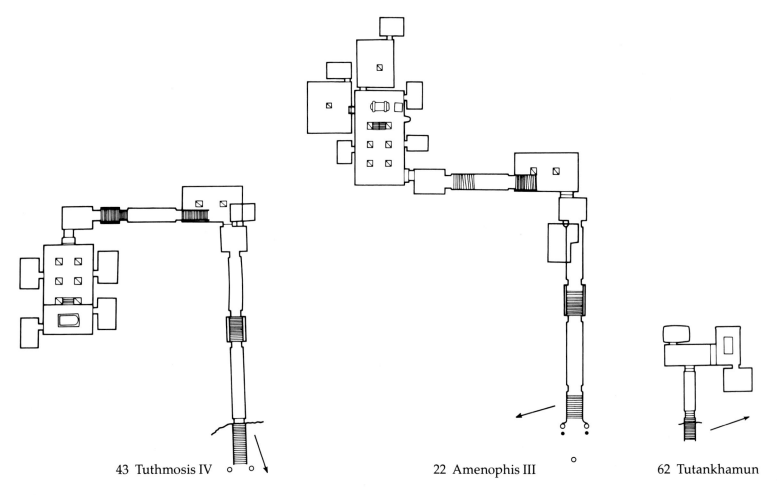

43 Tuthmosis IV

22 Amenophis III

62 Tutankhamun

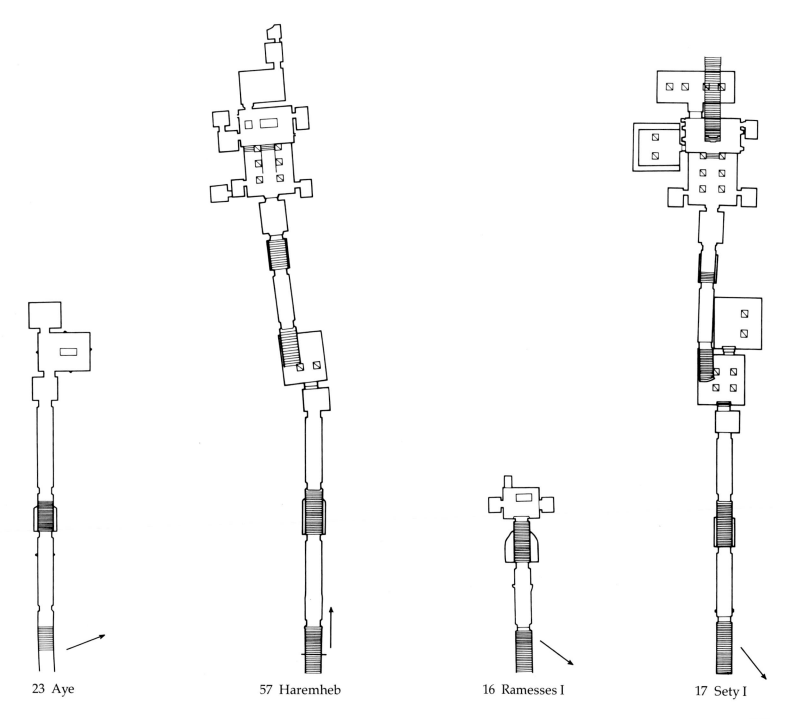

23 Aye

57 Haremheb

16 Ramesses I

17 Sety I

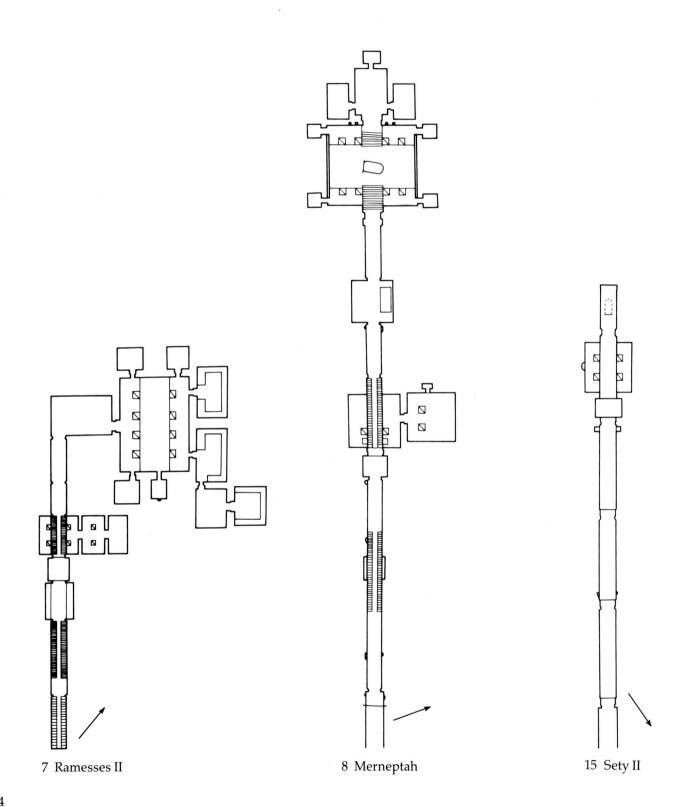

7 Ramesses II

8 Merneptah

15 Sety II

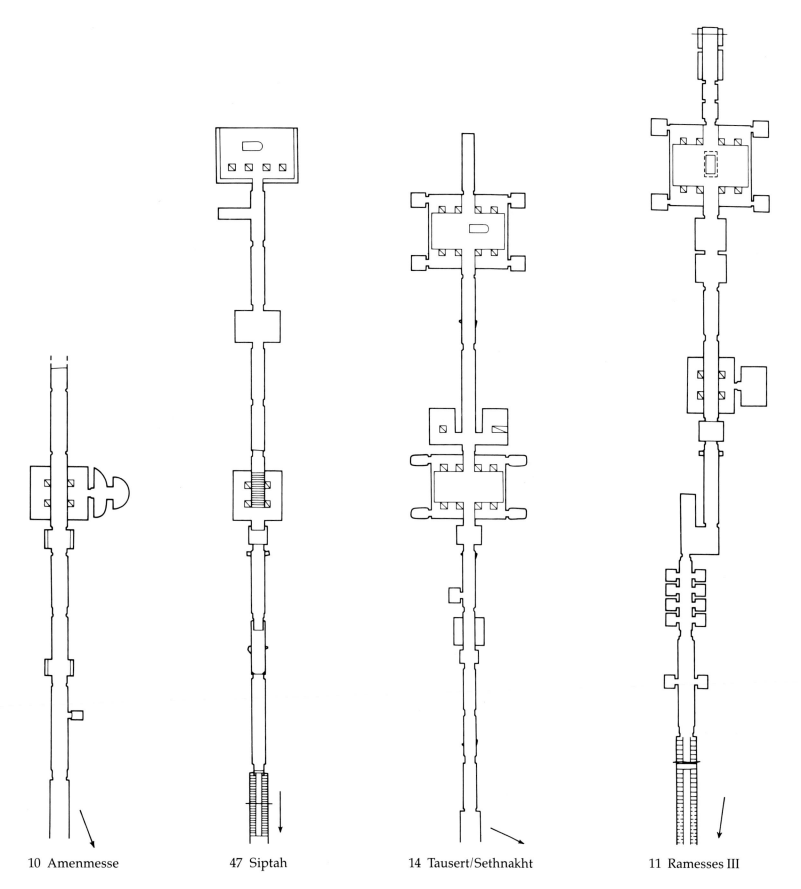

10 Amenmesse   47 Siptah   14 Tausert/Sethnakht   11 Ramesses III

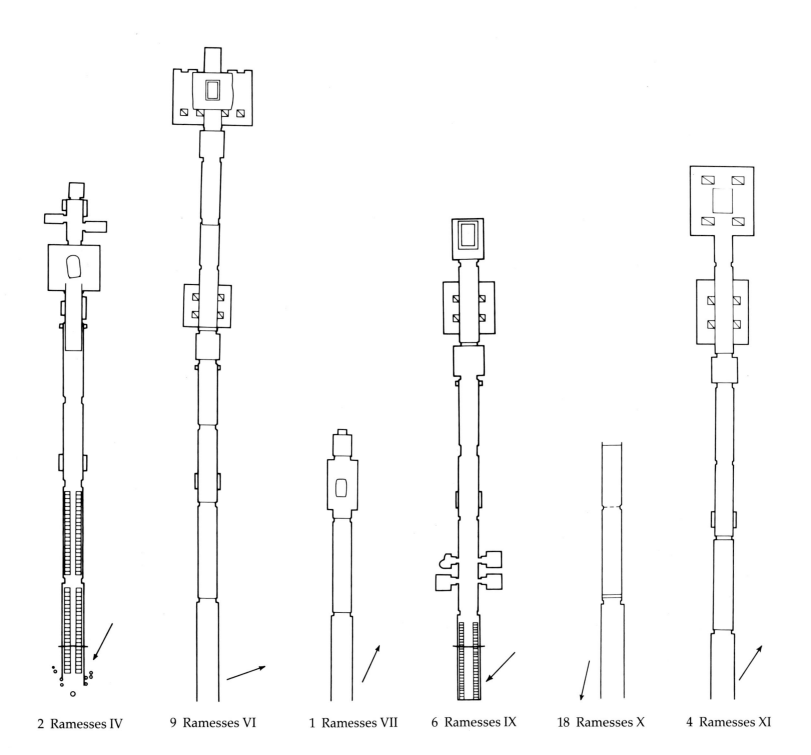

2 Ramesses IV   9 Ramesses VI   1 Ramesses VII   6 Ramesses IX   18 Ramesses X   4 Ramesses XI

Sources of the Black-and-White Illustrations

2 Photography by the Egyptian Expedition, The Metropolitan Museum of Art, New York.

6 Photography by the Egyptian Expedition, The Metropolitan Museum of Art, New York. The publisher thanks Dr. Dorothea Arnold of the Metropolitan Museum of Art for her help in obtaining these photographs as well as those on pages 125, 126, 172, 173, 174, and 196.

CHAPTER 1

10 *Wonderful Things: The Discovery of Tutankhamun's Tomb*, The Metropolitan Museum of Art (New York, 1976).

12 J. Baillet, *Inscriptions grecques et latines des tombeaux des rois ou syringes à Thèbes* (Cairo, 1925), no. 901, pl. 36.

13 R. Pococke, *Description of the East, Part I* (1743), pl. 29.

13 Ibid., pl. 30.

14 V. Denon, *Voyage dans la Basse et la Haute Égypte* (Paris, 1801), pl. 42.

15 *Description de l'Égypte*, pl. 91.

16 J.F. Champollion, *Monuments de l'Égypte et de la Nubie* III (Paris, 1845), pl. 232, 3.

17 *Die Gartenlaube* 32 (1884): 629.

18 Photograph, F. Teichmann.

19 H. Carter and A. C. Mace, *The Tomb of Tut.Ankh.Amen* I (London, 1923), p. 223.

20 Elizabeth Simpson from Charles Nims, *Thebes of the Pharaohs: Pattern for Every City* (London, 1965) p. 14.

21 Elizabeth Simpson from Elizabeth Thomas, *The Royal Necropoleis of Thebes* (Princeton, 1966) p. 60.

CHAPTER 2

23 W. B. Emery, *Great Tombs of the First Dynasty* I (Cairo, 1949), pl. 2.

24 Ground plan by J. Brinks, "Die Entwicklung der koniglichen Grabanlagen des Alten Reiches," HÄB 10 (1979): pl. 1. Reconstruction by J. P. Lauer, *La Pyramide à degrès* II (Cairo, 1936), pl. 4.

24 L. Borchardt, "Einiges zur dritten Bauperiode der grossen Pyramide bei Gise," Beiträge Bf I/3 (1932): pl. 1.

25 J. P. Lauer, *Les pyramides de Sakkarah* (Cairo, 1977), fig. 77.

26 G. Jéquier, *Le monument funéraire de Pepi II*, 3 (Cairo, 1940), p. 7, fig. 5.

26 D. Arnold, *Der Tempel des Königs Mentuhotep von Deir el-Bahari* (Mainz, AVDAIK 8, 1974), p. 6.

27 W. Wolf, *Funde in Ägypten* (Göttingen, 1966), p. 121, fig. 16.

27 S. Schott, "Die Schrift der verborgenen Kammer," NachAkGött (1958): 321, fig.5.

28 H. Grapow, ZÄS 72 (1936): 13, fig. 2.

30 G. Steindorff and W. Wolf, "Die thebanische Gräberwelt," LÄS 4 (1936): 85, fig. 32.

31 Ibid., p. 87, fig. 34.

CHAPTER 3

39 *Artefact. 150 jaar Rijksmuseum van Oudheden* (Leiden, 1968), pl. 49.

40 B. Bruyère, FIFAO, 16 (1939): pl. 7.

42 H. Carter and A.H. Gardiner, JEA 4 (1917): pl. 29.

42 Photograph from the Fitzwilliam Museum by arrangement with Mrs. E. Brunner-Traut.

43–45 Photographs, F. Teichmann.

44 below Photograph, A. Brodbeck.

46 J. Vandier and J. Vandier d'Abbadie, " La Tombe de Nefer–Abou," MIFAO 69 (1935): pl. 21.

46 Steindorff-Wolf, Theban. Graberwelt, p. 94, fig. 39.

47 J. Cerny, *Catalogue des ostraca hiératiques non littéraires de Deir el Médineh*, IV (Cairo,1939), p. 18, n. 303.

CHAPTER 4

55 F. Abd el Wahab, "La tombe de Sennedjem à Deir el Médineh," MIFAO 89 (1959): pl. 35.

56 E. Hornung, *Das Totenbuch der Ägypter* (Zurich and Munich, 1979), p. 116f, fig. 26.

57 Champollion, *Monuments* III, pl. 234, 3.

58 H. Schäfer, ZÄS 71 (1935): 18, fig. 1.

59 A. Piankoff and N. Rambova, *Mythological Papyri* (New York, BS 40, 3, 1957), p. 41, fig. 25.

60 E. Hornung, *Das Grab des Haremhab im Tal der Könige* (Bern 1971) p. 29, fig. 6.

60 Hornung, *Totenbuch*, p. 170, fig. 42.

61 F. Guilmant, "Le tombeau de Ramsès IX," MIFAO 15 (1907): pl. 85.

62 J. Champollion, *Monuments de L'Égypte et de la Nubie, Notices descriptives* I (Paris, 1835–1872), p. 418.

62 Hornung, *Totenbuch*, p. 389, fig. 90.

CHAPTER 5

71 A. de Buck, *The Egyptian Coffin Texts* VII, plan 14.

72 H. Bonnet, "Ägyptische Religion," in H. Haas, *Bilderatlas zur Religionsgeschichte*, part 2–4 (Leipzig, 1924), fig. 143.

72 Piankoff-Rambova, *Mythological Papyri*, p. 33, fig. 16.

73 A. Piankoff, "Les chapelles de Tout-Ankh-Amon," MIFAO 72 (1952): pl. 5.

76 Drawing, A. Brodbeck after the scene in the tomb of Sety II.

76 E. Hornung, *Ägyptische Unterweltsbücher* (Zurich and Munich, 1972), p. 142f., fig. 9.

77 W. M. F. Petrie, *Tombs of the Courtiers and Oxyrhynkhos* (London 1925), pl. 12, 5.

78 Guilmant, "Tombeau de Ramsès IX," pl. 49.

79 Ibid., pl. 88.

80 Hornung, *Unterweltsbücher*, p. 287, fig. 60.

CHAPTER 6

87 A. Erman, *Die Religion der Ägypter* (Berlin and Leipzig, 1934), p. 19, fig. 7.

88 Hornung, *Totenbuch*, p. 261, fig. 67.

88 A. Piankoff, *The Litany of Re* (New York, BS 40, 4, 1964) p. 14, fig. A.

89 Drawing, A. Brodbeck.

89 Hornung, *Totenbuch*, p. 58, fig. 7.

90 A. Piankoff, *Bulletin de la Société d'Archéologie Copte* 16 (1962): 261, fig.1.

90 Ibid., pl. 3, B. pp. 261–269.

91 H. Schäfer, ZÄS 71 (1935): 20, fig. 2.

93 Drawing, A. Brodbeck after Champollion, *Monuments* III, pl. 266.

94 Drawing, A. Brodbeck after Champollion, *Notices descriptives* I, p. 422f.

CHAPTER 7

103 Hornung, *Unterweltsbücher*, p. 215, fig. 23.

104 Ibid., p. 300, fig. 71.

105 Photograph, A. Brodbeck.

106 Hornung, *Totenbuch*, p. 69, fig. 8d.

106 E. Naville, *Texts relatifs au mythe d'Horus* (Geneva and Basel, 1870), p. VII.

107 Piankoff-Rambova, *Mythological Papyri*, p. 22, fig. 3.

108 Hornung, *Unterweltsbücher*, p. 186, fig. 14.

109 Hornung, *Totenbuch*, p. 98, fig. 17 (drawing by A. Brodbeck).

110 A. Piankoff, *The Shrines of Tut-Ankh-Amon* (New York, BS 40, 2, 1955) p. 142, fig. 46.

CHAPTER 8

115 E. Hornung, *Ältagypt. Höllenvorstellungen*, p. 39, after H. te Velde, *Seth, God of Confusion* (Leiden, 1967), p. 69, fig. 10.

116 Hornung, *Unterweltsbücher*, p. 459, fig. 97.

116 Ibid., p. 468, fig, 103.

117 Ibid., 407, fig. 81.

118 F. Le Corsu, *Isis. Mythe et mystères* (Paris, 1977), p. 14, fig. 8.

119 Drawing, A. Brodbeck after a photograph from the Fitzwilliam Museum.

120 Hornung, *Unterweltsbücher*, p. 430, fig. 83.

121 Piankoff-Rambova, *Mythological Papyri*, p. 60, fig. 47 and p. 91, fig. 58.

121 Piankoff, *The Shrines of Tut-Ankh-Amon*, p, 55, fig. 16.

123 Photography by the Egyptian Expedition, The Metropolitan Museum of Art, New York.

124 Drawing, A. Brodbeck after A. Piankoff, *Egyptian Religion* 4 (1936): 67, fig. 5.

125 Photography by the Egyptian Expedition, The Metropolitan Museum of Art, New York.

126 Photography by the Egyptian Expedition, The Metropolitan Museum of Art, New York.

CHAPTER 9

135 N. M. Davies, JEA 24 (1938): 30, fig. 9.

135 Hornung, *Totenbuch*, p. 205, fig. 55.

136 Ibid., p. 184, fig. 49.

136 Ibid., p. 94, fig. 15.

137 Hornung, *Unterweltsbücher*, p. 209, fig. 19.

137 I. Rosellini, *I monumenti dell'Egitto e della Nubia* (Pisa 1832–1844), II, pl. 125, which is identical with Champollion, *Monuments* III, pl. 270.

138 Hornung, *Unterweltsbücher*, p. 164f, fig. 11.

139 Hornung, *Totenbuch*, p. 216, fig. 58.

139 Hornung, *Unterweltsbücher*, p. 234, fig. 32.

141 Drawing, A. Brodbeck from the tomb of Amenophis II.

141 Photograph, A. Brodbeck.

CHAPTER 10

149 E. Naville, *Das aegyptische Todtenbuch* I (Berlin 1886), pl. 136.

151/153 Photographs, F. Teichmann.

154 A. Piankoff and N. Rambova, *The Tomb of Ramesses VI* (New York, BS 40, 1, 1954), p. 182, fig. 51.

154 Ibid., p. 371, fig. 123.

155 Ibid., p. 369, fig. 121.

156 Ibid., p. 437, fig. 141.

157 Photograph, F. Teichmann.

157 Hornung, *Altägypt. Höllenvorstellungen*, p. 26 (drawing by H. Fehre).

158 Drawing, A. Brodbeck.

CHAPTER 11

165 "'Grab und Wohnhaus': Die Anfange Agyptens," Exhibition of the University of Constance, 1980, p. 24, pl. 6 (drawing by F. Gerke).

166 W. M. F. Petrie, *Corpus of Prehistoric Pottery and Palettes* (London, 1921), pl. 34.

167 H. Junker, *Giza* I (Vienna, 1929), p. 175, fig. 31.

168 Hornung, *Totenbuch*, p. 44, fig. 1b.

169 T. M. Davis, *The Tomb of Iouiya and Touiyou* (London, 1907), p. 39, fig. 2 (drawing by H. Carter).

169 N. de G. Davies, *Two Ramesside Tombs at Thebes* (New York, 1927), pl. 37.

170 Photograph, A. Brodbeck.

171 Piankoff, *The Shrines of Tut-Ankh-Amon*, fig. 41.

172 Piankoff-Rambova, *Mythological Papyri*, p. 31, fig. 12.

172 Photography by the Egyptian Expedition, The Metropolitan Museum of Art, New York.

173 Photography by the Egyptian Expedition, The Metropolitan Museum of Art, New York.

174 Photography by the Egyptian Expedition, The Metropolitan Museum of Art, New York.

CHAPTER 12

183 A. Mariette, *Monuments divers recueillis en Égypte et en Nubie* (Paris, 1889), pl. 49.

184 Junker, *Giza I*, p. 182, fig. 34.

184 Erman, *Die Religion der Ägypter*, p. 250, fig. 94.

185 Brinks, *Entwicklung*, p. 73.

185 Photograph, A. Brodbeck.

186 T. M. Davies et al., *The Tomb of Iouiya and Touiyou*, p. XXIV.

186 Steindorff-Wolf, *Theban. Gräberwelt*, p. 93, fig. 36.

187 Porter-Moss, *Topographical Bibliography* I, 2nd ed. (Oxford, 1964), p. 510.

188 Drawing, A. Brodbeck

190 Hornung, *Totenbuch*, p. 318, fig. 77.

191 L. Borchardt et al, ZÄS 70 (1934): 29, fig. 5.

196 Photography by the Egyptian Expedition, The Metropolitan Museum of Art, New York.

210–215 Elizabeth Simpson from Elizabeth Thomas, *The Royal Necropoleis of Thebes* (Princeton, 1966), pp. 85f., 93f., 119f.

Color Plates according to Individual Tombs

Amenophis II   11, 13, 18, 43, 72, 75, 98

Haremheb   15, 17, 21, 23, 25–26, 34, 36–37, 39–40, 46, 84, 128

Merneptah   56–57, 65, 67, 74, 129

Nofretari   19, 85–86, 143–144, 150–151

Ramesses I   49

Ramesses III   42, 93, 107–109, 112

Ramesses VI   3, 12, 41, 48, 52–55, 68, 70, 73, 77, 79–80, 94, 100–111, 113, 116–117, 121–122, 124–125

Ramesses IX   38, 69, 102–103, 110, 119–120

Sennefer   106, 127, 145–149

Sety I   20, 24, 47, 50–51, 58–59, 60–61, 78, 81–83, 90–91, 95–97, 104–105, 114–115, 130–131, 140

Sety II   16, 133–138

Siptah   37, 66

Tausert   22, 30–33, 64, 71, 87–89, 99, 101, 123, 132, 139

Tuthmosis III   27, 44–45, 62–63, 76, 118

Tuthmosis IV   29

Tutankhamun   3, 126

Credits for the Color Illustrations

Artur Brack 3, 7, 11

British Library 34 (Add. Mss. 29 820, folio 81), 82 (ibid., folio 97), 83 (Add. Mss. 25 641, folio 53), 92 (ibid., folio 33), 93 (Add. Mss. 29 820, folio 99) Reproduced by permission of the British Library.

Hans Hauser 2, 9, 10, 20, 81

Gunther Lapp 71

Ursula Schweitzer 13, 28

Lotty Spycher 6

Elisabeth Staehelin 22, 90–91, 140

Frank Teichmann 15, 17, 21, 23, 25–26, 34, 36–37, 39–40, 46, 84, 128, 138

David Warburton 142

Plate 105 is taken from H. von Minutoli, *Reise zum Tempel des Jupiter Ammon in der Libyschen Wüste, Nachträge* (Berlin, 1827), Tab. III

The remaining photographs were taken by Andreas Brodbeck.

INDEX